LITTLE-KNOWN FACTS *about* JOSEPH SMITH

LITTLE-KNOWN FACTS *about* JOSEPH SMITH

WAYNE J LEWIS, JANA LEE COX
& LEE NELSON

ISBN 13: 978-1-4621-1524-2

Published by CFI, an imprint of Cedar Fort, Inc.
2373 W. 700 S., Springville, UT 84663
Distributed by Cedar Fort, Inc., www.cedarfort.com

LIBRARY OF CONGRESS CATALOGING-IN-PUBLICATION DATA

Lewis, Wayne J, 1941- author.
500 little-known facts about Joseph Smith / Wayne Lewis, Jana Cox, Lee Nelson.
pages cm
Jana Cox named as an editor in the back matter.
Includes bibliographical references and index.
ISBN 978-1-4621-1524-2 (alk. paper)
1. Smith, Joseph, Jr., 1805-1844--Miscellanea. I. Cox, Jana, 1964- editor. II. Nelson, Lee, author. III. Title. IV. Title: Five hundred little-known facts about Joseph Smith.
BX8695.S6L48 2014
289.3092--dc22
[B]

2014037203

Cover design by Shawnda T. Craig
Cover design © 2014 Lyle Mortimer
Edited and typeset by Jessica B. Ellingson

Printed in the United States of America

10 9 8 7 6 5 4 3 2 1

Printed on acid-free paper

Dedication

I dedicate this work to the wives of all the Prophets, ancient and modern, who have sacrificed so much so that their husbands would have the time necessary to serve mankind, and especially record doctrine and revelations for future generations.

This book is also dedicated to my wife Maren Barraclough Lewis, my best friend and mother of our twelve children who passed away December 2, 2012. Her support during our fifty years of marriage is the highest example of motherhood.

And to our children Kurt and Merie Lewis Kammerer, W. Jay and Darlene Lewis, Talmage and Robyn Lewis, Mark and Ginger Lewis Boyd, Pablo and Heidi Lewis Riboldi, David and LaLoni Lewis Stott, Steve and Mollie Lewis Remund, David and Audrey Lewis Maycock, Eddie Edison Lewis, Jenny Lynelle Lewis, Dee and Annie Lewis Montgomery, and Jacob CML and Noelle Lewis and to our fifty-three grandchildren and three great grandchildren.

And lastly, out of respect, to Joseph City, Arizona, a small northern Arizona town, originally called Saint Joseph, in honor of the Prophet Joseph Smith. Later the town's name was changed to Joseph City. This is the birthplace of my mother, Verna Bushman Lewis, and home of our family of Bushmans, Porters and Smiths.

—Wayne J Lewis

Contents

Abbreviations

of References Used

Affidavits	*Mormon Redress Petitions, Documents of the 1833–1838, Missouri Conflict*, edited by Clark V. Johnson, 1992, 830 pages, BYU, Religious Studies Center.
BD	*Biographical Directory from The Joseph Smith Papers*, Vol. 1, Church Historian's Office, pages 397–451, Church Historian's Press.
BR-1	*Biographical Register, Personal Writings of Joseph Smith* by Dean C. Jessee, 1984, Deseret Book pages, 625–704.
BR-2	*Biographical Directory from The Papers of Joseph Smith* by Dean C. Jessee 1989 Deseret Book Volume 1 pages 471–525.
BR-3	*Biographical Register from The Papers of Joseph Smith Vol. 2* by Dean C. Jessee, 1992, Deseret Book, pages 521–607.
Call to Arms	*A Call to Arms: the 1838 Mormon Defense of Northern Missouri* by Alexander L. Baugh, 2000, BYU PhD Dissertation.
CH	*A Comprehensive History of the Church of Jesus Christ of Latter-day Saints*, B. H. Roberts, Reprint 1968 Bookcraft, Volumes 1 (through Missouri), 2 (through Nauvoo), 3, 4, 5, 6, 7 (Utah).
D&CWW	*Doctrine & Covenants Who's Who: A Comprehensive Guide to the People in the Doctrine and Covenants* by Ed J. Pinegar & Richard J. Allen, 2008, Covenant, 201 pages.
ELDS	*Early Latter-day Saints, A Mormon Trail Pioneer Database*, Pioneer Research Group, Nauvoo & Winter Quarters, Nebraska, 1987.

Abbreviations

EPB	*Early Patriarchal Blessings of the Church of Jesus Christ of Latter-day Saints*, compiled by H. Michael Marguardt, 2007, 501 pages, Smith Pettit Foundation.
GD	*Guide to Mormon Diaries & Autobiographies*, Davis Bitton, 1977, BYU, 416 pages.
HC	*The History of the Church of Jesus Christ of Latter-day Saints by Joseph Smith*, edited by B. H. Roberts. Volumes 1–7, 1951, 1980, Deseret Book, 3,992 pages.
JD	*Journal of Discourses* by President Brigham Young, His Two Counselors, the Twelve Apostles and others, reported by G. D. Watt, and D. W. Evans, Liverpool, England 1867.
LDSBE	*Latter Day Saint Biographical Encyclopedia*, Volumes 1, 2, 3, 4, 2929 pages, Andrew Jensen 1914, Andrew Jensen History Company.
LDSCC	*LDS Church Chronology* 1805–1914 by Andrew Jensen, 1914, revised and reprinted J. R. C. Nebeker, 2002, 452 pages, reprinted Quick & Easy.
Martyred	*The Day They Martyred the Prophet* by Henry A. Smith
Mormon Land	*Mormon Land Ownership as a factor in evaluating the extent of Mormon Settlements and Influence in Missouri* 1831–1841 Wayne J. Lewis, Master Thesis, BYU, 1981, pages 88–166, BYU.
My Life's Review	*My Life's Review*, Autobiography of Benjamin F. Johnson, 404 pages. Johnson Family Organization.
Profile	*A Profile of Latter-Day Saints of Kirtland, Ohio and Members of Zion's Camp: Vital Statistics and Sources.* Compiled by Milton V. Backman, Jr., 1982, 165 pages, BYU Press.
Revelations	*The Revelations of the Prophet Joseph Smith* by Lyndon W. Cook, 1981, 380 pages, Deseret Book.
RJ	*Remembering Joseph* by Mark L. McConkie, 2003, 529 pages, Deseret Book.
SBR	*Selected Biographical Registry, Remembering Joseph*, p. 425–454, Mark L. McConkie, 2003, Deseret Book.

Compiler's Note

Documents and researched data on Joseph Smith have been placed in one book to provide easier access to information. By consolidating as much as possible it will eliminate the need to go to scores of libraries and hundreds of books to locate the enclosed information. The ever-increasing volume of information from many sources including the Joseph Smith Papers Project makes it even more important to simplify the data.

Biographical data has been added into these lists and stories by merging numerous sources. This should assist in helping to provide more accurate identification and help fit the pieces of the historical record together by adding birth, death, and baptism information together of those individuals who were so close to the Prophet.

Birthplace in Sharon Township, Vermont

This frame home was 22x24 feet and 1½ levels, built on the township lines of Sharon and Randolph Townships.

—*Richard L. Anderson, KBYU Joseph Smith Papers*, January 10, 2010

Debate club

Young Joseph Smith belonged to the local debate club in Palmyra, according to O. Turner.

—Pioneer History of Philips and Gorham Purchase

Leg surgery

Summer 1813: As young boy, Joseph Smith suffered from osteomyelitis brought on by typhus fever. He endured four surgeries to relieve the terrible pain. The first was in his shoulder; after it was lanced, it discharged a full quart of matter. The infection then went straight to his leg, where surgery was again required, and the surgeon made an eight–inch cut. During surgery number three, the same surgeon enlarged the wound, cutting clear to the bone. As the wound healed, the pain returned again, and about sixty days later, a council of surgeons was called in for surgery number four. Eleven doctors from Dartmouth College came and recommended amputation, to which Joseph's mother vehemently objected. Finally, without any pain medication, they bored into the bone and took out nine large pieces of bone, after which the symptoms were relieved and young Joseph recovered.

—Scot Facer Proctor and Maurine Jensen Proctor, eds., *History of Joseph Smith by His Mother Lucy Mack Smith*, 72–77; Norma Fischer, *Portrait of a Prophet*, 26–31

Joseph Smith's family lived in West Lebanon, just five miles away from where Dr. Nathan Smith practiced medicine in Hanover, New Hampshire. Dr. Nathan Smith was the only doctor in the United States who could have done the complicated surgery. He founded Dartmouth Medical School. An original first edition copy of the Book of Mormon is in this school library to this day.

—Scot Facer Proctor and Maurine Jensen Proctor, eds., *History of Joseph Smith by His Mother Lucy Mack Smith*, 77; Compiler's notes; Norma Fischer, *Portrait of a Prophet*, 26

Vermont famous maple syrup

When Joseph was very young, the family harvested 1,200–1,500 maple trees for maple syrup.

—*History of Joseph Smith by His Mother*, 88

Family

Alvin a Wrestler too

"My brother Alvin . . . was a very handsome man . . . and of great strength. When two Irishmen were fighting, and one was about to gouge the other's eyes, Alvin took him by his collar and breeches, and threw him over the ring . . . of men standing around to witness the fight."

—Recorded by Joseph Smith January 9, 1843; Cecilia Jensen, *Joseph in Palmyra*, XV

Cousins

Joseph never knew that these individuals were related to him, but it has now become known that he had some interesting cousins. Brigham Young was his fifth cousin. Oliver Cowdery was his sixth cousin. Parley Pratt, Orson Pratt, Wilford Woodruff, and Harold B. Lee were his cousins. Emma and Joseph shared the same fifth great-grandfather, John Howland, a Mayflower passenger.

—Ted Gibbons, *Sealing the Testimony: An Eyewitness Account of the Martyrdom*, 3–4

Famous relatives of Joseph Smith—a short list

This is a short list of Joseph's relatives through the connecting lines of his mother.

- Borden, Sir Robert Laird (1854–1937)—Prime Minister of Canada, Lathrop–Mayflower.
- Bush, George Herbert Walker (1924–)—41st US President, Hawland–Mayflower
- Bush, George Walker (1946–)—43rd US President, Hawland–Mayflower
- Churchill, Sir Winston (1874–1965)—Prime Minister of England, Hawland–Mayflower

- Cowdery, Oliver (1806–1846)—LDS Church Assistant President, Hawland–Mayflower
- Dewey, Thomas E. (1902–1971)—Governor of New York, Lathrop–Mayflower
- Dulles, Allen (1883–1969)—Director of CIA, Lathrop–Mayflower
- Dulles, John Foster (1890–1952)—Former Secretary of State, Lathrop– Mayflower
- Ford, Gerald (1913–)—40th US President, Hawland–Mayflower
- Fuller, Alfred Carl (1885–?)—Founder Fuller Brush, Lathrop–Mayflower
- Grant, Ulysses S. (1822–1935)—18th US President, Lathrop–Mayflower
- Holmes, Oliver Wendell (1841–1925)—US Supreme Court, Lathrop–Mayflower
- Lee, Harold B. (1899–1973)—LDS 11th Church President, Lathrop–Mayflower
- Longfellow, Henry Wadsworth (1807–1882)—Poet, Lathrop–Mayflower
- Marriott, David Daniel (1939–)—LDS Utah Congressman, Lathrop–Mayflower
- Morgan, John Pierpont (1876–1943)—Financier, Lathrop–Mayflower
- Nixon, Richard M. (1913–1994)—39th US President, Hawland–Mayflower
- Post, Marjorie M. (1889–1962)—Founder General Foods, Lathrop–Mayflower
- Pratt, Orson (1811–1881)—LDS Church Apostle, Lathrop–Mayflower
- Pratt, Parley (1806–1887)—LDS Church Apostle, Lathrop–Mayflower
- Romney, George (1907–1995)—LDS Governor of Michigan, Lathrop–Mayflower
- Romney, Mitt (1947–)—LDS Governor of Massachusetts, Lathrop–Mayflower
- Roosevelt, Franklin D. (1882–1945)—32nd US President, Lathrop–Mayflower
- Spock, Benjamin (1907–2003)—Physician and writer, Lathrop–Mayflower

- Stephenson, Adlai E. (1930–)—US Senator–Illinois, Lathrop–Mayflower
- Whitney, Eli (1765–1825)—Inventor of Cotton Gin, Lathrop–Mayflower
- Woodruff, Wilford (1807–1895)—4th LDS Church President, Lathrop–Mayflower

—Church Family History Library, December 23, 1978; *Church News,* December 23, 1978

Smith family

According to Joseph Smith Sr., the Smith family is as great as any family who ever lived.

—Richard E. Turley and Lael Littke, *Stories From the Life of Joseph Smith,* 154

The Smith family men worked as day laborers six days a week after running their own farm just to exist.

—*KBYU Joseph Smith Papers,* October 12, 2009

Smith family frame home

The Smith family frame home on their 100-acre farm in Manchester Township was the only home the Smith family built together. Their mortgage payment was $100 a year and they, along with eight other families in the area, had their home foreclosed on in the tough financial crisis of 1828–1829. They lost the home to Lemuel O' Durfey and then rented it back from him.

—*KBYU Joseph Smith Papers,* October 12, 2009

Smith family of Joseph Sr. and Lucy Mack

Note: Three boys, Samuel, Ephraim, and William, have the same birthday, March 13th.

- Son: Premature. Died at birth, 1796, at Tunbridge, Vermont.
- Alvin: Born February 11, 1798. Died November 19, 1823.
- Hyrum: Born February 9, 1800, at Tunbridge, New York. Murdered June 27, 1844, at Carthage, Hancock County, Illinois.
- Sophronia: Born May 17, 1803, at Tunbridge, Vermont. Died July 22, 1876.
- Joseph Jr.: Born December 23, 1805, at Sharon Township, Windsor County, Vermont. Murdered June 27, 1844 at Carthage, Hancock County, Illinois.
- Samuel Harrison: Born March 13, 1808, at Tunbridge, Vermont. He was six feet tall and was the first person besides Joseph to receive

the Melchizedek Priesthood in June 1830. He became the third martyr when he died on July 30, 1844.
- Ephraim: Born March 13, 1810. Died eleven days later in Tunbridge, Vermont.
- Willaim: Born at Royalton, Vermont, on March 13, 1811, was 6'3" tall and weighed 230 pounds. Died November 13, 1893.
- Katherine: Born July 28, 1813, at West Lebanon, New Hampshire. Died February 1, 1900. She was tall, more than six inches above other women.
- Don Carlos: Born March 25, 1816, at Norwich, Vermont. Died August 1, 1841.
- Lucy: Born at Farmington Township, New York, July 18, 1821. Died December 9, 1882.

—Richard Lloyd Dewey, *Joseph Smith: A Biography*, 4; Kyle R. Walker, *United by Faith*, 83, 123, 167, 205, 247, 310, 355, 399

"Joseph Smith's family had a history of storekeeping. Even before Joseph was born, his father had been one of the partners in a mercantile venture in the town of Randolph, Vermont." Later, the Smiths in the Palmyra area "ran a 'shop' of some kind . . . [and sold] 'gingerbread, pies, boiled eggs, root beer, and other like notions of traffic.'" On January 5, 1842, Joseph finally opened the Red Brick Store and received thirteen wagon loads of goods from New Orleans and St. Louis.

—Matthew B. Brown, *Joseph Smith: The Man, the Mission, the Message*, 61

Emma

Children of Joseph and Emma Smith

- Alvin Smith—Born June 15, 1828, in Harmony, Pennsylvania; died within a few hours of his birth. He was named after Joseph's brother who died while overworking to build a home for his parents in Manchester Township, New York.
- Thaddeus Smith—Born April 30, 1831, in Kirtland, Ohio (twin); died within three hours.
- Louisa Smith—Born April 30, 1831, in Kirtland, Ohio (twin); died within three hours.
- Julia Murdock Smith—Born May 1, 1831, in Kirtland (twin—adopted); died 1880.
- Joseph Murdock Smith—Born May 1, 1831, in Kirtland, Ohio (twin—adopted); died March 30, 1832, from exposure when Joseph was tarred and feathered by a mob in Hiram, Ohio.
- Joseph Smith III—Born November 6, 1832, in Kirtland, Ohio; died December 10, 1914. He became president of the RLDS Church in 1861.
- Frederick Granger Williams Smith—Born June 28, 1836, in Kirtland, Ohio; died April 13, 1862. He was named after Joseph Smith's close friend and counselor in the First Presidency, Frederick Granger Williams.
- Alexander Hale Smith—Born June 2, 1838, in Far West, Missouri; died August 12, 1909. He was named after Alexander W. Doniphan, a lawyer and friend who saved Joseph Smith's life during the surrender and betrayal at Far West, Missouri, in 1838.
- Don Carlos Smith—Born June 13, 1840, in Nauvoo, Illinois; died August 15, 1841. He was named after Joseph's beloved brother Don Carlos.

- Stillborn son—Born February 6, 1842, in Nauvoo, Illinois.
- David Hyrum Smith—Born November 17, 1844, in Nauvoo, Illinois; died August 29, 1904. He suffered from a mental collapse.

Note: Anyone inclined to censor or judge Emma Smith harshly might reflect upon the deaths of the six children and husband who preceded her in death.

Emma

Emma toiled thousands of extra hours so that Joseph Smith would have time to do all that was required of him: translate *the Book of Mormon;* restore the priesthood; organize the Church; receive all the revelations; print the Doctrine and Covenants, the Pearl of Great Price, and the Joseph Smith Translation of the Bible; serve as Prophet and President of the Church; and travel all over to assist the Church. According to her granddaughter, Gracia Jones, "[Emma] has been tossed upon the ocean of uncertainly—she has breasted the storms of persecutions, and buffeted the rage of men and devils."

—Gracia Jones, *Emma and Lucy,* 123; Compiler's note

Emma was fine looking, smart, a good singer, and had a beautiful soprano voice.

—Buddy Youngreen, *Reflections of Emma*; Gracia Jones, *Emma and Lucy*, 26, 87

Emma was pregnant for more than 6 years of her 17½ years of marriage to Joseph.

—Buddy Youngreen, *Reflections of Emma*

Emma an herb doctor

"Emma was considered an herb doctor and went among the sick [in Nauvoo] administering Sappington's pills, Dover's powder, and various medications [to those who were sick with typhoid and malaria]."

—Joseph Bates Noble, *Keeper of the Prophet's Sword*, Howard Carlos Smith, 45

Emma helped Joseph raise his sights

As in the Word of Wisdom revelation, Emma merely helped Joseph raise his sights when needed.

—Michael Kennedy, *Emma Smith: My Story,* 2007, movie

Emma never left the Church

Emma Hale Smith never left the Church, nor was she excommunicated.

—Historical Record

Emma undaunted, firm, and unwavering

"When I contemplated for a moment the many scenes we had been called to pass through, the fatigues and the toils, the sorrows and sufferings, and the joys and consolations, from time to time, which had strewed our paths. . . oh what a commingling of thought filled my mind for the moment, again she is here, even in the seventh trouble—undaunted, firm, and unwavering—unchangeable, affectionate Emma!"

—Joseph Smith, *HC*, 5:107

Emma's ancestors

Seven of Emma's ancestor were on the *Mayflower*. Joseph and Emma were actually distant cousins. Elizabeth Lewis Hale and Lucy Mack Smith were both descendants of John Howland, one of the 102 passengers on the *Mayflower*.

—Gracia Jones, *Emma and Lucy*, 223; Lori E. Woodland, *Beloved Emma: The Illuminated Life Story of Emma Smith*, 10

Emma's births

Of the nine children Emma gave birth to, "only in one instance did Emma bear a child in a home she could call her own, and that was David Hyrum, born after the Prophet's death."

—Truman G. Madsen, *Joseph Smith the Prophet*, 29

Emma's care of Joseph's mother Lucy Mack Smith

Emma cared for her mother–in–law, Lucy Mack Smith, for many of the fifteen years from the death of Joseph Smith Sr. until Lucy's death on May 14, 1856. Lucy was entirely bedridden for the last couple of years.

—Gracia N. Jones *Emma and Lucy*, 183, 219

Emma saw the Savior

A few days before her death in April 1879, Emma told her nurse, Elizabeth Revel, that Joseph came to her in a vision and said, "Emma, come with me, it is time for you to come with me." Emma related that she went with Joseph into a beautiful mansion, and in the nursery was her babe, Don Carlos, who had been taken from her. She wept with joy over the child then "turned to Joseph and said, 'Joseph, where are the rest of my children.' He said to her, 'Emma, be patient and you shall have all of your children.' [Then] Emma said she saw standing by Joseph's side a personage of light, even the Lord Jesus Christ."

—Gracia N. Jones, *Emma and Lucy*, 190

Emma's blessing

On June 24, 1844, at about 6:00 p.m., "Joseph goes . . . to bid farewell to his family. Before he leaves Emma the last time, she requests a blessing from him. He tells her to write the best one she can think of and he will sign it. In her long handwritten letter, she requests a 'fruitful, active mind,' 'the spirit of discernment,' 'wisdom to bring up all the children . . . in such a manner that they will be useful ornaments in the kingdom of God,' . . . '[and] that I may wear a cheerful countenance,' and several other things."

—J. Christopher Conkling, *A Joseph Smith Chronology*, 235–36

Emma's trials

Emma was ostracized by her family, lived about fifteen years in someone else's home, bore almost all of the nine children without Joseph there, worked tirelessly so Joseph would have time to be the Prophet, felt the plates but never saw them, and buried six of eleven babies. She cooked uncounted meals for unannounced guests and provided shelter for all those Joseph invited in for temporary assistance. She lived under constant uncertainty. She endured thirty-four years after Joseph was murdered. She had to keep many secrets.

—Compiler's note

Emma remained in Nauvoo with the debts of Joseph Smith and the Church. We now have documentation that Brigham Young sent her money several times through a Church attorney, which she never received. This attorney was Almon Whiting Babbitt, and he kept the money himself instead of taking it to Emma to pay the remaining debts of the Church in Nauvoo. Neither Brigham Young nor Emma Smith knew that this had happened. It is not surprising that Emma had some hurt feelings concerning Brigham Young.

—Compiler's note

Family prayers

Joseph and Emma's home life included prayers three times a day: morning, noon, and night.

—Eliza R. Snow, *Women of Mormonism*, 66

First home

Joseph was thirty-six years old when he was able to build his first real home for Emma. He moved in eleven months before he was murdered, in August of 1843.

—Scot F. Proctor and Maurine J. Proctor, eds., *History of Joseph Smith by His Mother*, 428

Gardening

Emma refused to let Joseph in the garden because dozens of people would gather just to be around him, and they would trample all the plants.

—Compiler's note

Joseph and Emma's posterity

The Joseph Smith Jr. and Emma Hale Smith family organization estimates that there are 1,600 descendants of Joseph Smith and Emma, of whom about 1,100 are living today. There are 130–40 confirmed Latter-day Saints among those 1,100 who are still living. Michael (third great-grandson of Joseph and Emma) and Darcy Kennedy have met 90 percent of these living descendants.

—Michael Kennedy, *The Family of Joseph and Emma Smith: The Untold Story,* DVD

Joseph and Emma's courtship

Joseph and Emma's courtship lasted fifteen months.

—Lori E. Woodland, *Beloved Emma: The Illuminated Life Story of Emma Smith*, 10

Love for Emma

Said Joseph, "What unspeakable delight, and what transports of joy swelled my bosom, when I took by the hand, on that night, my beloved Emma—she that was my wife, even the wife of my youth, and the choice of my heart. . . . [A]gain she is here, even in the seventh trouble—undaunted, firm and unwavering—unchangeable, affectionate Emma!"

—*HC*, 5:107

From Joseph's writings and journals there are entries day after day that tell of his tender feelings for Emma:

- "Walked to the store with Emma."

—*HC*, 5:21

- "I rode out with Emma in a sleigh."

—*HC*, 6:170

- "Emma is no better. I was with her all day."

—*HC*, 5:166

- "[I] rode out with Emma to the temple."

—*HC*, 5:183

Marriage

Joseph and Emma were married by justice of the peace Esquire Zachariah Tarble in South Bainbridge, New York, on January 18, 1827. They first met in 1825 when he boarded at Emma's house. He was sealed to Emma for time and all eternity on May 28, 1843, in the Red Brick Store.

—Norman Rothman, *The Unauthorized Biography of Joseph Smith, Mormon Prophet*, 69; Gracia Jones, *Emma and Lucy*, 26; John W. Welch, ed., *A Chronology of the Life of Joseph Smith,* BYU Studies, 148

Seventeen

Emma was seventeen months older than Joseph. They courted for seventeen months and were married seventeen years.

—Compiler's note

People Joseph Knew

Bodyguards of the Prophet Joseph Smith

The following is a list of Joseph's bodyguards, their birth and death dates, and the year of their baptism.

- James Allred (1784–1876) 1833—After his kidnapping by Missourians while in Nauvoo, Joseph Smith chose James as a personal bodyguard.

  —James Allred Family Organization; *Wikipedia*

- John Binley (1814–?) 1839—After moving to Nauvoo in 1840, he served as a bodyguard to Joseph Smith and as a Nauvoo policeman.

  —*LDSBE,* 4:733

- George Black (1823–1872) 1840—At age eighteen, he became a bodyguard to Joseph Smith.

  —*RJ,* 426; *EPB,* 330

- Israel Barlow (1806–1883) 1834—He acted as a bodyguard to Joseph.

  —*The Israel Barlow Story and Mormon Mores,* 24

- George Washington Brown (1827–1906) 1839—He served as bodyguard to Joseph Smith.

  —*LDSBE,* 3:609

- Seymour Brunson (1799–1840) 1831—He was a bodyguard to Joseph Smith.

  —D&C*WW*

- John Lowe Butler (1808–1861) 1835—He was ordained a bodyguard of Joseph Smith about 1842. He also helped to bury Joseph and Hyrum secretly.

  —*GD,* 52

- William Cherry (*est.*1800–?) *est.*1840—He was chosen by Joseph Smith to teach sword fighting to the twenty lifeguards who were chosen during Zion's Camp. Cherry was a native of Ireland and had served more than twenty years in the British Dragoons.

  —*HC*, 2:183–85; *Profile*, 16; compiler's note

- Zebedee Coltrin (1804–1887) 1831—He was a bodyguard to Joseph Smith.

  —*Wikipedia*

- Thomas Grover (1807–1886) 1834—He was a personal bodyguard to Joseph Smith.

  —D&C*WW*, 38, 126; *Wikipedia*

- Jesse Joseph Pierce Harmon (1795–1877) 1838—He was a bodyguard to Joseph Smith in Nauvoo. He was also a policeman.

  —*RJ*, 136

- Isaac Chauncey Haight (1813–1886) 1839—He was a bodyguard to Joseph Smith and a member of the police force in Nauvoo. He said he was one of forty bodyguards to Joseph Smith. He was later excommunicated and died in Thatcher, Arizona.

  —*Wikipedia*

- William Adams Hickman (1815–1883) 1838—"Personal bodyguard." Daughter's statement.

  —*HC*, 4:340

- Jonathan Herriman Holmes (1806–1880) 1832—He was a bodyguard to Joseph Smith. He later married a plural wife of Joseph's, Elvira A. Cowles.

  —*LDSBE*, 4:183

- Henry Bailey Jacobs (1817–1886) 1834—He stated he was a bodyguard to Joseph Smith.

  —*Wikipedia*

- Benjamin Franklin Johnson (1818–1905) 1835—He said he was one of the nineteen bodyguards chosen to protect the Prophet.

  —*My Life's Review*

- Heber Chase Kimball (1801–1868) 1832—He guarded Joseph Smith.

  —*GD*, 194; *Wikipedia*

- Newel Knight (1800–1847) 1830—His wife Lydia said, "He became a bodyguard of Joseph Smith." He died on the Iowa Trail.

  —*Wikipedia*

- John Lambert (1820–1893) *est.*1837—"Bodyguard of Joseph Smith in Nauvoo," according to his daughter Elena Dorothy Lambert Michie.

  —*Wikipedia*

- John D. Lee (1812–1877) 1836—He was a bodyguard to Joseph Smith.

  —*Wikipedia*

- Cornelius Peter Lott (1798–1850) *est.*1833—He was commander of Joseph Smith's bodyguards at Nauvoo.

  —*BR,* 566

- John Lytle (1803–1892) *est.*1835—He was a bodyguard to Joseph Smith.

  —*GD,* 216

- Moses Worthen Mecham (1804–1856) 1839—He was a policeman and bodyguard of Prophet.

  —*Mecham family records; Wikipedia*

- Philemon Christopher Merrill (1820–1856) 1839—He was a guard at Joseph Smith's speech before leaving for Carthage and part of Joseph Smith's rescue party in 1843.

  —*GD,* 239

- Joseph Bates Noble (1810–1900) 1832—He was a bodyguard to Joseph Smith.

  —*Mormon Times,* October 10, 2009, 5

- Roger Orton (1795–1851) *est.*1833—In Zion's Camp, he was chosen to be one of the twenty lifeguards for Joseph Smith and was the captain of one of the companies of ten men.

  —*Saints without Halos; Wikipedia*

- James Pace (1811–1888) 1839—He was a policeman and bodyguard to Joseph Smith and was a Nauvoo Legion member.

  —*GD,* 266; *LDSBE,* 4:759

- Thomas Rich (1817–1884) *est.*1836—He acted as a bodyguard to Joseph Smith.

  —*LDSBE,* 3:212

- Phineus Richards (1788–1874) 1837—He was a member of Joseph Smith's lifeguards.

—GD, 294

- Orrin Porter Rockwell (1813–1878) 1830—He was a bodyguard on several occasions. However, when Joseph went to Carthage, he requested Rockwell stay behind in Nauvoo and guard Emma and the children.

—D&C*WW*, *91; GD*, 300

- James Henry Rollins (1816–1899) 1832—He was a bodyguard and clerk.

—Wikipedia

- Shadrack Roundy (1789–1872) 1831—He was a bodyguard and policeman in Nauvoo in 1843.

—D&C*WW*, 149; *BR*, 588; *Revelations*, 273

- George Albert Smith (1817–1875) 1832—He was the armor bearer for the twenty men chosen in Zion's Camp in 1834. He was a bodyguard to Joseph Smith.

—D&C*WW*, 134; Ted Gibbons, *Sealing the Testimony*, 44–45; *GD*, 320

- Hyrum Smith (1800–1844) 1830—He was chosen as captain over ten of the twenty lifeguards of Joseph Smith during Zion's Camp.

—Wikipedia

- Sylvester Smith (*est.*1805–1880) *est.*1831—He was chosen as adjutant over the twenty lifeguards of Joseph Smith during Zion's Camp.

—Wikipedia

- John Snyder (1800–1975) 1836—He was revered as a bodyguard to Joseph Smith when the Prophet's body was returned to Nauvoo.

—D&C*WW*, 174.

- William Somerville (1817–1878) 1840—He slept on the floor near the Prophet in the Nauvoo Mansion and guarded Joseph by placing his feet against the door.

—RJ, 116.

- Zerubbabel Snow (1809–1888) 1832—He was chosen as commissary of the companies of ten bodyguards during Zion's Camp.

—Saints without Halos; Wikipedia; Parley Pratt article

- Allen Joseph Stout (1815–1848) 1837—In 1843, he was guarding the Prophet when John the Revelator came to Joseph Smith.

  —*RJ*, 210; *Wikipedia*

- Hosea Stout (1810–1889) 1838—He was chief of police in Nauvoo and considered a bodyguard to Joseph Smith.

  —*Wikipedia*

- Nathan Tanner (1815–1910) 1831—He was an assistant commissary of Joseph's bodyguards.

  —*Saints without Halos; Wikipedia*

- John Taylor (1808–1887) 1836—His wife Sarah Burket Taylor said he was a bodyguard to Joseph Smith.

  —*Wikipedia*

- Henry Thornber (*est.*1816–1887) 1839—It's stated in his family records that he was a bodyguard to Joseph Smith.

  —*Wikipedia*

- James Montgomery Whitmore (*est.*1800–1866) *est.*1840—He moved to Nauvoo and was a bodyguard to Joseph Smith. He later moved to Texas.

  —*Wikipedia*

- Frederick Granger Williams (1787–1842) 1830—He was chosen as quartermaster of the twenty lifeguards in Zion's Camp.

  —*Saints without Halos; Wikipedia*

- Lewis Dunbar Wilson (1805–1856) 1837—He was a bodyguard of Joseph Smith.

  —*Journal of Amaeda Wilson Daley Brown Standley; Wikipedia;* D&C*WW*, 174

- Anson Perry Winsor (1818–1917) 1842—He acted as one of the bodyguards of the Prophet Joseph Smith.

  —*LDSBE*, 3:569

Other Bodyguards who played various roles

- John S. Butler (est.1812–?) est.1835—He guarded Joseph's body on the return to Nauvoo.

  —*HC*, 7:135

- Barnett Cole (1796–1858) 1830—He was a bodyguard at the time of Joseph Smith's death.

  —*Barnett Cole Family;* Internet

- John Solomon Fullmer (1807–1883) 1839—He stayed at Carthage for awhile to help protect the Smiths' bodies.

—*24 Hours to Martyrdom* by Reed Blake, 78

- John Portineus Greene (1793–1844) 1832—He stayed at Carthage for a while to help protect the Smiths' bodies.

—*24 Hours to Martyrdom* by Reed Blake, 78

- Amos C. Hodge (est.1800–?) est.1840—He was a bodyguard to return Joseph's body to Nauvoo.

—*HC*, 7:135

- Dan Jones (1810–1862) 1843—He was a bodyguard and walked with sticks with Stephen Markham to guard the Prophet at Carthage.

—D&C*WW*

- Christian Kreymer (est.1800–?) est.1840—He was a bodyguard to return Joseph's body to Nauvoo.

—*HC*, 7:135

- Stephen Markham (1800–1878) 1837—He was a bodyguard at Carthage Jail. He was a huge strong man.

—*Martyred*, 199

- William Marks (1792–1872) 1835—He was a bodyguard to return Joseph's body to Nauvoo.

—*HC*, 7:135

- Dr. Willard Richards (1804–1854) 1836—He helped bring the Smiths' bodies back to Nauvoo.

—*Martyred*, 199

- Samuel Harrison Smith (1808–1844) 1829 and 1830—He brought the bodies back to Nauvoo.

—*Martyred*, 199

- Lorenzo D. Wasson (1818–1857) 1842—He stayed in Carthage for a while to help protect the Smiths.

—Reed Blake, *24 Hours to Martyrdom*, 78

Bodyguards who acted as pallbearers for the Smith brothers after their death

- Alpheus Cutler (1784–1864) 1833—He was trusted to help secretly bury Joseph Smith.

—*Wikipedia*

- Gilbert Goldsmith (1811–?) est.1833
- Abraham Clause Hodge (1806–1882) 1840—He secretly helped to bury Joseph and Hyrum Smith.

—*Wikipedia*

- Dimick Baker Huntington (1808–1979) 1835
- Edward Hunter (1793–1883) 1840
- William Dresser Huntington (1818–1881) 1835
- Philip Bessom Lewis (1804–1879) 1842
- Henry Garlie Sherwood (1785–1862) 1832—He secretly helped bury Joseph and Hyrum Smith.

—*Wikipedia*

- James Emmett (1803–1852) 1831—He was armed with a musket and acted as the guard during the secret burial of the Smith brothers.

—*Martyred*, 202

- Anson Call (1810–1890) 1834

—Call Family Records

Enemies

Joseph was a licensed minister himself, and yet the large majority of Joseph's enemies were ministers and preachers. In Palmyra, they were Methodist minister George Lane, a Presbyterian preacher, a Baptist preacher, and an Episcopalian preacher. In Coleville, they were Presbyterians like Cyrus McMaster, Seymour, Byington, and Benton. In Kirtland, they were Cambellite preacher Symonds Ryder and Methodist preacher Ezra Booth. In Missouri, they were Presbyterians Sashiel Woods, Phineus Ewing, and Samuel Bogart, and preachers Dixon, Cavanaugh, Hunter, Isaac, McCoy, Fitzhugh, Liens, Riley, Pixley, and Lovelady. In Illinois, they were Preacher Levi Williams and Thomas S. Brockman.

—LeGrande Richards, *A Marvelous Work and a Wonder*, 55; Compiler's note

The devil had a firm hold on Joseph's enemies. "They were always bitter, who, wolf–like toward the lamb, hated him not so much as they thirsted for his blood, because their deeds were evil and their natures and their appetites had fallen to crave for violence and delight in vengeance."

—Mercy R. Thompson, *They Knew the Prophet*, Hyrum L. Andrus, 135

Josiah Stowell

Squire Josiah Stowell (1770–1844) came to the Joseph Smith Sr. home with Joseph Knight and contracted to buy wheat from them in 1825. During 1826, Joseph Smith Jr. worked for Squire Stowell temporarily, digging for a presumed treasure and later farming for him. During this time, he met Emma Hale and married her on January 18, 1827. Stowell invited this newly married couple to spend their honeymoon at his home and provided the means for their move to live with Joseph's parents near Palmyra. Later, Stowell and Knight came to visit the Smiths at the time Joseph was to get the gold plates. Joseph and Emma borrowed Knight's horse and Stowell's spring wagon to go to the Hill Cumorah early in the morning of September 22, 1827. Among Mr. Stowell's children was a son, Simpson Stowell, who lived in Palmyra. He had a daughter Rhoda (1805–1844) and a son Josiah Stowell Jr.

—William G. Hartley, *Stand By My Servant Joseph: The Story of the Joseph Knight Family and the Restoration*, 6–8, 32–33

Martin Harris

Martin Harris had been a Quaker, a Universalist, a Baptist, and a Presbyterian. He helped select the first Twelve Apostles. Although Martin served on the high council, he never had further leadership positions in the Church, which was a disappointment to him. He once saw his dead father in a vision and became convinced of baptism for the dead. He later associated with apostate James Strang, Shakerism, and William Smith's Church of Christ. He was 5' 8" tall. He finally came west to Utah in August 31, 1870, was rebaptized September 17, 1870, by Edward Stevenson. He died July 10, 1875, after bearing his testimony again and was buried in Clarkston, Utah. Among Martin Harris's descendants are Elder Dallin Harris Oaks.

—Robert V. Remini, *Joseph Smith*, 54; Madge Harris Tuckett and Belle Harris Wilson, *The Martin Harris Story: Special Witness to the Book of Mormon*, 63–67, 86, 100, 187

Oliver Hervy Piney Cowdery

Oliver's full name was Oliver Hervy Piney Cowdery, according to Wikipedia. He knew the Whitmer family and introduced Joseph to them. He married Elizabeth Ann Whitmer (1815–1892) and was a brother-in-law to Phineas H. Young (brother of Brigham Young, who married his sister Lucy Cowdery).

—John W. Welch and Larry E. Morris, *Oliver Cowdery: Scribe, Elder, Witness*, 10, 351; *Wikipedia*

Porter Rockwell

At Joseph's instruction, Orrin Porter Rockwell, one of Joseph's bodyguards, did not go to Carthage. He stayed in Nauvoo to guard and protect Emma and the family.

—Howard Carlos Smith, *Keeper of the Prophet's Sword*, 69

"Sunday Morning, June 28," says Anson Call, "O. Rockwell rode into Nauvoo at full speed, with the [sweat] dripping from his horse, shouting, 'Joseph is killed—Joseph is killed; they have killed him—they have killed him!"

—Anson Call, *RJ*, 377

Scribes and Secretaries of the Prophet Joseph Smith

A comprehensive list of those who served the Church and Prophet as scribes, secretaries, and historians, with their birth, death, and baptism dates.

- Bernhisel, John Milton (1799–1881) 1841—Secretary to Joseph Smith in 1843. Copied the Joseph Smith Translation manuscript of the Inspired Version of the Bible.

  —*Prominent Characters,* xxxvi

- Burdick, Thomas (1795–1877) *est.*1835—Clerk to President Joseph Smith in recording membership licenses in 1836.

  —*BD,* 402

- Bullock, Thomas (1816–1885) 1841—Scribe to Joseph Smith's office in Nauvoo. Recorded speeches of Joseph Smith in shorthand. Hauled freight on Mississippi.

  —*GD,* 47

- Clayton, William (1814–1879) 1837—Secretary and clerk to Joseph Smith, 1842–1844.

  —*HC,* 3

- Coray, Howard (1817–1883) 1840—Clerk to Joseph Smith. Assisted Lucy Mack Smith in writing history of Joseph Smith. He was a teacher.

  —*GD,* 75

- Corrill, John (1799–1842) 1831—Church historian 1838. Excommunicated 1839. Carriage maker and builder.

  —*LDSBE,* 1:241

- Cowdery, Oliver Hervey Piney (1806–1850) 1829 and 1830—Scribe, secretary, historian, and printer, 1827–1829. Excommunicated in 1838. Rebaptized 1848.

  —*Church Almanac 2011*

- Cowdery, Warren A. (1799–1851) 1830—Secretary, printer, and clerk to Joseph Smith. First General Church Recorder. Left Church in 1838.

  —*LDSBE,* 1:246; *BR,* 667

- Fullmer, John Solomon (1807–1883) 1839—Secretary and clerk to Joseph Smith for one year.

  —*History of John Solomon Fullmer,* 2

- Gilbert, Algernon Sidney (1789–1834) 1830—Church agent, operated Church store in Kirtland and later in Independence, Missouri.

  —*HC,* 1, 2, 3

- Granger, Oliver (1794–1841) 1830—Attorney-in-fact and agent for Joseph Smith in Ohio 1838.

  —*HC,* 3

- Harris, Martin (1783–1875) 1830—Scribe during part of the translation of the first 116 pages of the Book of Mormon in 1838.

  —*LDSBE,* 1:271

- Higbee, Elias (1795–1843) 1832—Church recorder and historian 1838–1843.

  —*LDSBE,* 1:242

- Hyde, Orson (1805–1878) 1831—Editor and clerk to First Presidency 1833.

  —*HC,* 1

- Johnson, Benjamin Franklin (1818–1905) 1835—Private secretary to Joseph Smith; power of attorney for Joseph Smith, 1842–1844.

  —*My Life's Review*

- Kingsbury, Joseph Corodon (1812–1898) 1832—Clerk who copied down section 132 of the Doctrine and Covenants under the direction of Bishop Newel K. Whitney.

  —*LDSBE,* 1: 227

- Marks, William (1792–1872) 1830—Editor of *Messenger & Advocate* in 1837; agent to Bishop Newel K. Whitney.

  —*BR*, 568

- Mulholland, James (1804–1839) 1831—Clerk at Far West in 1838, scribe for Joseph Smith's journals 1838–9, scribe for Joseph Smith's history, and clerk for land.

  —*BR*, 574

- Page, John Edward (1799–1867) 1833—Editor of *The Gospel Light* in 1843. Followed Stangites and Hedrickites, and died in Illinois.

  —*BD*, 428

- Parrish, Warren Farr (1803–1877) 1833—Clerk and scribe to Joseph Smith 1835–1836, secretary of Kirtland Safety Society. Excommunicated 1837.

  —*BR*, 577

- Peck, Reed (1814–1894) 1830—Agent for Nauvoo Temple fund.

  —*HC*, 5

- Phelps, William Wines (1792–1872) 1831—Editor, printer and scribe to Joseph for the book of Abraham, clerk to Joseph Smith in 1841–1844, editor of *Evening & Morning Star.*

  —*BR*, 580

- Pratt, Orson (1811–1881) 1830—Copied revelations for Joseph Smith in 1834. Worked in printing office.

  —*GD*, 281

- Pratt, Parley Parker (1807–1857) 1830—Editor of *Millennial Star*

  —*LDSBE*, 1:84

- Richards, Willard (1804–1854) 1836—Recorder, scribe, clerk of court, Church historian, private secretary to Joseph Smith, and scribe for personal history of Joseph Smith.

  —*BR*, 584; *GD*, 295

- Rigdon, Sidney (1793–1876) 1830—Scribe for Joseph Smith in 1830 for the Joseph Smith Translation and the Doctrine and Covenants.

  —*HC*, 1–3

- Robinson, George W. (1814–1878) *est.*1837—General Church recorder and clerk to First Presidency in 1837–1840; replaced

Oliver Cowdery. Left Church in 1841. Followed Sidney Rigdon (father-in-law).

—*LDSBE,* 1:253; *BD,* 435

- Robinson, Ebenezer (1816–1891) 1835—Printer, clerk, recorder, *Times & Seasons* and *Millennial Star.* Went on trip to Salem, Massachusetts, to look for buried treasure.

—*GD,* 298

- Rollins, James Henry (1816–1899) 1830—Clerk to Joseph Smith.

—*Autobiography of James Rollins; Wikipedia*

- Smith, Don Carlos (1816–1841) 1830—Printer of *Elder's Journal* in 1837 and *Times & Seasons* in 1839–1841.

—*BR,* 592

- Smith, Emma Hale (1804–1879) 1830—Scribe to Joseph Smith in translating some of the Book of Mormon.

—*Revelations,* 3, 7; *HC,* 2, 3

- Smith, Hyrum (1800–1844) 1830—Secretary in helping with publication of Book of Mormon in 1829–30.

—*HC,* 1

- Smith, Joseph Sr. (1771–1840) 1830—Secretary to Joseph Smith.

—*HC,* 1

- Smith, Sylvester (1806–1880) 1831—Scribe to Joseph Smith in 1836.

—*Revelations,* 156; *HC,* 3

- Taylor, John (1808–1887) 1836—Editor of *Times & Seasons* and *Nauvoo Neighbor.*

—*BR,* 598

- Thompson, Robert Blashel (1811–1841) 1836—General Church recorder and clerk in 1840–1841; editor of *Times & Seasons* in 1841. Wrote *Proclamation to Kings.*

—*LDSBE,* 1:254; *Revelations,* 278

- Wandell, Charles Wesley (1815–1875) 1837—Clerk for Willard Richards in charge of Mormon Historical Records.

—*GD,* 370

- Whitmer, John (1802–1878) 1829 and 1830—Scribe in June 1829, during translation of Book of Mormon; Church historian, 1831. Excommunicated in 1838.

—*LDSBE,* 1:251

- Williams, Frederick Granger (1787–1842) 1830—Clerk and scribe to Joseph Smith in 1832. Editor of *Times & Seasons,* trustee of School of the Prophets, and justice of the peace.

—*LDSBE,* 1:51

Seventeen-year-old home teacher

William F. Cahoon relates that he was called to be a ward teacher to the Prophet Joseph Smith's family when he was seventeen. On his first visit, "[Joseph] said, 'Brother William, I submit myself and family into your hands. . . . Ask all the questions you feel like.' . . . I said, 'Brother Joseph, are you trying to live your religion?' He answered, 'Yes.' I then said, 'Do you pray in your family?' He answered, 'Yes.' 'Do you teach your family the principles of the gospel?' He replied, 'Yes, I am trying to do it.' 'Do you ask a blessing on your food?' He said he did. 'Are you trying to live in peace and harmony with all your family?' He said that he was. I turned to Sister Emma, his wife, and said, 'Sister Emma, are you trying to live your religion? Do you teach your children to obey their parents? Do you try to teach them to pray?' To all these questions she answered, 'Yes, I am trying to do so.' I then left my parting blessing upon him and his family, as a teacher, and departed."

—*RJ*, 67–68

Willard Richards

Willard Richards was a personal secretary to Joseph and was with him at the martyrdom. He wrote more of the history of the Church than any other man.

—Dean Jessee, *KBYU Joseph Smith Papers*, November 30, 2009

William E. McLellin

William E. McLellin had more formal education than any of the other early leaders, and he challenged the Prophet's ability to receive revelation. He attempted to write a revelation and was a complete failure. The next day, he apologized to the youthful prophet.

—Leon Hartshorn, *Joseph Smith: Prophet of the Restoration*, 77

Abraham Lincoln

Abraham Lincoln checked out a copy of the Book of Mormon from the Library of Congress. According to Byron C. Andreasen, there is a possibility or likelihood that Joseph Smith and Abraham Lincoln met in Springfield, Illinois, in 1842, when Joseph went there for a hearing before Judge Nathaniel Pope and was acquitted. Abraham's wife, Mary Ann Todd Lincoln, was in the courtroom for the hearing. In the 1840 US presidential election in Illinois, all of the votes went to Ralston and not one vote for Lincoln.

—*Church News,* May 30, 2009, 3–4; *A Joseph Smith Chronology,* 145

If Abraham Lincoln had died at age thirty–eight (like Joseph Smith did), he would have never been renowned like he is today.

—Compiler's note

Josiah Quincy Adams

On May 15, 1844, Josiah Quincy Adams, former mayor of Boston, visited Joseph in Nauvoo. He said, "It is by no means improbable that some future textbook for the use of generations yet unborn will contain a question something like this: What historical American of the nineteenth century has exerted the most powerful influence upon the destinies of his countrymen? And it is by no means impossible that the answer to the interrogatory may be thus written: Joseph Smith, the Mormon prophet."

—J. Christopher Conkling, *A Chronology of the Life of Joseph Smith,* 165; Josiah Quincy Adams, *Leaves From My Journal*

Stephen A. Douglas

On March 18, 1843, "Joseph Smith dined with Judge Stephen A. Douglas and prophesied that the judge would aspire to the presidency of the United States but that if he ever turned against the Saints, he would feel the hand of the Almighty." He did turn against the Saints, and he lost the presidential election to an unknown named Abraham Lincoln.

—John W. Welch, ed., *A Chronology of the Life of Joseph Smith,* BYU Studies, 148–49; *HC,* 5:393–4; Compiler's note

Women

Emma Hale Smith

1804–1879—Baptized 1830 (convert #47)

This courageous wife of Joseph Smith was in tune with God, was able to believe young Joseph's story, and knew that she was to marry him. She believed, with faith, all that Joseph told her about seeing divine beings, angels, and the gold plates. She assumed much of Joseph's everyday work so he could have time to translate and work to restore the Church. She no doubt chopped extra wood, planted and harvested the crops, and encouraged Joseph through any self-doubts. She defended Joseph against all the false charges brought against him by friends and foes for seventeen years.

—*BD*-2, 438; *EPB*, 30; *PC*, xlvii; Wayne J. Lewis, *Early Converts of the First 14 years of the Restoration*

Lucy Mack Smith

1775–1856—Baptized 1830 (convert #15)

The mother of Joseph Smith Jr. helped to set the stage for a righteous family and had a huge influence on her sons. She was in tune with God and able to influence her husband. She believed her son Joseph and encouraged him to follow the instructions of angels and Deity. She supported her sons in their missions in the Restoration. She influenced one of the greatest families in the history of the world.

—*BD*, 440; *GD*, 326; *RJ*, 73; *HC*, 1:2; *Mormon Land*, 131; *ELDS, Index*; *LDSBE*, 1:590; William G. Hartley, *Stand By My Servant Joseph*, 60; Wayne J. Lewis, *Early Converts of the First 14 years of the Restoration*

Eliza Roxcy Snow

1804–1887—Baptized 1835 (convert #2730)

Eliza had great faith in the Church and in Joseph Smith through all his claims and trials. She was a defender of the Restoration in many ways, and especially with her gift of writing. She served with Emma Smith in the first Relief Society Presidency. She went West and added great wisdom in counsel to Brigham Young in managing his household.

—*HC*, 6:192; *BR*, 433; *Affidavits*, 608; *GD*, 331; *Profile*, 65; Wayne J. Lewis, *Early Converts of the First 14 years of the Restoration*

Mary Fielding Smith

1801–1852—Baptized 1836 (convert #1600)

She was the wife of Hyrum Smith who assisted him through many trials after his first wife died. She gave birth to Joseph Fielding Smith, who became the sixth President of the Church, and walked to the Salt Lake Valley after her husband was murdered.

—*Mormon Land,* 150; *Profile,* 63; HC, 2:492; Wayne J. Lewis, *Early Converts of the First 14 years of the Restoration*

Mary Elizabeth Rollins Lightner

1818–1913—Baptized 1830 (convert #65)

She was an early Rollins family supporter of Joseph Smith. She borrowed a Book of Mormon as a young girl and received a testimony. She was a niece of Algernon Sidney Gilbert of the Gilbert and Whitney store.

—*BR,* 486; *RJ,* 77; *GD,* 212; *ELDS*; *Autobiography of Mary Elizabeth Rollins Lightner*

Mary Ann Angell Young

1803–1882—Baptized 1830 (convert #137)

She was the wife of Brigham Young after his first wife died. She faithfully supported Brigham through all his trials in Ohio, Missouri, Illinois, and crossing the plains. She supported him with all of his duties.

—*Missouri Mormon Burials,* 193; Wayne J. Lewis, *Early Converts of the First 14 years of the Restoration*

Elizabeth Ann Smith Whitney

1800–1881—Baptized 1830 (convert #86)

Wife of Newel K. Whitney, she had spiritual experiences before they joined the Church. In her home, many saw the Savior in the School of the Prophets. She supported her husband as he gave his all to the Church in Kirtland, and later in Missouri, Nauvoo, and Utah, until his death in 1850 in Salt Lake City.

—*HC,* 1:146; *Profile,* 76; Wayne J. Lewis, *Early Converts of the First 14 years of the Restoration*

Julia Ellis Hills Johnson

1783–1853—Baptized 1831 (convert #234)

She was a mother of fifteen children. Although her husband, Ezekiel, never joined the Church, most of her children joined the Church. Her sons Benjamin Franklin Johnson and Joel Hills Johnson were close friends with Joseph Smith. It is estimated that hers is the largest family in the Church today, with well over 100,000 members.

—Orva Jeanne Cluff, *Our Family Heritage,* 41; Linda J. Thayne, *My Soul Rejoiced,* 63; *My Life's Review,* 40; Wayne J. Lewis, *Early Converts of the First 14 years of the Restoration*

Rebecca Swain Williams

1798–1861—Baptized 1830 (convert #97)

She was the wife of President Frederick G. Williams, a close friend of the Prophet. She supported her husband through numerous trials in

Kirtland (including the Kirtland Safety Society failure) and Missouri, as he gave his all to the kingdom of God. After her husband's death, she influenced her children to go West with Brigham Young.

—*RJ*, 502; *EPB*, 44; *ELDS*; *Ensign*, April 2011, 38–41; Wayne J. Lewis, *Early Converts of the First 14 years of the Restoration*

Elizabeth Van Benthusen Gilbert

1800–1891—Baptized 1831 (convert #231)

She was the wife of Algernon Sidney Gilbert of the Gilbert and Whitney store. She followed her husband to Jackson County, Missouri, in 1831, where he set up a Church store. They were driven from Jackson County in 1833. Later, in 1834, Zion's Camp stayed at the Gilbert home in Clay County, Missouri, where her husband was exposed to cholera and died June 29, 1834. She remained faithful, went West with the Saints, and died in Utah. She was an aunt of Mary Elizabeth Rollins Lightner.

—*BA*, 9; *Profile*, 28; Wayne J. Lewis, *Early Converts of the First 14 years of the Restoration*

Vienna Jacques

1787–1884—Baptized 1831 (convert #273)

She walked from Portage, Ohio, to Kirtland at age forty-five to meet Joseph Smith, was baptized in 1831, and went to Missouri in 1833. She was a nurse. She gave all she had ($1,400 in savings) to the Church in 1833. She drove a wagon to Utah in 1847.

—D&C 90:28–32; HC, 1:331; *Mormon Land*, 125; D&C*WW*, 59; Wayne J. Lewis, *Early Converts of the First 14 years of the Restoration*

Laura Clark Phelps

1805–1842—Baptized 1831 (convert #223)

She was the wife of Morris Phelps. She assisted the Saints and her husband through six states for the gospel's sake. She hid the Prophet in their Far West, Missouri, home. While in Missouri, her husband was falsely charged and held in a Boone County jail. He courageously helped with the escape of her husband Morris, Parley Pratt, and King Follett in 1838 from the Boone County, Missouri, jail.

—*HC*, 4:150; *ELDS*; Phelps family records; Wayne J. Lewis, *Early Converts of the First 14 years of the Restoration*

Polly Peck Knight

1774–1831—Baptized 1830 (convert #42)

She was the wife of Joseph Knight. She was the matriarch of the great Knight family who embraced the Church in Coleville, New York, and which became a nucleus for the early Church. She and her husband provided food for Joseph and Emma Smith and Oliver Cowdery during the translation of the Book of Mormon. Her greatest desire was to set her foot in the newly revealed Zion of Missouri. She died just two weeks after arriving in Jackson County, Missouri, on July 6, 1831, and became the first Latter-day Saint to die in Missouri.

—*HC*, 1:296; *RJ*, 249; *EPB*, 214; Wayne J. Lewis, *Early Converts of the First 14 years of the Restoration* by Wayne J Lewis

Vilate Murray Kimball

1806–1867—Baptized 1832 (convert #425)

She was the wife of Heber C. Kimball. She was spiritually in tune and able to see a vision of an innumerable army of spirits on September 22, 1827, who marched to defend Joseph Smith when he received the gold plates from the angel Moroni. She somehow mustered the strength to support her husband on his epic mission to England in 1837, which helped to save the early infant Church through the trials and apostasy of the Kirtland and Missouri period of 1837–1839.

—*HC*, 1:296; *RJ*, 249; *EPB*, 214; Wayne J. Lewis, *Early Converts of the First 14 years of the Restoration*

Jane Elizabeth Manning James

1813–1908—Baptized 1840 (convert #4390)

She was a black convert who walked 1,000 miles to meet Joseph Smith, much of the trip with bare feet. She had eight children, of which all but two died before she did. She followed the Saints to Utah in 1847. Her daughter Mary Ann was the first black person born in Utah. Her husband left her in 1869. She stayed valiant to the gospel and was a very great and courageous woman.

—Wayne J. Lewis, *Early Converts of the First 14 years of the Restoration*; *RJ*, 31, 437; *GD*, 174; *Wikipedia*

Other great woman of the Restoration

- Bathsheba Wilson Bigler Smith, 1822–1910
- Julia Clapp Murdock, 1796–1831 (wife of John Murdock, 1792–1871)
- Emmeline Blanche Woodward Wells, 1828–1921
- Mercy Rachel Fielding Smith Thompson, 1807–1893
- Lydia Goldthwaite Bailey Knight, 1812–1884 (wife of Newel Knight, 1800–1847)
- Martha Jane Knowlton Coray, 1822–1881 (wife of Howard Coray)
- Clarissa Reed Hancock, 1790–1870 (wife of Levi Ward Hancock, 1803–1882)
- Delcena Diadamia Johnson Sherman, 1804–1854

- Zina Diantha Huntington, 1821–1901
- Presendia Lathrup Huntington, 1810–1892
- Eliza Maria Partridge, 1820–1885
- Helen Mar Kimball, 1828–1896
- Desdmona Catlin Wadsworth Fullmer, 1809–1886
- Emily Dow Partridge, 1824–1899
- Fanny Young, 1787–1859

—Wayne J. Lewis, *Early Converts of the First 14 years of the Restoration*

Note: Hundreds of great LDS women could be added to this list; this is not a complete listing of the heroines of the Restoration. But from the forty years of research the compiler has completed, these women stand out in their support to their husbands and early leaders of the Church.

Angelic Visitors

A comprehensive list of the 139 angels and gods who taught, tutored, restored keys to the young prophet—Joseph Smith, the most visionary prophet and seer who ever lived.

The following is a probable list. In some cases, there is only one source of reference to the vision that was being reported. Those source references noted by prophets and apostles are given more credence. In other cases, several individuals recorded that Joseph Smith had these angelic visitations and experiences. By making this list, it is intended that other scholars will help refine it.

Godhood Members

- Heavenly Father, Elohim—At least five times.
  - (1) First Vision in the spring of 1820—Joseph saw and heard His voice as recorded in Pearl of Great Price, Joseph Smith—History.
  - (2) June 3–6, 1831—Joseph saw Heavenly Father and the Savior.
  - (3) February 16, 1832—Joseph and Sidney Rigdon saw the Savior on the right hand of God (similar to Stephen in Acts 7:55–56).
  - (4–5) March 18, 1833—Joseph identified the presence of God and Christ in the School of the Prophets and again, later, when God and Christ walked through the back of the room at a meeting of the brethren in Kirtland, Ohio, in 1836.

—HC; John W. Welch, Opening the Heavens, 311–18

- The Savior Jesus Christ—recorded ten or more times.
  - (1) Spring of 1820—Joseph saw the Savior with Heavenly Father during the First Vision.
  - (2) June 3–6, 1831—Joseph saw Heavenly Father and the Savior.

(3) April, 1834—Joseph saw Heavenly Father and the Savior in Pontiac, Michigan.
(4) 1831—Joseph identified the Savior in a meeting of the Saints.
(5) February 16, 1832—Joseph and Sidney Rigdon saw the Son of Man on the right hand of God.
(6) March 18, 1833—Joseph identified the presence of God and Christ in the School of the Prophets.
(7) December 18, 1833—Joseph saw Jehovah appear to Adam.
(8) January 21, 1836—Joseph saw the celestial kingdom with Christ standing in the midst.
(9) March 30, 1836—Joseph saw Jesus Christ and other angels, including John the Beloved.
(10) April 3, 1836—Joseph and Oliver Cowdery saw Jesus Christ in the Kirtland Temple.

HC; John W. Welch, Opening the Heavens, 311–18*; Ronald Vern Jackson, The Seer,* 65

Angels—resurrected or translated beings

- Moroni—Celestial resurrected angel. Was Joseph's primary tutor. Visited Joseph Smith up to twenty–seven times. Dates of many of these times are know, as follows:
  (1–3) September 21–22, 1823—In the Smith log home in Farmington Township (later became Manchester township).
  (4) September 21–22, 1823—Next to the fence at the field near the Smith log home.
  (5) September 22, 1923—At Hill Cumorah.
  (6) September 1823—At Hill Cumorah again, to teach Joseph about good and evil.
  (7–11) September 1823–September 1827—Many visits.
  (12) September 22, 1824—At Hill Cumorah.
  (13) September 22, 1825—At Hill Cumorah.
  (14) September 22, 1826—At Hill Cumorah.
  (15) September 22, 1827—At Hill Cumorah; Joseph received the gold plates early, just after midnight, to avoid his enemies.
  (16) May–June 1828—At Harmony, Pennsylvania, in Joseph and Emma's log cabin; when the 116 pages were lost, Moroni picked up the gold plates and the Urim and Thummim.
  (17) Early July, 1828—At Harmony, Pennsylvania; Moroni returned the plates.
  (18) Late July 1828—Moroni took the plates.

(19) July 1828—At Manchester Township; Moroni returned the plates and Urim and Thummim.
(20) 1828—Moroni was seen walking on the road to the Whitmers' in Fayette Township by Joseph, Oliver Cowdery, and David Whitmer.
(21) 1829—Moroni took the plates.
(22) 1829—Moroni returned the plates.
(23–27) 1829–1830—Many visits to warn of impending danger to the plates and manuscript.

—Truman Madsen Tapes; *A Chronology of Joseph Smith,* BYU Studies

- John the Baptist—Celestial resurrected personage—Aaronic Priesthood restoration.

—D&C 13

- Apostle Peter—Celestial resurrected personage—Was seen more than once; at Missouri and the Kirtland Temple dedication.

—Hyrum L. Andrus, Joseph Smith, the Man and the Seer, 81, 86

- Apostle James—Celestial resurrected angel—Was seen at Kirtland Temple dedication.

—Hyrum L. Andrus, Joseph Smith, the Man and the Seer, 86

- Apostle John the Beloved, or Revelator—Translated angel—Melchizedek Priesthood restoration; at Kirtland Temple dedication.

—Joseph Smith, the Man and the Seer by Hyrum L. Andrus, 86

- Apostle Paul—Celestial resurrected angel.

—Joseph Fielding Smith, Teachings of the Prophet Joseph Smith, 180; *Teachings of Joseph Smith,* 2008–09, 493

- Adam, or Michael—Celestial resurrected god—Several times.

—HC, 2:380; D&C 128:21; *JD* 9

- Seth—Celestial resurrected angel.

—JD 21:94; Hyrum L. Andrus, *Joseph Smith, the Man and the Seer,* 81

- Abraham—Celestial resurrected god.

—HC, 2:380; D&C 27:10; *JD* 21:94

- Isaac—Celestial resurrected god.

—JD 21:94; Hyrum L. Andrus, *Joseph Smith, the Man and the Seer,* 81

- Jacob, or Israel—Celestial resurrected god.

—JD 21:94; Hyrum L. Andrus, *Joseph Smith, the Man and the Seer*

- Elijah—Translated angel or resurrected personage.

—D&C 110

- Elias—Celestial resurrected personage.

—D&C 110

- Moses—Translated angel or resurrected personage.

—D&C 110:11

- Enoch—Translated angel.

—*JD* 21:94; Hyrum L. Andrus, *Joseph Smith, the Man and the Seer*, 81

- Alma—Translated angel.

—*JD* 27:374; *JD* 13:47; Hyrum L. Andrus, *Joseph Smith, the Man and the Seer*

- The Three Nephites—Translated angels—More than once.

—*HC; JD*

- Alma the Younger

—*JD* 27:374; *JD* 13:47; Hyrum L. Andrus, *Joseph Smith, the Man and the Seer*

- Mormon

—*JD* 27:374; *JD* 17:374; Hyrum L. Andrus, *Joseph Smith, the Man and the Seer*

- Twelve Ancient Apostles of the Savior—Peter, James, John (listed previously), Andrew, Matthew, Philip, Bartholomew, Thomas, James, Simon, Judas the brother of James (not Iscariot), and perhaps Matthias (who replaced Judas Iscariot).

—*Matthew* and *Acts*

- Twelve Nephite Apostles—Nephi, Timothy, Jonas, Mathoni, Mathonihah, Kumen, Zedekiah, Kumenonhi, Jeremiah, Jonas, Shemnon, and Isaiah.

—*3 Nephi* 19:4

- Raphael

—D&C 128

- Noah

—D&C 128:21; *JD* 21:94; Hyrum L. Andrus, *Joseph Smith, the Man and the Seer*

- Cainan

—*HC*, 3:338; D&C 107:53–57

- Abel

—*HC*, 3:388; *JD* 18:325

- Enos

—*HC*, 3:388; *JD* 21:94

- Jared (of the Bible)

—*HC*, 3:388; D&C 107:53–57

- Joseph of Egypt

—D&C 27:10; Brian L. Smith, *Joseph Smith and the Doctrinal Restoration: The Annual Sidney B. Sperry Symposium,* 344

- Lamech

—*JD* 18:325

- Lehi

—*JD* 16:265–266; Brian L. Smith, *Joseph Smith and the Doctrinal Restoration: The Annual Sidney B. Sperry Symposium,* 343

- Mahalaleel

—*JD* 18:325; *HC*, 3:388

- Methuselah

—*JD* 18:325; *HC*, 3:388

- Zelph the white Lamanite

—*HC*, 2:79; *Times and Seasons,* 6:788

- Eve

—*RJ*, 187

- Unidentified Angel—A heavenly messenger who appeared to Joseph in August 1830 while he was on his way to get wine for the sacrament.

—D&C 27

- Prophet leaders of each Dispensation

—D&C 128

- Nephi and others

—*JD* 27:94, 17:374; Hyrum L. Andrus, *Joseph Smith, the Man and the Seer*, 81

- An additional forty-nine angels—Came to Joseph, according to Ronald Vern Jackson. Included in the Jackson list are:
  - Jacob (son of Lehi)
  - King Benjamin
  - Alma the Elder
  - Captain Moroni
  - Jarom
  - Mosiah
  - Helaman
  - Nephi

- Samuel the Lamanite
- Melchizedek
- Mahonri Moriancumer
- Zenock
- Joshua
- David
- Solomon
- Jeremiah
- Daniel
- Joel
- Obadiah
- Micah
- Zechariah
- Zephaniah
- Nahum
- Manasseh
- Benjamin
- Gad
- Judah
- Rueben
- Zebulon
- Abinadi
- Jared
- Zenos
- Isaiah
- Samuel
- Saul
- Job
- Ezekiel
- Hosea
- Amos
- Jonah
- Malachi
- Haggai
- Habakkuk
- Ephraim
- Asher
- Dan
- Issachar
- Naphtali
- Simeon

—*Ronald V. Jackson, The Seer*, 95–96, 165–66. LDS writer Ronald Vern Jackson names another fifty-eight angels of the Old Testament, New Testament, and Book of Mormon. Although the names are given by this writer, there are no specific references or documentation of how this is known. Therefore, it is with reservation that this list is included.

Groups of Angels

- Unidentified angels

  —D&C 128:21; *Life of Heber C. Kimball; Temples of the Most High*

- Many angels—1823–1827

  —*JD* 25:185; Hyrum L. Andrus, *Joseph Smith, the Man and the Seer*, 81

- Angels—January 28, 1836—In the unfinished Kirtland Temple.

  —*HC*, 2:428

- Multitude of angels—March 27, 1836—In the Kirtland Temple during the dedication. They were seen by Joseph and hundreds of other Saints.

  —*HC*, 2:428

- Angels—March 30, 1836—Administered to Joseph and others in the Kirtland Temple.

  —*HC*, 2:381

- Thousands of Nephites, Lamanites, and Jaredites

—*History of the Prophet Joseph Smith by His Mother Lucy Mack Smith,* 82–83; *Hyrum L. Andrus, Joseph Smith, the Man and the Seer,* 80

First evidence of a resurrected being besides Jesus

Moroni's appearance to Joseph was the first appearance of a resurrected being other than the Savior.

—Mark L. McConkie tapes

John the Revelator

Allen Stout was walking with Joseph on the west side of the Mississippi River. They saw a man walking along the road, and Joseph told Allen to remain where he was while he stepped over to speak with this pedestrian. Finally, "the Prophet [came back and] said, 'We must return immediately to Nauvoo." . . . [Allen began to weep and] confessed, 'I am an insufficient bodyguard—criminally neglectful of your welfare. I allowed that man you met to speak with you without even being ready to defend if he attacked you. He could have killed you. . . . [Y]our life is too precious to be trusted to my care.'

"The Prophet then said, 'That man would not harm me. You saw John the Revelator.' "

—*RJ,* 210–11

Saw angels constantly

"[Joseph] was visited constantly by angels," said George Q. Cannon.

—Hyrum L. Andrus, *Joseph Smith: The Man and the Seer,* 80

Other angels Joseph saw

- Joseph saw Cainan.

—HC, 3: 388; D&C 107:53–57

- At the dedication of the Kirtland Temple, Elias appeared to Joseph and Oliver.

—D&C 110

- At the dedication of the Kirtland Temple, Elijah appeared to Joseph and Oliver.

—D&C 110

- "[Joseph] communicated with Enoch."

—John Taylor, *JD,* 21:94; D&C 107:53–57

- Joseph saw Enos.

—*JD,* 21:94; *HC,* 3:388; D&C 107:53–57

- Joseph, with Oliver Cowdery and Zebedee Coltrin, saw Adam and Eve in a vision.

—*RJ*, 187

- Joseph communicated with Isaac.

—D&C 27:10; John Taylor, *JD*, 21:94; Brian L. Smith, ed., *Joseph Smith and the Doctrinal Restoration: The 34th Annual Sidney B. Sperry Symposium*, 343

- Joseph communicated with Jacob.

—D&C 27:10; John Taylor, *JD*, 21:94: Brian L. Smith, ed., *Joseph Smith and the Doctrinal Restoration: The 34th Annual Sidney B. Sperry Symposium*, 343

- Saw Jared of the Bible.

—*HC*, 3:388; D&C 107:53–57

- Saw John and Peter at Kirtland Temple dedication. Heber C. Kimball declared that there were twenty witnesses that "John stood in their midst" while Peter was "in the stand."

—Hyrum L. Andrus, *Joseph Smith: The Man and the Seer*, 86

- Saw John the Baptist. John the Baptist restored the Aaronic Priesthood on May 15, 1829.

—D&C 13

- Joseph of Egypt appeared to Joseph Smith.

—D&C 27:10; Brian L. Smith, ed., *Joseph Smith and the Doctrinal Restoration: The 34th Annual Sidney B. Sperry Symposium*, 344

- Joseph saw Lamech.

—*JD*, 18:325; Brian L. Smith, ed., *Joseph Smith and the Doctrinal Restoration: The 34th Annual Sidney B. Sperry Symposium*, 343

- Lehi appeared to Joseph Smith and ministered to him.

—*JD*, 16:265–66; Brian L. Smith, ed., *Joseph Smith and the Doctrinal Restoration: The 34th Annual Sidney B. Sperry Symposium*, 343

- Joseph Smith saw Mahalaleel.

—*JD*, 18:325; *HC*, 3:388; D&C 107:53–57

- "During those four years [1823–1827] he [Joseph] was often ministered to by the angels of God, and received instructions."

—Orson Pratt, *JD*, 25:185; Hyrum L. Andrus, *Joseph Smith: The Man and the Seer*, 81

- Joseph Smith saw Methuselah.

—*JD*, 18:325; *HC*, 3:388; D&C 107:53–57

- John Taylor stated that "when Joseph Smith was raised up as a

Prophet of God, Mormon, Moroni, Nephi, and others . . . came to him and communicated certain principles pertaining to the gospel."

—*JD*, 27:374; Hyrum L. Andrus, *Joseph Smith: The Man and the Seer*, 81; *JD*, 17:374

- Joseph saw Moroni at least twenty-one times.

—Truman Madsen tapes

- Joseph saw Moses. Moses appeared in the Kirtland Temple dedication and restored the keys of the gathering.

—D&C 110:11

- Joseph saw Nephi and others. After the appearance of Moroni, "then came Nephi," said John Taylor.

—*JD*, 27:374; Hyrum L. Andrus, *Joseph Smith: The Man and the Seer*, 81; *JD*, 17:374

- Joseph communicated with the Twelve Nephite apostles (including the Three Nephites).

—John Taylor, *JD*, 21:94; Brian L. Smith, ed., *Joseph Smith and the Doctrinal Restoration: The 34th Annual Sidney B. Sperry Symposium*, 343

- Joseph communicated with Noah.

—John Taylor, *JD*, 21:94; D&C 128:21

- Joseph saw and could describe Paul in detail.

—Joseph Fielding Smith, *Teachings of the Prophet Joseph Smith*, 180; *Teachings of the Prophet Joseph Smith, manual, 2008–2009*, 493

- "Later, when the Prophet was in Missouri, he reportedly stated that he had 'a conversation a few days ago' with the Apostle Peter," said Heber C. Kimball.

Note: This seems to be before 1836 and may have been during Zion's Camp.

—Hyrum L. Andrus, *Joseph Smith: The Man and the Seer*, 86; Compiler's note

- Joseph saw Peter, James, and John. Peter, James, and John appeared to and ordained Joseph and Oliver, restored the Melchizedek Priesthood, and ordained the two apostles in 1829.

—D&C 27:12

- Joseph communicated with Seth.

—John Taylor, *JD*, 21:94; D&C 107:53–57; HC, 3:388; Brian L. Smith, ed., *Joseph Smith and the Doctrinal Restoration: The 34th Annual Sidney B. Sperry Symposium*, 343

Saw unidentified angels

- Angels administered to Joseph and the Twelve on January 22, 1836.
- Joseph saw angels in the Kirtland Temple.
- Joseph saw an angel three times with a drawn sword commanding plural marriage.
- Joseph saw various angels.
- Angels were present for dedication of the Kirtland Temple.

—D&C 27, 128:21; *Life of Heber C. Kimball; Temples of the Most High*

Saw Heavenly Father

- First Vision, Spring of 1820; Joseph saw and heard the voice of Heavenly Father.
- June 3–6, 1831; Joseph saw Heavenly Father and the Savior.
- February 16, 1832; Joseph and Sidney Rigdon saw the Savior on the right hand of God (similar to Stephen in Acts 7:55–56).
- March 18, 1833; Joseph identified the presence of God and Christ in the School of the Prophets.

—*Opening the Heavens* by John W. Welch, pp. 311–318

Saw his brother Alvin (in the future)

In a vision of the celestial kingdom (in the future), Joseph relates, "I saw. . . my brother Alvin, that had long since slept."

—*HC*, 2:380

Saw his father and mother (in the future)

In a vision of the celestial kingdom (in the future), Joseph relates, "I saw. . . my father and mother." (They were currently living.)

—*HC*, 2:380

Saw Jesus Christ

- Spring 1820; Joseph saw the Savior with God the Father.
- June 3–6, 1831; Joseph saw Heavenly Father and the Savior.
- 1831; Joseph identified the Savior in a meeting of the Saints.
- February 16, 1832; Joseph and Sidney Rigdon saw the Son of Man on the right hand of God.
- March 18, 1833; Joseph identified the presence of God and Christ in the School of the Prophets.
- December 18, 1833; Joseph saw Jehovah appear to Adam.
- January 21, 1836; Joseph saw the celestial kingdom with Christ standing in the midst.

- March 30, 1836; Joseph saw Jesus Christ and angels, including John the Beloved.
- April 3, 1836; Joseph and Oliver Cowdery saw Jesus Christ in the Kirtland Temple.

—John W. Welch, *Opening the Heavens*, 311–18

Saw Zelph the white Lamanite

While on a Zion's Camp march in 1835, Joseph saw Zelph the white Lamanite in a vision and described him in detail to the members of Zion's Camp.

—*Times and Seasons*, 6:788; HC, 2:79–80

Marrow of bones would melt

Joseph with several of the brethren at the School of the Prophets in the upper room of the Newel K. Whitney store simultaneously saw the Father and the Son. "Zebedee Coltrin recalled that when the Father appeared he felt as though the marrow in his bones would melt."

—Matthew B. Brown, *Joseph Smith: the Man, the Mission, the Message*, 74–76

Nephite Angels

Emma Smith said, "Nephite angels were there at the Restoration."

—Mark L. McConkie tapes

Singing with angels

"The heavens were opened and angels ministered unto us. . . . [They] mingled their voices with ours, while their presence was in our midst," said Joseph Smith.

—John W. Welch, *Opening the Heavens*, 286

The Three Nephites

Heber C. Kimball reported the appearance of one of the Three Nephites near the Hill Cumorah. He also reported to have seen them when the Saints were making a defense of Far West.

—James Byrd and Oliver Huntington, *Joseph Smith: The Man and the Seer*, Hyrum L. Andrus, 95

"Others who administered to Joseph Smith were the three Nephites. Heber C. Kimball reported the appearance of one of them to the Prophet in the early days of the Church, near the Hill Cumorah. . . . The Prophet is also reported to have seen the three Nephites when the Saints were making a defense of Far West."

—Hyrum L. Andrus, *Joseph Smith, the Man and the Seer*, 95

Moroni

Angel Moroni's first visit was on a Sunday, September 21, 1823. Imagine what type of a spiritual day Joseph and the Smith family must have had.

—Compiler's note

David Whitmer relates that while traveling with Joseph and Oliver, "traveling along in a clear open place, a very pleasant, nice looking old man suddenly appeared by the side of our wagon and saluted us with, 'Good morning, it is very warm,' at the same time wiping his face or forehead with his hand. We returned the salutation, and by a sign from Joseph, I invited him to ride if he was going our way. But he said very pleasantly, 'No, I am going to Cumorah.'" This was the first time David had heard the word *Cumorah* and did not know what it meant. The old man instantly disappeared. Joseph explained to them that this man was a Nephite prophet (presumably Moroni).

—Susan Easton Black and Andrew C. Skinner, *Joseph Smith: Exploring the Life and Ministry of the Prophet*, 74 (H. Dean Garrett)

When Joseph and Emma borrowed a horse and wagon to go get the plates on September 22, 1827, Joseph took the one lamp to the top of the hill to meet the angel Moroni. Emma was left at the bottom of the hill in the dark. It turned out that Joseph was able to see the plates from the "glow" of the angel Moroni.

—Richard E. Turley Jr. and Lael Littke, *Stories From the Life of Joseph Smith*, 42

Adam and Eve: Joseph Helped Others to See

Oliver Cowdery, Zebedee Coltrin, and Joseph Smith walked to a place with beautiful grass. Joseph Smith then said, "Let us pray."

All three prayed in turn—Joseph, Oliver, and Zebedee. Brother Joseph said, "Now brethren, we will see some visions."

"Joseph lay down on the ground on his back and stretched out his arms, and we laid on them. The Heavens gradually opened, and we saw a golden throne, on a circular foundation, and on the throne sat a man and a woman, having white hair and clothed in white garments. Their heads were white as snow, and their faces shone with immortal youth. They were the two most beautiful and perfect specimens of mankind I ever saw," said Zebedee. Joseph said, "They are our first parents, Adam and Eve."

"Adam was a large broad shouldered man, and Eve, as a woman, was as large in proportion."

—Zebedee Coltrin, *They Knew the Prophet,* by Hyrum L. Andrus, 31–32

Other Visions that Joseph Smith saw

- Satan and his numerous followers

  —*Messenger and Advocate,* October 1835; *JD* 3:229–30; *JSH* 1:15–16; Hyrum L. Andrus, *Joseph Smith, the Man and the Seer,* 74, 81

- The Book of Mormon people and events

  —*History of the Prophet Joseph Smith by His Mother Lucy Mack Smith,* 82–83; Hyrum L. Andrus, *Joseph Smith, the Man and the Seer,* 94

- Adam admitting the faithful into the celestial kingdom

  —*JD* 9; Hyrum L. Andrus, *Joseph Smith, the Man and the Seer,* 72

- Celestial kingdom—Joseph first saw this in the attic of the printing office on January 21, 1836. It was received again on February 16, 1836, when he and Sidney Rigdon had six visions of the kingdoms that await all mankind, which was written as section 76 of the Doctrine and Covenants.

—D&C 76

- The gates of the celestial kingdom

—*HC*, 2:380

- Alvin Smith and Don Carlos (Joseph's brothers) after their deaths.

—*HC*, 2:380

- Father Joseph Smith Sr. and mother Lucy Mack Smith in the celestial kingdom
- Adam and Eve on their thrones—With Oliver Cowdery and Zebedee Coltrin.

—*Hyrum L. Andrus, They Knew the Prophet*, 30–32

- Heavens—April 3, 1836—Dedication of the Kirtland Temple.

—*HC*, 2

- Thousands of angels—October 1838—defended the Saints at Far West when thousands of General Clark's army (mob) approached. Joseph Smith told Brother James Bird that the Three Nephites were there as well, and they were armed and ready.

—*HC*, 3

Voices that Joseph Smith heard

Joseph told various brethren that he knew the voices of most of those angels who visited him so well that he knew who was visiting him before he saw them. An example of this is, "He [Joseph] told me that the voices of the angels became so familiar that he knew their names before he saw them."

—Joseph B. Noble, *RJ*, 195

Other Things that Joseph Smith saw

- A cave in the Hill Cumorah—Joseph went inside this room or cave on numerous occasions and took with him Oliver Cowdery, Hyrum Smith, and Don Carlos Smith.

—*Joseph Fielding Smith, Documentary History of the Doctrine and Covenants*, 54

- Brass plates

—*History of Joseph Smith by His Mother, Lucy Mack Smith*, 127

Armies of spirits seen by Joseph Smith and others

When Joseph Smith received the gold plates on September 22, 1827, evil spirits were seen attempting to stop the coming forth of the Book of Mormon:

"While thus he stood gazing and admiring, [Moroni] said, 'Look!' and as he thus spake [Joseph] beheld the prince of darkness, surrounded by his innumerable train of associates. . . . [Moroni] said, 'All this is shown, the good and the evil, the holy and the impure, the glory of God, the power of darkness, that ye may know hereafter the two powers and never be influenced or overcome by that wicked one.' "

—*Messenger and Advocate*, October 1835; Hyrum L. Andrus, *Joseph Smith: The Man and the Seer*, 4; *JST* 1:15–16; *JD* 3:229–30

A army of righteous spirits fought to defend Joseph Smith while he received the gold plates on September 22, 1827.

Vilate M. Kimball records, "On the night of the 22nd of September, 1827, while living in the town of Menden (Ohio), after we retired to bed, John Greene, who was then a traveling Reformed Methodist preacher, living within one hundred steps of our house, came and called my husband to come out and see the sight in the heavens. Heber awoke me, and Sister Fannie Young (sister of Brigham) who was living with us, and we all went out-of-doors.

It was one of the most beautiful starlit nights so clear we could see to pick up a pin. We looked to the eastern horizon, and beheld a white smoke arise towards the heavens. As it ascended, it formed into a belt, and made a noise like the rushing wind, and continued southwest, forming a regular bow, dipping in the western horizon.

After the bow had formed, it began to widen out, growing transparent, of a bluish cast. It grew wide enough to contain twelve men abreast. In this bow an army moved, commencing from the east and marching to the west. They continued moving until they reached the western horizon. They moved in platoons, and walked so close the rear ranks trod in the steps of their file leaders, until the whole bow was literally crowded with soldiers.

We could distinctly see the muskets, bayonets, and knapsacks of the men, who wore caps and feathers like those used by the American soldiers in the last war with Great Britain. We also saw their officers with their swords and equipage and heard the clashing and jingling of their instruments of war, and could discern the form and features of the men. The most profound order existed throughout the entire army. When the foremost man stepped, every man stepped at the same time. We could hear their steps.

When the front rank reached the western horizon, a battle ensued, as we could hear the report of the arms, and the rush.

None can judge of our feelings as we beheld this army of spirits as plainly as ever armies of men were seen in the flesh. Every hair of our heads seemed alive.

We gazed upon this scenery for hours, until it began to disappear.

After we became acquainted with Mormonism, we learned that this took place the same evening that Joseph Smith received the records of the Book of Mormon from the Angel Moroni, who had held those records in his possession. . . .

The next night a similar scene was beheld in the west, by the neighbors, representing armies of men engaged in battle."

Note: When Joseph got the plates, Moroni said to him, "Look," and he beheld that Satan and all of his angels were very upset to see the Book of Mormon come forth, and a spiritual army protected Joseph Smith and the plates.

—Vilate M. Kimball, *RJ*, 249

Bible proceedings viewed

Joseph said, "After I got through translating the Book of Mormon, I took up the Bible to read with the Urim and Thummim. I read the first chapter of Genesis and I saw the things as they were done. I turned over the next and the next, and the whole passed before me like a grand panorama; and so on chapter after chapter until I read the whole of it. I saw it all!"

—Lorenzo Brown, *RJ*, 210

Described the Nephites

"Sometimes Joseph would describe the appearance of the Nephites, their mode of dress and warfare, their implements of husbandry, etc., and many things he had seen in vision."

—Wandle Mace, *They Knew the Prophet,* Hyrum L. Andrus, 131

The devil

When Joseph received the gold plates, Moroni said to Joseph, "Look!" Joseph looked and saw the prince of darkness and all his host who were angry that the Book of Mormon would be coming forth.

—John W. Welch, *Opening the Heavens,* John W. Welch, 278

Heber C. Kimball relates that shortly after the Prophet moved into his home in Far West, Missouri (between March–October 1838), after an administration to one of his children, "[Joseph Smith] had an open vision, and saw the devil in person, who contended with Joseph, face to face, for some time. [The devil] said it was his house, it belonged to him, and Joseph had no right there. Then Joseph rebuked Satan in the name of the Lord, and he departed."

—John W. Welch, *Opening the Heavens*, 88, 315

"He said the devil contended with him face to face."

—Helen Mar Kimball Whitney, *They Knew the Prophet*, Hyrum L. Andrus, 198

Calvin W. Moore said, "One time in the Kirtland Temple, at a fast meeting, Charles Hyde got up to talk, and the devil took hold of him and stopped him. Joseph laid his hands on him and rebuked the evil one, and Brother Hyde went on talking."

—Calvin W. Moore, *They Knew the Prophet,* Hyrum L. Andrus, 89

Another time, "The devil . . . bound Harvey Whitlock and John Murdock so they could not speak. Joseph cast the devil out of these brethren."

—Whitlock and Murdock, *Sacred Places: Ohio and Illinois,* Lamar C. Berrett, 19–20

Joseph's Last Dream

"Joseph related to me . . . the following dream:

'While I was at Jordan's in Iowa the other night I dreamed that myself and my brother Hyrum went on board a large steamboat lying in a small bay near the great ocean. Shortly after we went on board there was an alarm of fire, and I discovered that the boat had been anchored some distance from the shore out in the bay, and that an escape from the fire in the confusion appeared hazardous. But as delay was folly, I and Hyrum jumped overboard and tried our faith at walking upon the water. At first we sank in the water nearly to our knees, but as we proceeded we increased in faith and were soon able to walk upon the water.

'Looking towards the burning boat in the east, we saw that it was drifting towards the wharf and the town with a great flame and clouds of smoke, and as if by whirlwind the town was taking fire too, so that the scene of destruction and horrors of the frightened inhabitants was terrible. We proceeded on the bosom of the mighty deep and were soon out of sight of land. The ocean was still, the rays of the sun were bright, and we forgot all the troubles of our Mother Earth.

'Just at that moment I heard the sound of a human voice, and turning round saw my brother Samuel H. approaching towards us from the east. We stopped and he came up. After a moment's conversation he informed me that he had been lonesome and had made up his mind to go with me across the mighty deep.

'We all started again and in a short time were blessed with the first sight of a city, whose silver steeples and towers were more beautiful than any I had ever seen or heard of on earth. It stood, as it were, upon the western shore of the mighty deep we [were] walking on, and its order and glory seemed far beyond the wisdom of man. While we were gazing upon the perfection of the city, a small boat launched off from the port and almost as quick as thought came to us. In an instant they took us on board and saluted, with welcome and with music, such as is not of earth.

'The next scene on landing was more than I can describe. The greetings and the music from a thousand towers, and the light of God himself at the return of these three of his sons, soothed my soul into [such] quiet and joy that I felt as if I were truly in Heaven. I gazed upon the splendor. I greeted my friends.

'I awoke, and lo, it was a dream.'

"I will say that Joseph never told this dream again, as he was martyred about two days after."

—William W. Phelps, *RJ*, 390–91

First Vision

"The First Vision is the single most important thing that happened in the world since the Resurrection of Christ."

"It hallowed young Joseph."

—Truman G. Madsen tapes

Heavenly visions

On March 30, 1836, Harrison Burgess stated that in a meeting with about a hundred priesthood members, "I beheld the room lightened up with a peculiar light. . . . It was soft and clear and the room looked to me as though it had neither roof nor floor. . . . I beheld the Prophet Joseph and Hyrum Smith and Roger Orton enveloped in the light: Joseph exclaimed aloud, 'I behold the Savior, the Son of God.' Hyrum said, 'I behold the angels of heaven.' Brother Orton exclaimed, 'I behold the chariots of Israel.' . . . [T]he remembrance . . . will remain with me while I live upon the earth."

—Harrison Burgess, *Opening the Heavens,* John W. Welch, 284

"On January 21, 1836, Joseph Smith was more in heaven than on earth. That day he received at least two, and possibly three, visions of different events. In one of these visions, he saw 'the blazing throne of God, whereon was seated the Father and the Son.' "

—John W. Welch, *Opening the Heavens,* John W. Welch, 282–83

"I saw the transcendent beauty of the gate through which the heirs of that kingdom will enter."

—Joseph Smith, *HC,* 2:380

"I saw the beautiful streets of that kingdom, which had the appearance of being paved with gold."

—Joseph Smith, *HC,* 2:380

Independence, Missouri—New Jerusalem

Joseph was "shown in vision where the temple at Independence and the city of Zion would be located." A master plan of the city of Zion was laid out on 64 acres with 24 temples on two 15–acre parcels.

—*HC,* 1:188; *A Chronology of the Life of Joseph Smith,* BYU Studies, 29; LaMar C. Barrett, *Sacred Places: Missouri,* 22–23

Last days will be intense

"[Joseph] saw that the Spirit of God should be withdrawn from the inhabitants of the earth, in consequence of which there should be blood upon the face of the whole earth, except among the people of the Most High. The Prophet gazed upon the scene his vision represented, until his heart sickened and he besought the Lord to close it up again."

—*JD,* 2:146–47; Hyrum L. Andrus, *Joseph Smith the Man and the Seer,* 120

Martyrs of old seen

Edward Stevenson remembered Joseph looking at the *Book of the Martyrs*. In doing so, Joseph said many of those who suffered death at the fiery stake were honest, true Christians according to the light they possessed. He requested to have the loan of this book. He returned it at Far West, Missouri. Joseph said at that time, "I have seen those martyrs by aid of the Urim and Thummim; God has a salvation for them."

—*RJ,* 112

Other members had visions and were witnesses

James Henry Rollins had a vision where he saw Joseph and Hyrum in December 1830.

—*RJ,* 220

Sanford Porter Sr. had a vision in 1816 and was told that the true

Church was not on the earth but would be and he would partake of it.

—Sanford Porter family papers; Joseph Grant Stevenson, *Porter Family History*, 87–88

Resurrection seen

Wilford Woodruff said that Joseph saw in vision the resurrection of the dead. (Before April 16, 1843.)

—John W. Welch, *Opening the Heavens*, 316

Satan and all his hosts beheld by Joseph Smith

"While thus he stood gazing and admiring, the angel [Moroni] said, 'Look!' and as he thus spake he beheld the prince of darkness surrounded by his innumerable train of associates. . . . [Moroni] said, 'All this is shown, the good and the evil, the holy and the impure, the glory of God, the power of darkness, that ye may know hereafter the two powers and never be influenced or overcome by that wicked one.' "

—*Messenger and Advocate*, October 1835; Hyrum L. Andrus, *Joseph Smith: The Man and the Seer*, 74; *JST*, 1:15–16; *JD*, 3:229–30

Seventh Heaven

"[Joseph] said, 'John the Revelator was caught up to the third heaven, but I know one who was caught up to the seventh heaven and saw and heard things not lawful for me to utter.' "

—Mary Elizabeth Rollins Lightner, *They Knew the Prophet*, Hyrum L. Andrus, 27

Shared visitations

Joseph Smith shared many visions with others. He and Oliver Cowdery shared in the Aaronic and Melchizedek Priesthood restoration with John the Baptist and Peter, James, and John. He shared the angel Moroni visitation with the three witnesses. He shared the vision of the Savior with Frederick G. Williams, Sidney Rigdon, and others. The vision of Christ, Moses, Elijah, and Elias occurred at the dedication of the Kirtland Temple and was shared with the attending company. He shared the vision of Adam and Eve with Oliver Cowdery and Zebedee Coltrin. In the School of the Prophets in the Newel K. Whitney store, several men, along with Joseph, simultaneously saw the Father and the Son.

—Matthew B. Brown, *Joseph Smith: The Man, The Mission, The Message*, 74–76

Cloud of glory

Newel K. and Elizabeth Whitney had a vision of a cloud of glory resting upon their house just before they met the Prophet in 1831. Later in the upstairs of this same house in the School of the Prophets, the Savior was seen by ten of the brethren, and Heavenly Father was seen four times.

—Hyrum L. Andrus, *They Knew the Prophet*, 44–45

Thousands of visions

Just one vision like some of the other famous prophets had would have made Joseph Smith great forever; yet he had thousands of these flashes of intelligence and light.

—Compiler's note

Three degrees of glory

The vision of the three degrees of glory was, in reality, a series of visions. Joseph and Sidney saw six different visions over a 2½-hour period in Hiram, Ohio, and were commanded four different times during these visions to "write it down." Other brethren were with them in the room. One of these, Philo Dibble, reported that he "saw the glory and felt the power, but did not see the vision."

—Hyrum L. Andrus, *Joseph Smith, the Man and the Seer*, 107

Saw martyrs

"He requested to have [me] loan [him] the book [I had] of 'the Martyrs.' . . . [H]e returned it at Far West, Missouri, remarking as he did so, 'I have seen those Martyrs by aid of the Urim and Thummim; God has a salvation for them.' "

—Edward Stephenson, *RJ*, 112

Vision defined

Joseph told Martha Thomas, "When a true spirit makes known anything to you, in the daytime, we call it a vision. If it is a true spirit it will never leave you, every particular will be as plain fifty years hence as now."

—*RJ*, 192

Vision of a resurrection

Joseph said, "I actually saw men, before they had ascended from the tomb, as though they were getting up slowly. They took each other by the hand and said to each other, "My father, my son, my mother, my daughter, my brother, my sister."

—Lorenzo D. Barnes, *Opening the Heavens*, John W. Welch, 293

Vision of Adam several times

A sister had a vision of an angel. Joseph told her it was Michael the Archangel and it was a true vision, for he had seen the same angel several times.

—Daniel Tyler, *They Knew the Prophet*, Hyrum L. Andrus, 56

Vision of celestial kingdom

On January 21, 1836, while in the Kirtland Temple with the First Presidency, Joseph saw the Father and the Son in the celestial kingdom. The account of this experience was recorded in section 137 of the *Doctrine and Covenants.*

—John W. Welch, ed., *A Chronology of the Life of Joseph Smith,* BYU Studies, 80

Vision of God

"Visions of God attended Joseph Smith from the night of [January] 22 [1836,] until the early morning of the 23rd.

—John W. Welch, ed., *A Chronology of the Life of Joseph Smith,* BYU Studies, 81

Vision of Missouri in high state of cultivation

Said Nathan Tanner during Zion's Camp in 1834, in Missouri, "I had the pleasure of seeing [Joseph Smith, while he was having] a vision, when he saw the country over which we were traveling in a high state of cultivation. He told us what he had seen while in the Spirit. It was glorious and grand to hear."

—John W. Welch, *Opening the Heavens,* 290–91

Vision of Zion shown

"By Heavenly Vision Joseph Smith was commanded to travel to western Missouri and there designate the location of a temple and central gathering place of Zion." (June 1831)

"Joseph Smith and others were shown where the Temple at Independence and the City of Zion would be located." (July 1831)

—John W. Welch, *Opening the Heavens,* 311–12

Visions by the thousands were seen by Joseph

The Prophet had a gift that he would see a vision of events that had happened, were happening, or would yet happen. One example was when Israel Barlow delivered a message to Joseph Smith, who was in hiding. Upon leaving, he was told to " 'listen to the direction of the Spirit.' While riding on his horse, a voice said to [him], 'Ride faster,' and later, 'Ride for your life,' and 'Turn to the right.' In this manner the Spirit guided him and preserved him from a mob lying in wait. Later, when he began to tell the Prophet of his experience, the Prophet stopped him and stated, 'I saw it all; you have no need to tell me.' "

—Israel Barlow, "Ride Faster," *Church News,* October 17, 2009, 16

Visons greater than any other prophet

The visions that Joseph Smith received were greater in number and scope than those received by Isaiah, John the Revelator, Paul, Moses, or Abraham.

—Compiler's note

Visions of Adam

Father Adam was one of Joseph Smith's most frequent heavenly visitors. Joseph saw Adam in at least three instances in the 1830s. First, Adam helped him detect Satan as an angel of light (1820–1830). Second, he saw Adam give all his posterity a blessing three years before his (Adam's) death. Third, he saw Adam and Eve in a vision with Oliver Cowdery and Zebedee Coltrin.

—John W. Welch, *Opening the Heavens*, 285

Visions of the Savior

Joseph saw Jesus Christ at least five times.

—Truman G. Madsen tapes

Visions trained his mind

This line upon line tutoring, from the First Vision, to the seer stone, to the Urim and Thummim and Moroni's teaching, trained Joseph's mind until he became the most visionary mortal man to ever grace planet earth, except for the Savior.

—Compiler's note

Visions versus presence of heavenly being

Joseph saw God and Christ in 1820. They were present. Stephen in the New Testament (Acts 7:55–56) had a vision of God and Christ in Heaven. There is a difference.

—Compiler's note

Westward trek motivated by Joseph Smith

Joseph's life and teachings motivated the Saints to have the strength to cross the great distance to the great Salt Lake Valley. Even though over 4,000 died in this great westward trek, over 80,000 made the journey. When Joseph viewed the vision of the Saints going to the Rocky Mountains, he said, "Oh the death and apostasy that awaits the Saints."

—Calvin R. Stephens, BYU Education Week, 2009, speech

Whitney family was prepared

When Joseph Smith was brought to the Whitney home, "I remarked to my husband that this was the fulfillment of the vision we had seen of a cloud as of glory resting upon our house."

—Elizabeth Ann Whitney, *They Knew the Prophet,* Hyrum L. Andrus, 44

Zion's Camp members who died seen in vision

Joseph Smith saw a vision of the thirteen men and one woman who died in the Zion's Camp cholera epidemic and said, "If I get a mansion as bright as theirs, I ask no more."

—*HC*, 2:180–81

Baptism for the dead

The principle of baptism for the dead was revealed on August 10, 1840, at Seymore Brunson's funeral, and baptisms were performed in the Mississippi River. Another account says it was on August 15, 1840. On November 21, 1841, the first baptisms for the dead were performed in the Nauvoo Temple. Wilford Woodruff said, "It was like a shaft of light from the throne of God to our hearts. It opened a field wide as eternity to our minds."

—*J. Christopher Conkling, A Joseph Smith Chronology*, 146; Susan Easton Black, *Setting the Record Straight: Joseph Smith the Mormon Prophet*, 12, 91

Gazelem

Gazelem is Joseph Smith's code name in the Doctrine and Covenants; another time he identified himself as Enoch.

—D&C

God would not reveal two things

There were two things that God would not reveal to the Prophet:

- The time of the second coming.
- The specific reason why the Saints were driven from Missouri.

—Calvin R. Stephens, 2009 BYU Education Week Speech

Grammar correction attempted

"At Father Billings' home, a revelation was given where some of the men undertook to correct the language of a revelation as being ungrammatical. Joseph rebuked them and said that every word of that revelation had been dictated by Jesus Christ."

—Zebedee Coltrin, *They Knew the Prophet,* Hyrum L. Andrus, 30–31

Description of heaven

Joseph gave a comprehensive description of the degrees of glory. Paul only gave a hint of them in three verses of 1 Corinthians 15:40–42. Joseph received revelations totaling hundreds of verses about heaven and the various degrees. Paul revealed a sum total of three inches of description, while Joseph's descriptions would equal a document measuring eighteen feet of revelation about heaven.

—D&C 76, 88, 105

Indians of Missouri

Joseph was told to go to the Missouri Indians. The word *Missouri* means "house of the long canoe."

—Missouri tribes, Osage, Mississippi; Compiler's note

Isaiah: Joseph's courage to translate

God inspired Joseph Smith to translate Isaiah with changes from the way it is in the Bible.

At first glance, when one sees the notation in the Book of Mormon ("see Isaiah 48," for example), a logical person might suppose that Joseph and Oliver copied the words straight from the Bible. There are twenty full chapters of Isaiah quoted in the Book of Mormon by four individuals: Nephi, Jacob, Abinadi, and the Savior Jesus Christ.

Careful comparison of these twenty chapters side by side with the Bible and the Book of Mormon reveals there were remarkable changes in all but two chapters. Each change makes it clearer. We might ask: How would this young man be so bold as to make changes to the text of Isaiah? The answer is: God was in charge of the translation.

The following is a summary of those changes by chapter and is quite revealing as to the integrity of Joseph Smith.

	Book of Mormon	Person quoting Isaiah	Chapter in Bible	Number of changes	Punctuation changes
1.	1 Nephi 20	Nephi	Isaiah 48	105 changes	9
2.	1 Nephi 21	Nephi	Isaiah 49	109 changes	13
3.	2 Nephi 7	Jacob	Isaiah 50	75 changes	8
4.	2 Nephi 8	Jacob	Isaiah 52	29 changes	23
5.	2 Nephi 12	Nephi	Isaiah 2	85 changes	2
6.	2 Nephi 13	Nephi	Isaiah 3	36 changes	15
7.	2 Nephi 14	Nephi	Isaiah 4	11 changes	1

8.	2 Nephi 15	Nephi	Isaiah 5	16 changes	5
9.	2 Nephi 16	Nephi	Isaiah 6	23 changes	6
10.	2 Nephi 17	Nephi	Isaiah 7	6 changes	1
11.	2 Nephi 18	Nephi	Isaiah 8	6 changes	2
12.	2 Nephi 19	Nephi	Isaiah 9	13 changes	4
13.	2 Nephi 20	Nephi	Isaiah 10	4 changes	1
14.	2 Nephi 21	Nephi	Isaiah 11	None	0
15.	2 Nephi 22	Nephi	Isaiah 12	None	0
16.	2 Nephi 23	Nephi	Isaiah 13	45 changes	2
17.	2 Nephi 24	Nephi	Isaiah 14	33 changes	2
18.	2 Nephi 27	Nephi	Isaiah 29	865 changes	7
19.	Mosiah 14	Abinadi	Isaiah 53	7 changes	0
20.	3 Nephi 22	Jesus Christ	Isaiah 54	10 changes	0

Word changes = 1,445   Punctuation changes = 101
Total changes = 1,546

JST (Joseph Smith Translation)

Joseph Smith was commanded to make over 3,300 inspired corrections in the Old and New Testaments of the Bible. Emma, with newly born Alexander and three other children, carried two bundles across the frozen Mississippi containing the Bible manuscripts.

—Mark L. McConkie tapes; Robert Remini, *Joseph Smith*, 137

Language

Joseph Smith received some new words that were from the pure language of God, and verified others:

- Deseret (honeybee)
- Jehovah
- Adam-ondi-Ahman
- Michael
- Urim and Thummim
- Alpha and Omega
- gnolaum (eternal)
- Elohim (God the Father)
- Ahman
- Idumea (the world)
- Raphael
- Olea (moon)
- Kolob (governing planet)
- kokaubeam (stars)

—Abraham 3; Compiler's note

At the age of twenty-five, Joseph was in Hiram, Ohio, and had received several revelations. Some of the older, more educated men challenged him with: "How do we know that the revelations are of God? The language sounds so very much like the language of Joseph Smith." He did not become offended or take offense but simply said, "'I don't know. . . . Let's ask the Lord.' They all knelt with him and he petitioned God for the answer. . . . [He then] said to his scribe, 'Please record the following.'" He then dictated section 1 of the Doctrine and Covenants. In verses 24–27, God answered their question: "Behold, I am God and have spoken it; these commandments are of me, and were given unto my servants in their weakness, after the manner of their language."

—Leon R. Hartshorn, *Joseph Smith: Prophet of the Restoration*, 76–77

Long sermons

On December 29, 1835, Joseph preached for three hours to a large crowd at the Kirtland School, some of whom were Presbyterians. The King Follett sermon was seven hours long.

—John W. Welch, ed., *A Chronology of the Life of Joseph Smith,* BYU Studies, 78

Longest verse

The longest verse in the scriptures was given to Joseph Smith on September 6, 1842, as Doctrine and Covenants 128:18.

—Compiler's note

Mahonri Moriancumer

Mahonri Moriancumer was the name of the brother of Jared. Joseph was asked by Reynolds Cahoon (1790–1861) to bless and name their baby. "Joseph did so and gave the boy the name of Mahonri Moriancumer [Cahoon]." (July 27, 1834, Kirtland, Ohio; died Murray, Utah, 1888). "Turning to Elder Cahoon, [Joseph] said, 'The name I have given your son is the name of the Brother of Jared; the Lord has just shown (or revealed) it to me.' . . . [T]his was the first time the name of the Brother of Jared was known in the Church in this dispensation."

—George Reynolds, *RJ*, 275

Melchizedek Priesthood restoration

The circumstances when Peter, James, and John gave the Melchizedek Priesthood: "[Joseph] and Oliver were under arrest on charges of deceiving the people [in Colesville, New York]. When they were at the justice's house for trial in the evening, all were waiting for Mr. Reid, Joseph's lawyer. . . . Mr. Reed came in and said he wanted to speak to his clients in private. . . . As soon as they got into the room, the lawyer said there was a mob outside in front of the house, 'and if they get hold of you they will perhaps do you bodily injury; and I think the best way for you to get out of this is to get right out there,' pointing to the window and hoisting it. They got into the wood in going a few rods from the house—it was night and they traveled through brush and water and mud, fell over logs, etc., until Oliver . . . gave out entirely and exclaimed, 'Oh Lord! Brother Joseph, how long have we got to endure this thing?' They sat down on a log to rest and Joseph said at that very time Peter, James, and John came to them and ordained them to the Apostleship. They had sixteen or seventeen miles to travel to get back to Mr. Hale's, his father–in–law's, but Oliver did not complain any more of fatigue."

—Addison Everett, *RJ*, 326

Noted researcher and LDS historian Larry C. Porter, PhD, believes that the Melchizedek Priesthood was restored on May 28, 1829. BYU Studies puts the date as about May 24, 1829.

—Records of Larry C. Porter, *A Chronology of the Life of Joseph Smith*, BYU Studies, John W. Welch, ed., 14

Patriarchal blessings

Joseph Smith gave the first patriarchal blessing on Wednesday, December 18, 1833, in an upstairs room of the John Johnson Inn in Kirtland, Ohio. He gave a blessing to his father, mother, brothers, and sisters. Oliver Cowdery was the scribe. Few, if any, other Christian Churches understand and empower their members to give blessings.

—*EPB*, 3; Compiler's note

Patriarchal blessing of Joseph Smith Jr.

This blessing was given by Joseph Smith Sr. on December 9, 1834 in Kirtland, Ohio (Oliver Cowdery, scribe).

Joseph, my son, I lay my hands upon thy head in the name of the Lord Jesus Christ, to confirm upon thee a father's blessing. The Lord thy God has called thee by name out of the heavens: thou hast heard his voice from on high from time to time, even in thy youth. The hand of the angel of his presence has been extended toward thee by which thou hast been lifted up and sustained; yea, the Lord has delivered thee from the hands of thine enemies and thou hast been made to rejoice in his salvation: thou hast sought to know his ways, and from thy childhood thou hast meditated much upon the great things of his law. Thou hast suffered much in thy youth, and the poverty and afflictions of thy father's family have been a grief to thy soul. Thou hast desired to see them delivered from bondage, for thou hast loved them with a perfect love. Thou hast stood by thy father, and like Shem, would have covered his nakedness, rather than see him exposed to shame: when the daughters of the Gentiles laughed, thy heart has been moved with a just anger to avenge thy kindred.

Thou hast been an obedient son: the commands of thy father and the reproofs of thy mother, thou hast respected and obeyed—for all these things the Lord my God will bless thee. Thou hast been called, even in thy youth to the great work of the Lord: to do a work in this generation which no man would do as thyself, in all things according to the will of the Lord. A marvelous work and a wonder has the Lord wrought by thy hand, even that which shall prepare the way for the remnants of his people to come in among the Gentiles, with their fullness, as the tribes of Israel are restored.

I bless thee with the blessings of thy fathers Abraham, Isaac and Jacob, and even the blessings of thy father Joseph, the son of Jacob. Behold, he looked after his posterity in the last days, when they should be scattered and driven by the Gentiles, and wept before the Lord: he sought diligently to know from whence the son should come who should bring forth the word of the Lord, by which they might be enlightened, and brought back to the true fold, and his eyes beheld thee, my son: his heart rejoiced and his soul was satisfied, and he said:

"As my blessings are to extend to the utmost bounds of the everlasting hills, as my father's blessing prevailed above the blessings of his progen[i]tor, and as my branches are to run over the wall, and my seed are to inherit the choice land whereon the Zion of God shall stand in the last days, from among my seed, scattered with the Gentiles, shall a choice Seer arise whose bowels shall be as a fountain of truth, whose loins shall be girded with the girdle of righteousness, whose hands shall be lifted with acceptance before the God of Jacob to turn away his anger from his annointed, whose heart shall meditate great wisdom, whose intelligence shall circumscribe and comprehend the deep things of God, and whose mouth shall utter the law of the just: His feet shall stand upon the neck of his enemies, and he shall walk upon the ashes of those who seek his destruction: with wine and oil shall he be sustained, and he shall feed upon the heritage of Jacob his father: the just shall desire his society, and the upright in heart shall be his companions: No weapon formed against him shall prosper, and though the wicked mar him for a little season, he shall be like one rising up in the heat of wine—he shall roar in his strength, and the Lord shall put to flight his persecutors: he shall be blessed like the fruitful olive, and his memory shall be as sweet as the choice cluster of the first ripe grapes. Like a shief [sheaf] fully ripe, gathered into the garner, so shall he stand before the Lord, having produced a hundred fold." Thus spake my father Joseph.

Therefore, my son, I know for a surety that those things will be fulfilled, and I confirm upon thee all these blessings. Thou shalt like to do the work which the Lord shall command thee: Thou shalt hold the Keys of this ministry, even the presidency of this church, both in time and in eternity. Thy heart shall be enlarged, and thou shalt be able to fill up the measure of thy days according to the will of the Lord. Thou shalt speak the word of the Lord and the earth shall tremble; the mountains shall move and the rivers shall turn out of their course. Thou shalt escape the edge of the sword, and put to flight the armies of the wicked. At thy word the lame shall walk, the deaf shall hear and the blind shall see. Thou shalt be gathered to Zion and in the goodly land thou shalt enjoy thine inheritance; thy children and thy children's children to the latest generation; for thy name and the names of thy posterity shall be recorded in the book of the Lord, even in the book of blessings and genealogies, for their joy and benefit forever.

And now, my son, what more shall I say? Thou art as a fruitful olive and a choice vine: thou shalt be laden with precious fruit. Thousands and tens of thousands shall come to a knowledge of the truth through thy ministry, and thou shalt rejoice with them in the Celestial Kingdom:

Thou shalt stand upon the earth when it shall reel to and fro as a drunken man, and be removed out of its place: thou shalt stand when the mighty judgments go forth to the destruction of the wicked: thou shalt stand on Mount Zion when the tribes of Jacob come shouting from the north, and with thy brethren, the sons of Ephraim, crown them in the name of Jesus Christ: Thou shalt see thy Redeemer come in the clouds of heaven, and with the just receive the hallowed throng with shouts of hallalujahs, praise the Lord. Amen.

—H. Michael Marquardt, comp., *Early Patriarchal Blessings of the Church of Jesus Christ of Latter Day Saints*, Salt Lake City, Utah, Smith–Pettit Foundation, 2007

Last father's and patriarchal blessing from Joseph Smith Sr. to Joseph Smith Jr.

At Joseph Smith Sr.'s deathbed in 1840 in Nauvoo:

"Joseph, my son, thou art called to a high and holy calling. Thou art even called to do the work of the Lord. Hold out faithful and you shall be blessed and your children after you. You shall live to finish your work."

"At this Joseph cried out, weeping, 'Oh my father, will I?' 'Yes,' said his father, 'you shall live to lay out the plan of all the work which God has given you to do. This is my dying blessing on your head in the name of Jesus.' "

—*History of Lucy Smith, Mother of the Prophet,* 1845 manuscript, 298, Church Archives

First Patriarchal Blessing

Blessings by Joseph Smith Jr. to his family, dated December 18, 1833; revised and recorded approximately September 15–October 2, 1835

Thus spake the Seer, and these are the words which fell from his lips while the visions of the Almighty were open to his view, saying:

Blessed of the Lord is my father, for he shall stand in the midst of his posterity and shall be comforted by their blessings when he is old and bowed down with years, and shall be called a prince over them, and shall be numbered among those who hold the right of patriarchal priesthood, even the keys of that ministry: for he shall assemble together his posterity like unto Adam; and the assembly which he called shall be an ensample for my father, for thus it is written of him:

Three years previous to the death of Adam, he called Seth, Enos, Cainan, Mahalaleel, Jared, Enoch and Methuselah, who were High Priests, with the residue of his posterity, who were righteous, into the valley of Adam-ondi-Ahman, and there bestowed upon them his last blessing. And the Lord appeared unto them, and they rose up and blessed Adam, and called him Michael, the Prince, the Archangel. And the Lord administered comfort unto Adam, and said unto him, I have set thee to be at the head; a multitude of nations shall come of thee, and thou art a Prince over them forever.

So shall it be with my father: he shall be called a prince over his posterity, holding the keys of the Patriarchal Priesthood over the kingdom of God on earth, even the Church of the Latter-day Saints, and he shall sit in the general assembly of Patriarchs, even in council with the Ancient of Days when he shall sit and all the Patriarchs with him and shall enjoy his right and authority under the direction of the Ancient of Days.

And blessed also, is my mother, for she is a mother in Israel, and shall be a partaker with my father in all his patriarchal blessings.

And blessed, also, are my brothers and my sisters, for they shall yet find redemption in the house of the Lord, and their offsprings shall be a blessing, a joy and a comfort unto them.

Blessed is my mother, for her soul is ever filled with benevolence and philanthropy; and notwithstanding her age, she shall yet receive strength and be comforted in the midst of her house: and thus saith the Lord, She shall have eternal life.

And again, blessed is my father, for the hand of the Lord shall be over him, and he shall be full of the Holy Ghost: for he shall predict whatsoever shall befall his posterity unto the latest generation, and shall see the affliction of his children pass away, and their enemies under their feet: and when his head is fully ripe he shall behold himself as an olive tree whose branches are bowed down with much fruit. Behold, the blessings of Joseph by the hand of his progenitor, shall come upon the head of my father and his seed after him, to the uttermost, even he shall be a fruitful bough: he shall be as a fruitful bough, even a fruitful bough by a well whose branches run over the wall, and his seed shall abide in strength, and the arms of their hands shall be made strong by the hands of the mighty God of Jacob, and the God of his fathers: even the God of Abraham, Isaac and Jacob, shall help him and his seed after him: even the Almighty shall bless him with blessings of heaven above and his seed after him, and the blessings of the deep that lieth under: and his seed shall rise up and call him blessed. He shall be as the vine of the choice grape when her clusters are fully ripe: and he shall also possess a mansion on high, even in the Celestial Kingdom. His counsel shall be sought for by thousands, and he shall have place in the house of the Lord; for he shall be mighty in the council of the elders, and his days shall yet be lengthened out: and when he shall go hence he shall go in peace, and his rest shall be glorious; and his name shall be had in remembrance to the end. Amen.

Blessing from Joseph Smith Jr. to Hyrum Smith

Blessed of the Lord is brother Hyrum for the integrity of his heart; he shall be girt about with strength, and faithfulness shall be the strength of his loins. From generation to generation he shall be a shaft in the hand of his God to execute judgment upon his enemies, and he shall be hid by the hand of the Lord that none of his secret pacts shall be discovered unto his enemies unto his hurt. His name shall be called a blessing among men. His acquaintance shall be among kings; and he shall be sought for that he may sit in council, by nations and kings afar off and to thousands of souls shall he be an instrument in the hand of his God in bringing unto salvation. And when he is in trouble and great tribulation has come upon him, he shall remember the God of Jacob and he shall shield him from the power of Satan. He shall receive counsel in the house of the Most High that he may be strengthened in hope. He shall be as a cooling spring that breaketh forth at the foot of the mountain, one shadowed with choice trees bowed down with ripe fruit that yieldeth both nourishment to the appetite and quencheth the thirst, thereby yielding refreshment to the weary traveler; and the goings of his feet shall ever be by streams of living water. He shall not toil nor want for knowledge for the Lord his God shall put forth his hand and lift him up and shall call upon him with his voice in the way wherein he is traveling, that he may be established forever. He shall stand in the rocks of his father and be numbered among those who hold the right of patriarchal priesthood, even the evangelical priesthood, and power shall be upon him that in his old age his name may be magnified on the earth. Behold he shall be blessed with an abundance of riches of the earth: gold, silver, and treasures of precious stones, of diamonds and patina. His chariots shall be numerous and his cattle shall multiply abundantly: horses, mules, asses, camels, dromedaries, and swift beasts that he may magnify the name of the Lord and benefit the poor: yea this shall be the desire of his soul, to comfort the needy and bind up the broken in heart. His children shall be many and his posterity numerous, and they shall rise up and call him blessed. And he shall have eternal life. Amen.

—Given in Kirtland, December 18, 1933, and recorded September 1835. Oliver Cowdery, clerk and recorder

Patriarchal blessing of Emma Smith

"Emma, my daughter-in-law, thou art blessed of the Lord, for thy faithfulness and truth, thou shalt be blessed with thy husband, and rejoice in the glory which shall come upon him. Thy soul has been afflicted because of the wickedness of men in seeking the destruction of thy companion, and thy whole soul has been drawn out in prayer for his deliverance; rejoice, for the Lord thy God has heard thy supplication. Thou hast grieved for the hardness of the hearts of thy father's house, and thou hast longed for their salvation. The Lord will have respect to thy cries, and by His judgments He will cause some of them to see their folly and repent of their sins; but it will be by affliction that they will be saved. Thou shalt see many days, yea, the Lord will spare thee till thou art satisfied, for thou shalt see thy Redeemer. Thy heart shall rejoice in the great work of the Lord, and no one shall take thy rejoicing from thee. Thou shalt ever remember the great condescension of thy God in permitting thee to accompany my son [Joseph] when the angel delivered the record of the Nephites to his care. Thou hast seen much sorrow because the Lord has taken from thee three of thy children: in this thou art not to be blamed, for He knows thy pure desires to raise up a family, that the name of my son might be blessed. And now, behold, I say unto thee, that thus says the Lord, if thou will believe, thou shalt yet be blessed in this thing and thou shalt bring forth other children, to the joy and satisfaction of thy soul and to the rejoicing of thy friends. Thou shalt be blessed with understanding, and have power to instruct thy sex, teach thy family righteousness, and thy little ones the way of life, and the holy angels shall watch over thee and thou shalt be saved in the kingdom of God, even so, Amen.

—Oliver Cowdery, clerk and recorder. Kirtland, December 9, 1834. [Patriarchal Blessing Book 1:4–5]

Polygamy

Eliza R. Snow relates, "The Prophet Joseph . . . described the trying mental ordeal he experienced in overcoming the repugnance of his feelings (regarding the practice of plural marriage) . . . but God . . . had given the commandment, and He must be obeyed. Yet the Prophet hesitated and deferred from time to time, until an angel of God stood by him with a drawn sword, and told him that, unless he moved forward and established plural marriage, his priesthood would be taken from him and he should be destroyed!" This happened at least three times since 1834. Several early prominent members attested to this, including Joseph Noble and Benjamin F. Johnson.

—Hyrum L. Andrus, *They Knew the Prophet*, 65, 106

"I heard him preach that the *ancient order of Abraham* should be restored," recorded Bathsheba W. Smith. "He counseled the sisters not to trouble themselves in consequence of plural marriage, that all would be right, and the result would be for their glory and exaltation."

—Hyrum L. Andrus, *They Knew the Prophet*, 139

There are over twenty accounts that tell of the angel commanding the practice of polygamy.

— Joseph Smith Papers

Polygamy was only practiced when God commanded it, and only when authorized by the General Authorities.

—John W. Welch, *Opening the Heavens*, 287–88, 316; Compiler's note

Note: It is the intent of the compiler of this book to purposely leave out the list of Joseph Smith's plural wives. It is certainly not a secret that he practiced polygamy, but it is a sacred subject and personal to the life of Joseph Smith. This type of information can easily be found in the Church Family Search records. Books have been written specifically about this to satisfy people's curiosity. Personally, I have a testimony that it was commanded by God Almighty, but I have never cared to search such private matters of Joseph's life. I desire to live worthy of meeting the Prophet Joseph Smith one day on the other side of the veil. I do not want to be asked to explain mistakes I might have made in describing private matters when we do not have all the records to understand them completely.

Scripture pages

The Prophet brought us more than 35 percent of all the scripture available to mankind. Of the 2,497 pages of scripture (includes more than 25 pages of Joseph Smith Translation), the Prophet provided over 900 pages. The Book of Mormon has 531 pages, the Doctrine and Covenants has 280 pages, the Pearl of Great Price has 61 pages, and the Joseph Smith Translation of the Bible has over 30 pages of corrections.

—Compiler's note

Seven principles Moroni taught Joseph

"The seven principles Moroni taught Joseph are as follows: first principle, one does not speak too openly about sacred things; second principle, one must learn how to recognize the feeling that identifies the Holy Ghost; third principle, integrity is keeping one's covenants with God; fourth principle, sometimes prophets must make their own decisions; fifth principle, friendships, however important, are not as important as keeping God's commandments; sixth principle, the Lord has already planned for his children's success; seventh principle, the Lord provides whatever help he understands we need."

—LeGrand L. Baker, *Joseph and Moroni: The 7 Principles Moroni Taught Joseph Smith*, 2

Singing brought a revelation

"He had a revelation while we were singing to him."

—Brigham Young, *They Knew the Prophet*, Hyrum L. Andrus, 39

Songwriter

Joseph, through revelation, became a songwriter while he received section 84 of the Doctrine and Covenants. He received a "New Song," four verses and 141 words, as recorded in Doctrine and Covenants 84:99–102:

99 The Lord hath brought again Zion;
The Lord hath redeemed his people, Israel,
According to the election of grace,
Which was brought to pass by the faith
And covenant of their fathers.

100 *The Lord hath redeemed his people;*
And Satan is bound and time is no longer.
The Lord hath gathered all things in one.
The Lord hath brought down Zion from above.
The Lord hath brought up Zion from beneath.

101 *The earth hath travailed and brought forth her strength;*
And truth is established in her bowels;
And the heavens have smiled upon her;
And she is clothed with the glory of her God;
For he stands in the midst of his people.

102 *Glory, and honor, and power, and might,*
Be ascribed to our God; for he is full of mercy,
Justice, grace and truth, and peace,
Forever and ever, Amen.

Spiritual truths by-product of visions

"Joseph Smith's insight into spiritual truth came largely as a by-product of the things he saw in vision."

—Hyrum L. Andrus, *Joseph Smith, the Man and the Seer*, 63

Stone seen in vision was stationary

The Prophet, speaking at Far West, Missouri, said, "I will correct the idea in regard to the little stone rolling forth, as foretold in Daniel, chapter 2. This is not so. It is stationary, like a grind stone, and revolves. (He made a motion with his hands showing how it turned.) When the Elders go abroad to preach the Gospel, and the people become believers in the Book of Mormon and are baptized, they are added to the little stone. Thus, they are gathered around it so that it grows larger and larger until it begins to pinch the toes of the image, and finally breaks it into pieces to be carried away like the chaff of a summer's threshing, while the stone will keep growing until it fills the whole earth."

—Henry William Bigler, *They Knew the Prophet*, Hyrum L. Andrus, 113

Verses that quote the Savior's words and teachings

Joseph Smith has given a wonderful gift to mankind by providing 3,852 verses (67 percent) of the 5,779 verses ever recorded of the Savior's words and teachings.

Recorded by two apostles and two disciples of the Lord

Bible:

Bible contributor	Number of verses quoting Savior	When written
Matthew	630	70 AD
Luke	595	67 AD
John	408	90 AD
Mark	289	70 AD

Total: 1,922 verses

Given through the Prophet Joseph Smith.

Book of Mormon and Doctrine and Covenants:

Reference	Number of verses quoting Savior	When written
3 Nephi	393	33–34 AD
Doctrine and Covenants	3459	1830–1844 AD

Total: 3,852 verses by Joseph Smith

Note: 3 Nephi is sometimes called the Fifth Gospel and was recorded immediately after the Savior visited the American Continent. The Savior reproved Nephi and the other apostles for words He had given about "other sheep" that were missing from the record they were keeping.

Wicked man's prayer

Willard Richards asked Joseph if he wanted to have a wicked man pray for him. He replied, "Yes; if the fervent affectionate prayer of the righteous man availeth much, a wicked man may avail a little when praying for a righteous man. There is none good but One. The better a man is, the more his prayer will avail. . . . The prayer of a wicked man may do a righteous man good."

—*HC*, 5:208

Word of Wisdom was 130 years ahead of its time

When the US Surgeon General report was released in the early 1960s on tobacco, it verified what the Lord told Joseph on February 27, 1833. An equivalent to two jumbo jets full of people die every day from tobacco, in addition to the devastation that alcohol causes.

—Compiler's note; Internet

Zion

While Joseph Smith was translating the Book of Mormon, it was revealed to him that there was to be a city of Zion on the American continent. It was also revealed in the book of Moses, within the Pearl of Great Price, where additional information was given about Zion and the Zion of Enoch:

- Zion will be built upon the American continent.
- Zion is all of North and South America.
- Zion is the pure in heart. Therefore, Zion includes all the Saints anywhere in their own "little Zion" of perfection in their heart and soul, no matter where that may be on the earth.
- The center of Zion is to include the New Jerusalem built in Jackson County, Missouri, where Adam and Eve once lived in what was the Garden of Eden.
- Christ will rule and reign on earth from both the New Jerusalem and the Old Jerusalem as King of kings, for a thousand years in the millennium.

Zion was very much upon the mind of Joseph Smith. He taught about Zion, as denoted in over four hundred references in the *History of the Church*, *Teachings of Joseph Smith* and *Writings of Joseph Smith*.

—Truman G. Madsen, *The Concordance of the Doctrinal Statements of Joseph Smith*, 454–55

Come and get more

The Prophet taught, "We don't ask men to give up any good they have, we only ask them to come and get more."

—*Michael Kennedy, Emma Smith: My Story*, 2007, movie

Counsel to missionaries

Henry W. Bigler heard Joseph Smith give counsel to some elders going on a mission. "Make short prayers and short sermons, and let [the] mysteries alone."

—*RJ*, 221

Discouragement

"Never be discouraged," Joseph once said to George A. Smith. "If I were sunk in the lowest pits of Nova Scotia, with the Rocky Mountains piled on me, I would hang on, exercise faith, and keep up good courage, and I would come out on top."

—John Henry Evans, *Joseph Smith an American Prophet*, 9

Value of the Doctrine and Covenants

Joseph stated that the value of the Doctrine and Covenants is worth more than the sum total of the earth's riches.

—J. Christopher Conkling, *A Joseph Smith Chronology*, 28

Knowledge about Enoch

From the Bible, we have about four inches of written information about Enoch. Joseph revealed over eleven feet in length of information about this prophet, found in Moses 7 of the *Joseph Smith Translation* and seven sections of the Doctrine and Covenants.

—Compiler's note

Friendship

Joseph taught that "friendship is one of the grand fundamental principles of 'Mormonism'; [it is designed] to revolutionize and civilize the world, and cause wars and contentions to cease and men to become friends and brothers."

—Wilford Woodruff, *Joseph Smith, the Man, the Seer,* Hyrum L. Andrus, 40

Greatness

Joseph taught on March 4, 1843, that for a man to achieve greatness, he cannot dwell on small things.

—*A Chronology of the Life of Joseph Smith,* BYU Studies, 145; *HC,* 5:298

Ignorance is an enemy

Joseph said, "We cannot be saved until we have risen above all our enemies, not the least of which is ignorance."

—*Richard L. Evans Quote Book,* 73

Learn more in 5 minutes

"Could you gaze into heaven five minutes, you would know more than you would by reading all that ever was written on the subject."

—Joseph Smith, *Joseph Smith, the Man and the Seer,* Hyrum L. Andrus, 135

Life's purpose

Life's test, the Prophet taught, was to "[prove] our strength to overcome the wiles and devices of Lucifer, the great prince and power on this earth at the present day."

—John M. Bernhisel, *They Knew the Prophet,* Hyrum L. Andrus, 199

"The Prophet said: 'We . . . [are] to serve an allotted time on this earth, in order to test our integrity and determine the fact of our faith.' "

—John M. Bernhisel, *They Knew the Prophet,* Hyrum L. Andrus, 199

Light is the glory of God

Joseph taught Benjamin F. Johnson, "All light and heat are the 'glory of God,' which is His power, that fills the 'immensity of space,' and is the life of all things, and permeates with latent life, and heat, every particle of which all worlds are composed; that light or spirit, and gross matter, are the two first great primary principles of the universe, or of being; that they are self-existent, co-existent, indestructible, and eternal, and from these two elements both our spirits and our bodies were formulated."

—Hyrum L. Andrus, *They Knew the Prophet,* 107

Love as a principle

"The Prophet's 'teaching of love' was not to work upon the sympathies and sensibilities of the people, rather it was his great example and self-sacrifice, and his showing us that while all the world was against us, our only hope was in our union, and that union was only possible as the fruit of our love for each other. . . . We should 'love God supremely, and our brothers as ourselves.' "

—Benjamin F. Johnson, *They Knew the Prophet,* Hyrum L. Andrus, 107

Matter has no beginning or end

Benjamin F. Johnson said he heard the Prophet teach "the eternity of matter, that no part or particle of the great universe could become annihilated or destroyed."

—Hyrum L. Andrus, *They Knew the Prophet,* 107

Merciful to enemies

"[Joseph] then said, 'Brethren and sisters, love one another; love one another and be merciful to your enemies.' "

—Lucy M. Smith, *They Knew the Prophet,* Hyrum L. Andrus, 170

No man knows my history

In the King Follett discourse, Joseph said, "You don't know me, you never knew my heart. I don't blame any one for not believing my history. If I had not experienced what I have, I could not have believed it myself."

—King Follett Discourse; Truman G. Madsen, *Joseph Smith the Prophet,* 29

Not humanize God but deify man

"Joseph Smith did 'not wish to humanize God but to deify man, not as he now is, but as he may become.' "

—Lowell L. Bennion, *Images of the Prophet Joseph Smith,* Davis Bitton, 136; Lowell L. Bennion, *The Religion of the Latter-day Saints,* 31

Not perfect but doctrine is perfect

Joseph stated, "I never told you I was perfect—but there is no error in the revelations which I have taught," and, "The doctrine I teach is true."

—Susan Easton Black and Andrew C. Skinner, *Joseph Smith: Exploring the Life and Ministry of the Prophet,* 370; Andrew F. Ehat and Lyndon W. Cook, *Words of Joseph Smith,* 369

One rule

"I made this one rule: When the Lord commands, do it."

—Joseph Smith, *Emma Smith: My Story, Michael Kennedy,* 2007, movie

People don't know me

Mary Elizabeth Rollins Lightner recorded this comment of Joseph Smith's: " 'People little know who I am when they talk about me, and they never will know until they see weighed in the balance in the kingdom of God. Then they will know who I am, and see me as I am. I dare not tell them and they do not know me.' These words were spoken with such power that they penetrated the heart of every soul that believed on him."

—Hyrum L. Andrus, *They Knew the Prophet* by Hyrum L. Andrus, 289–300

Perfection

"He greeted us warmly and told us that we must not look for perfection in him. If we did he would look for perfection in us."

—John Oakley, *RJ*, 95

Prosperity could be people's downfall

"In the day of prosperity now the people are slow to follow the Lord. If He were now to bless this people with gold and silver, houses and lands, with everything to make them wealthy and comfortable . . . a great many would turn away from Him to worship their idols."

—Brigham Young, *RJ*, 218

Purpose of life

"He offered to the people of the frontier in the nineteenth century a knowledge of where they had come from, what the purpose of life was, and where they could go in the eternities and what they could become. And I think for those people it was tremendously significant to have a destiny, a divine destiny."

—Ross Peterson, *American Prophet: The Story of Joseph Smith*, Lee Groberg and Heidi S. Swinton, 126

Rejected Joseph's counsel

It was a heartbreak to Joseph when he recommended to the Saints that Sidney Rigdon be removed from his place. The members overwhelmingly voted to reject Joseph Smith's counsel and voted to sustain Sidney Rigdon. Joseph was hurt and pleaded, "Remove the weak, give me strength."

—Leon Hartshorn, *Joseph Smith: Prophet of the Restoration*, 97

Revelation comes by "sudden strokes of ideas"

Joseph taught that revelation comes by "sudden strokes of ideas" and is more than just the turning on of a light where it was once dark. It is a "quickening of understanding as feeling 'pure intelligence flowing into you.' "

—Joseph Fielding McConkie, *Prophets and Prophecy*, 166

Revelatory abilities

Joseph said at the funeral of Lorenzo D. Barnes on April 15, 1843, "It is my meditation all the day, and more than my meat and drink, to know how I shall make the Saints of God comprehend the visions that roll like an overflowing surge before my mind."

—Susan Easton Black, *Setting the Record Straight: Joseph Smith the Mormon Prophet*, 34

Revolutionize the whole world

"I intend to lay a foundation that will revolutionize the whole world. . . . It will not be by sword or gun that this kingdom will roll on: the power of truth is such that all nations will be under the necessity of obeying the Gospel."

—*Joseph Smith*, May 12, 1844; *HC*, 6:365; Donna Hill, *Joseph Smith: The First Mormon*, 371

Riches

Joseph Smith urged his people to realize that, "God does not judge men by the size of their purse. A poor man may be righteous or unrighteous. The rich man likewise."

—William E. Barrett, *Contributions of Joseph Smith,* William E. Berrett, Lowell L. Bennion, and T. Edgar Lyon, radio talks, 60–61

Savior's first miracle

Someone once asked the Prophet Joseph Smith, "What was the first miracle Jesus performed?" He answered, "He made this world, and what followed we are not told."

—Truman G. Madsen, *Joseph Smith the Prophet*, 49

Scientific things taught by Joseph Smith Jr.

- Matter has no beginning or end.
- Kolob is the governing star, next to God's planet.
- God's time is one day to every thousand years in earth time.
- God organized the elements (not created them) in the Creation; also, it was all done spiritually before it was done physically.
- Celestial beings look like people, not like green creatures from Mars or anything like that.
- The nature of light and all about it.
- The Word of Wisdom and harmfulness of tobacco, alcohol, tea, and coffee.
- The fundamental concepts of the universe.
- Elements are eternal.
- The indestructibility of matter.

- The indestructibility of energy.
- Organized intelligences with their many grades.
- The Fall.
- The reign of law.
- The law of evolution, worlds without end, and there is no end.
- Spiritual matter.
- All space is filled with substance.
- Universal ether.
- Creative periods were called "days."
- The nature of God and His creations are endless.

—John A. Widtsoe, *Joseph Smith as Scientist*, 3–13, 16, 51; Compiler's note

Secret keeper

Joseph taught, "The reason we do not have the secrets of the Lord revealed unto us is because we do not keep them but reveal them . . . even to our enemies. I can keep a secret till Doomsday."

—Truman G. Madsen, *Joseph Smith the Prophet*, 29

Sermons and discourses

There were 177 separate discourses of Joseph Smith's, recorded by 36 individuals in 43 records. The more complete texts were the works of Wilford Woodruff.

—Andrew Ehat and Lyndon W. Cook, *The Words of Joseph Smith: Contemporary Accounts of the Nauvoo Discourses of Joseph Smith*, 1, 2

Slavery problem

Joseph said, "Break the shackles from the poor black man. The slave states should abolish slavery by 1850 . . . [and petition] Congress to pay every man a reasonable price for his slaves."

—John Henry Evans, *Joseph Smith an American Prophet*, 256–57

"He stated that slavery was wrong, but that the slaves should be bought from their owners, by the United States Government [using money raised by the sale of government land] and set free. Had this been done, the terrible Civil War might have been avoided."

—Dela Peterson and Nathan Glen Neeley, *A Child's Story of the Prophet Joseph Smith*, 149

Spiritual knowledge a tool against devil

Joseph taught, "If you don't continue to learn spiritual knowledge, the devil will gain in power against you."

—Randy Bott, *KBYU Discussions on the Doctrine and Covenants*, October 28, 2009

Stand fast

"Stand fast, ye Saints of God, hold on a little while longer, and the storm of life will be past, and you will be rewarded by that God whose servants you are," said Joseph Smith.

—Lee Groberg and Heidi Swinton, *American Prophet: The Story of Joseph Smith*, 147

Subjects he spoke of most in his sermons:

Revelation, the book of Abraham, and obedience were the top three subjects addressed in Joseph Smith's sermons. Others were God the Father, the Savior, and charity.

—Richard Horsley, interview

Taught from the Bible

"It is interesting to note that although the Prophet bore testimony of the Book of Mormon and the revelations in the Doctrine and Covenants, he almost never incorporated passages from them into his sermons. Instead, he taught out of the Bible." Here are the Bible books he quoted and the number of times:

- Matthew (41)
- John (14)
- I Corinthians (13)
- Isaiah (11)
- Luke (10)
- Genesis (26)
- Revelation (14)
- Hebrews (12)
- Acts (11)
- Malachi (8)

—Kent Jackson, *Joseph Smith: Exploring the Life and Ministry of the Prophet*, Susan Easton Black and Andrew C. Skinner, 371

Teachings about Deity

Kent Jackson listed some of the teachings that Joseph Smith taught about Deity:

- The Father, the Son, and the Holy Ghost are three separate beings.
- The Father and the Son have bodies of flesh and bones.
- The Holy Ghost has a body of spirit.
- God is a (glorified) man.
- God was once as we are now.
- We are spirit children of God.
- We may become as God.

—Susan Easton Black and Andrew C. Skinner, *Joseph Smith: Exploring the Life and Ministry of the Prophet*, 371–76

Down to earth teachings

"Complainers cannot be exalted."

—Mark L. McConkie tapes

There is no end

W. W. Phelps was taught by Joseph that there is no end to love, light, spirit, matter, glory, space, grace, priesthood, family, peace, intelligence, virtue, might, being, truth, wisdom, union, youth, race, progress, creations, improvement, or eternity. He later compiled this concept in the popular hymn, "If You Could Hie to Kolob."

—"If You Could Hie to Kolob," *Hymns*, no. 284

Truth defined

The only accurate definition of truth was given to Joseph by the Lord in *Doctrine and Covenants* 93:24: "And truth is knowledge of things as they are, and as they were, and as they are to come." In a university upper-level philosophy class, a lecture room full of students labored for weeks and could not come up with an accurate definition of truth.

—D&C 93:24; Compiler's note

Truth governs

According to Howard Coray, Stephen A. Douglas asked Joseph how he governed a people so diverse, coming from so many countries with their particular manners and customs. "Well," he said, "I simply teach them the truth, and they govern themselves."

—*RJ*, 49

Truth is independent

Truth is independent in its nature.

—D&C 93:24

Truth will survive

"I went one day to the Prophet with a sister. She had a charge to make against one of the brethren for scandal. When her complaint had been heard the Prophet asked her if she was quite sure that what the brother had said of her was utterly untrue. She was quite sure that it was. He then told her to think no more about it, for it could not harm her. If untrue it could not live, but the truth will survive."

—Jesse W. Crosby, *They Knew the Prophet*, Hyrum L. Andrus, 162

Wanted young men to go to the mountains and talk with God face to face

"[Joseph] wanted young men of faith who could go upon the mountains and talk with God face to face as Moses did on Mount Sinai, and learn from Him where His people should make a home. . . . I went home and upon my knees by my bedside I prayed [to know] what I should do. . . . In vision I performed the entire journey successfully . . . and saw the future of my entire life."

—Samuel F. Richards, *RJ*, 360

Wealth

"Joseph said to me in Kirtland, 'Brother Brigham, if I was to reveal to this people what the Lord has revealed to me, there is not a man or a woman would stay with me.' In the day of prosperity now the people are slow to follow the Lord. If He were now to bless this people with gold and silver, houses and lands, with everything to make them wealthy and comfortable here in Deseret or Utah, a great many would turn away from Him to worship their idols."

—Brigham Young, *JD* 9:294

Wife's true role

Parley Pratt expressed that his love for his wife was moved into a completely different paradigm of appreciation and importance when he was taught by Joseph.

—*Autobiography of Parley Parker Pratt*

Wives should be the dearest objects on earth

"The Prophet Joseph Smith . . . [said] wives should be [man's] bosom companions, the nearest and dearest objects on earth in every sense of the word. He said men should beware how they treat their wives, that they were given them for a holy purpose. . . . [M]any would awake on the morning of the resurrection sadly disappointed, for they, by transgression, would have neither wives nor children, for they surely would be taken from them and given to those who should prove themselves worthy. Again, he said, a woman would have her choice; this was a privilege that could not be denied her."

—Lucy Walker Kimball, *They Knew the Prophet*, Hyrum L. Andrus, 157–58

Worth of human personality

Joseph taught that "the whole purpose of man's existence is the development of personality, its enfoldment in joyous living, that eventually man may become like unto God."

—William E. Berrett, *Contributions of Joseph Smith: A series of Radio Talks*, William E. Berrett, Lowell L. Bennion, T. Edgar Lyon, 31

Mapped out the rest of Brigham Young's life

Twenty–five "staunch Saints" were at the "home of Stephen Winchester when Joseph spoke of his coming martyrdom; and 'then and there he mapped [out] the life and acts of Brigham Young until [his] death.'" William Henry Kimball testified that all of the prophecy was fulfilled to a letter and act.

—Hyrum L. Andrus, *Joseph Smith, the Man and the Seer*, 116

Missouri

Once Joseph escaped from Missouri, he prophesied on January 2, 1843, that he would not go back to Missouri "dead or alive."

—*HC*, 5:216

A prophecy about Missouri stated that before the Saints would return, not even a yellow dog would be able to wag its tail because of the great destruction there would be because of the treatment they gave the Saints. "This prophecy was literally fulfilled during the Civil War when Gen. Ewing ordered the Missourians to vacate several counties, including the very ones where these same Missourians and their fathers robbed, murdered, and exiled the Mormons. . . . [T]he Union Army pushed them out and burned every house, barn, and stack." Several accounts state that only chimneys were left standing in Jackson County.

—Catherine Smith Salisbury, *RJ*, 155–56

Never taste of death prophecy

"Joseph once told W. W. Phelps and his wife that they would never taste of death. Well, they died. . . . [H]ere is the explanation later given. Before Brother Phelps died he lost all his judgment, and lost all his mind, reason, consciousness, and sense. He knew nothing, not even his name, nor how to eat, thus being unable to taste anything; not even death. His wife was killed instantly, so quickly that she had not time to taste of death. She was killed as she was dipping up a bucket of water from the ditch, a gust of wind hurled a board from a house and it struck her on the neck breaking it instantly. She never tasted of death nor even felt the blow."

Oliver B. Huntington, *Images of the Prophet Joseph Smith* by Davis Bitton, 94

Prophesies not in our scriptures

There are hundreds of these prophesies by Joseph Smith, and we rely on the memories of those who recorded them. Thus, care should be taken in accepting these as doctrine.

"The time would come when none but the women of the Latter-day Saints would be willing to bear children."

—Lizzie Freeze, *RJ,* 135

"If they would let us alone, we would spread the gospel all over the world, and if they did not let us alone, we would spread it anyhow, only a little quicker."

—George A Smith, *RJ,* 156

"We may build as many houses as we would, and we should never get one big enough to hold the Saints."

—George A. Smith, *RJ,* 157

"The Prophet told General Doniphan . . . not to invest in the lands [in Missouri], as the time would come when all improvements would be destroyed and not one building stone would be left standing upon another." (During the Civil War, every house and barn was destroyed as both armies fought back and forth on Missouri's soil.)

—Catherine Smith Salisbury, *RJ,* 155

"The place or country where Noah's ark was built was designated in my hearing by the Prophet Joseph Smith as being in or near South Carolina."

—Oliver B. Huntington, *They Knew the Prophet,* Hyrum L. Andrus, 73

Note: Thirty-five uncanonized revelations by Joseph Smith (1831–44) are listed and described by Lyndon W. Cook in Appendix B of The Revelations of The Prophet Joseph Smith: A Historical and Biographical Commentary of the Doctrine and Covenants, *361–64.*

Prophecy of Brigham Young

When Joseph first met Brigham Young in 1832, he said, "Brigham Young is a great man and one day the whole Kingdom will rest upon him."

—Levi W. Hancock, *RJ*, 136

Prophesies seemed impossible

"I heard Joseph say . . . the revelations the Lord gave through him—it seemed to be so impossible for them to be fulfilled." However, they all came true.

—Heber C. Kimball, *RJ*, 211

Joseph's last Prophecy

In Carthage Jail, the night before Joseph and Hyrum were killed, "and when all were apparently asleep, Joseph (Smith) whispered to (Captain) Dan Jones, 'Are you afraid to die?' Dan answered: 'Has that time come, think you? Engaged in such a cause, I do not think that death would have many terrors.' Joseph replied (with what many have identified as his last prophecy): 'You will yet see Wales and fulfill the mission appointed you before you die.'" "The following morning, June 27, 1844, Smith asked Jones to deliver a letter on his behalf to Orville H. Browning in Quincy, Illinois, requesting that Browning act as the Smiths' lawyer in their upcoming trial. As Jones departed the jail on horseback, bullets were fired at him, but none struck him. In his haste and panic, Jones took the wrong road to Quincy and became lost. It was later learned that an anti-Mormon mob had been waiting to intercept him on the correct road to Quincy. When Jones finally reached Quincy later in the afternoon, he learned that Joseph and Hyrum Smith had been killed by a mob at the jail in Carthage, Illinois." In 1845, Captain Jones went on a mission to Wales (his native country), founded the Welsh mission, and converted about two thousand souls.

—*Wikipedia; LDSBE,* 3:658; *GD*, 185

Prophecy of his blood being spilt and of war

On June 16, 1844, "drawing his sword, he [Joseph] declared, 'I call God and angels to witness that this people shall have their legal rights or my blood shall be spilt upon the ground and my body consigned to the tomb, but if there is one drop of blood shed on this occasion, the sword shall never again be sheathed until Christ comes to reign over the earth. Peace shall be taken from the land which permits these crimes against the Saints to go unavenged.'"

—Christopher Layton, *They Knew the Prophet*, Hyrum L. Andrus, 196

Prophecy of Saints living safely in the mountains

"[The Saints] would have to go and find a place in the mountains, where they could find a place to live in peace, and in five years they would not be disturbed or driven away again."

—Andrew J. Stewart, *They Knew the Prophet*, Hyrum L. Andrus, 201

Prophecy to epileptic

"[Asa Lyman] was one of the stonemasons who built the Kirtland Temple. He had been afflicted with epileptic fits for two years. The Prophet Joseph told him if he went to work on that temple he should not be afflicted with a fit. He accordingly went to work, when it was six feet high, and continued until the top stone, fifty feet high, was put on, and all the time did not have one fit."

—Matthew B. Brown, *Joseph Smith: The Man, The Mission, The Message*, 78

Prophesy when in deep trouble

Joseph Smith said, "The Lord once told me that if at any time I got into deep trouble and could see no way out of it, if I would prophesy in His name, he would fulfill my words."

—Daniel Tyler, *RJ*, 224

Rocky Mountain prophecy

Wilford Woodruff tells that, at Isaac Morley's schoolhouse in June of 1831, Joseph prophesied, "There will be tens of thousands of Latter-day Saints who will be gathered to the Rocky Mountains. . . . [T]his people will go to the Rocky Mountains; they will build temples to the Most High."

—Conference Reports, April 1898, 57

"I was a little girl when the Prophet Joseph came to Jackson county, and distinctly remember attending a meeting . . . at which he was present. At this meeting the Prophet Joseph blessed the children who were present, and I was one of them. In blessing me he said that I should live to go to the Rocky Mountains. I did not know at the time what the term Rocky Mountains meant," said Paulina Lyman.

—*RJ*, 150

In conversation with Oliver B. Huntington, Joseph Smith Sr. said, "We will just stay here (in Nauvoo) seven years. . . . The Lord has told Joseph [Smith Jr.] that when we leave here we will go into the Rocky Mountains; right into the midst of the Lamanites."

—*RJ*, 139

"The nations of the earth shall be astonished and many of them will be gathered in that land [Rocky Mountains] and assist in building cities and temples, and Israel shall be made to rejoice," said Joseph Smith on July 14, 1843, in Montrose, Iowa, at Anson Calls' home.

—*Autobiography of Anson Call*, BYU Library, 6–7, 18–20; Hyrum L. Andrus, *They Knew the Prophet*, 121

Southern States did call on other nations

"The Southern States did call upon other nations"—upon Great Britain and France to help them in the Civil War.

—D&C 87:3; Hyrum L. Andrus, *Doctrinal Themes of the Doctrine and Covenants*, 139

Tabernacle in Salt Lake

Joseph Smith told Brigham Young that he should build a temple in the Rocky Mountains, and to the west of this temple they should build a tabernacle in size 250x150 feet. Thus it was done just as Joseph Smith had instructed to Brigham Young.

—Compiler's note

Hang by a hair

According to Mosiah Hancock, Joseph Smith said, "There will be two great political parties in this country. One will be called the Republican, and the other the Democrat party. These two parties will go to war and out of these two parties will spring another party which will be the Independent American Party. The United States will spend her strength and means warring in foreign lands until other nations will say, 'Let's divide up the lands of the United States,' then the people of the U. S. will unite and swear by the blood of their fore-fathers, that the land shall not be divided. Then the country will go to war, and they will fight until one half of the U. S. army will give up, and the rest will continue to struggle. They will keep on until they are very ragged and discouraged, and almost ready to give up—when the boys from the mountains will rush forth in time to save the American Army from defeat and ruin. And they will say, 'Brethren, we are glad you have come; give us men, henceforth, who can talk with God.' Then you will have friends, but you will save the country when it's liberty hangs by a hair, as it were. "

—*Life Story of Mosiah Lyman Hancock*, 1834–1835

Hang by a thread

About July 19, 1840, Joseph prophesied that the " 'time would come when the nations of the whole earth, even this nation [the United States], will be on the very verge of crumbling to pieces,' and the United States Constitution would hang by a thread."

—John W. Welch, ed., *A Chronology of the Life of Joseph Smith*, BYU Studies, 114–15

Said Brigham Young, "Will the Constitution be destroyed: No; it will be held inviolate by this people; and, as Joseph Smith said, 'The time will come when the destiny of the nation will hang upon a single thread. At that critical juncture, this people will step forth and save it from the threatened destruction.' It will be so."

—*JD*, 7:15

Constitution of United States

Said Joseph Smith, "Even this nation will be on the verge of crumbling to pieces and tumbling to the ground, and when the Constitution is upon the brink of ruin, this people will be the Staff upon which the Nation shall lean, and they shall bear the Constitution away from the very verge of destruction."

—Alma Burton, *Discourses of the Prophet Joseph Smith*, 304

Zion—only place of peace

In 1839, the Prophet made reference to the universal chaos and said, "The time is soon coming, when no man will have any peace but in Zion and her stakes. I saw men hunting the lives of their own sons, and brother murdering brother, women killing their own daughters, and daughters seeking the lives of their mothers. I saw armies arrayed against armies. I saw blood, desolation, fires."

—*HC*, 3:390–91

Blind received their sight

Jared Carter told of Joseph healing his baby. On the same day, one of the sisters was healed from blindness by Joseph's instrumentality.

—*RJ*, 118

Dead raised

William Huntington was very sick and his spirit left his body. He "found that he was in the upper part of the room near the ceiling, and could see the body he had occupied lying on the bed, with weeping friends standing around. About this time he saw Joseph Smith and two other brethren come into the room. . . . They stepped to the bed and laid their hands upon the head of his body. . . . [W]hen Joseph said 'amen,' he heard and could see and feel with his body. . . . [A] few minutes before, [he] was dead, really and truly dead!" William called for his clothes and ate a bowl of bread and milk. He remarked, "I testify that Joseph Smith was a prophet of God."

—William Huntington, *They Knew the Prophet,* Hyrum L. Andrus, 145–46

Handkerchief of the Prophet

Wilford Woodruff was involved with Joseph Smith helping to heal all the sick Saints in Nauvoo and Montrose, Iowa, in July 1839. When Joseph was unable to go with a man to heal his twins, "he took a red silk handkerchief out of his pocket and gave it to me (Elder Woodruff), and told me to wipe their faces with the handkerchief when I administered to them, and they should be healed. He also said unto me, 'As long as you will keep that handkerchief, it shall remain a league between you and me.' I went with the man, and did as the Prophet commanded me, and the children were healed. I have possession of the handkerchief unto this day."

—*Leaves From My Journal,* 62–65; Hyrum L. Andrus, *They Knew the Prophet,* 95

Healed a lame arm

Elsa Jacobs Johnson, wife of John Johnson, "had been afflicted for some time with a lame arm, and was not able . . . to lift her hand to her head. [While Joseph was visiting this family, he] rose, and walking across the room, taking Mrs. Johnson by the hand, said in the most solemn and impressive manner, 'Woman, in the name of the Lord Jesus Christ I command thee to be whole.' The sudden mental and moral shock . . . electrified the rheumatic arm. Mrs. Johnson at once lifted it up with ease, and on her return home the next day she was able to do her washing without difficulty or pain." A Methodist preacher and a doctor were there, making a total of eight persons present.

—Scot Facer Proctor and Maurine Jensen Proctor, eds., *History of Joseph Smith by His Mother*, 311; *RJ*, 122

Healings

Joseph healed hundreds of individuals by the power of his faith and priesthood. On January 1, 1836, he healed George A. Smith of inflammatory rheumatism. One of the more famous healings was on July 22, 1839, where Joseph and Wilford Woodruff miraculously healed sick on both sides of the Mississippi river.

—*HC*, 2:354; Compiler's note

Storm calmed during King Follett discourse

Mary C. Westover remembers that during the King Follett (1788–1844) service in the grove that a heavy thunderstorm arose and the people became frightened and were starting for home. The Prophet told them to remain still and pray in their hearts and the storm would not molest them in their service. "They did as they were bidden, the storm divided over the grove. I well remember how it was storming on all sides of the grove, yet it was as calm around us as if there was no sign of a storm so nearby."

—*RJ*, 117

Majesty: Like that of Godhead

Wilford Woodruff gave insight into Joseph's power in the healing of Elijah Fordham. "Joseph . . . said, 'Do you believe that Jesus is the Christ?' 'I do, Brother Joseph,' was the response. Then the Prophet of God spoke with a loud voice, as in the majesty of the Godhead, 'Elijah, I command you, in the name of Jesus of Nazareth, to arise and be made whole.' The words of the prophet were not like the words of man, but like the voice of God. It seemed to me that the house shook from its foundation. Elijah Fordham leaped from his bed like a man raised from the dead. . . . [He] called for his clothes . . . [and] asked for a bowl of bread and milk and ate it. Then he put on his hat and followed us into the street to visit others who were sick."

—Hyrum L. Andrus, *They Knew the Prophet*, 93–94

First miracle

The first miracle of the Church was in August 1830 when Joseph cast the devil out of Newel Knight.

—J. Christopher Conkling, *A Joseph Smith Chronology*, 17

Nigh unto death

The wife of Charles R. Dana was sick, "nigh unto death." He went in search of Joseph and, with eyes full of tears, asked him to come administer to her. At first, Joseph, who was preoccupied with another matter, said he could not. But on second thought, he said he would come presently. Said Brother Dana, "My heart leaped for joy. I hurried home. I had not much more than got there before Bro. Joseph came bounding over the bottom like a chased roe. . . . [He] laid his hands on her, and while in the midst of his administering to her he seemed to be baffled. The disease or evil spirit rested upon him, but he overpowered it and pronounced great blessings upon her. After he took off his hands he turned to me and said, 'That sister will get well, take good care of her.' . . . She began to amend from that hour. I firmly believe that if he had not been called in that she would have died."

—Davis Bitton, *Images of the Prophet Joseph Smith*, 88; Charles R. Dana Autobiography

Singing inspirationally

"In this meeting I [Elizabeth Ann Whitney] received the gift of singing inspirationally, and the first song of Zion ever given in the pure language was sung by me then, and interpreted by Parley Pratt. . . . The Prophet Joseph promised me that I should never lose this gift if I would be wise in using it; and his words have been verified."

—Elizabeth Ann Whitney, *They Knew the Prophet*, Hyrum L. Andrus, 45

Speaking in tongues

- Brigham spoke in tongues when he first met Joseph.
- Joseph, while preaching to an Indian tribe, spoke in their tongue after the Indian agent spoke untruths while pretending to be Joseph's interpreter.
- Hundreds of Saints were speaking in tongues during the dedication experience in the Kirtland Temple, when the temple was filled with angels.

—*History of Joseph Smith by His Mother*, 340; Norman Rothman, *The Unauthorized Biography of Joseph Smith*, 126

On September 8, 1834, Joseph taught that the gift of speaking in tongues was particularly instituted for the preaching of the gospel to other nations.

—John W. Welch, ed., *A Chronology of the Life of Joseph Smith,* BYU Studies, 64

Strengthen my lungs

In a day before microphones, at a conference held in Nauvoo on April 8, 1843, the Prophet asked "that I may have your prayers that the Lord will strengthen my lungs, so that I may be able to make you all hear."

—*Teachings of the Prophet Joseph Smith,* 2008–2009, 493

Zion's camp water miracle like Moses's

In June of 1834, when the camp was without water, Joseph sat in the tent door and called for a spade. He selected a spot, the most convenient in the camp for men and teams to get water. Then he dug a shallow well, and immediately the water came bubbling up into it and filled it. The two hundred men and their animals all drank from this while they camped there.

—John W. Welch, ed., *A Chronology of the Life of Joseph Smith,* BYU Studies, 54–57; George Q. Cannon, *Life of Joseph Smith the Prophet*, 532

The Book of Mormon

In 1830, it cost $3,000 (guaranteed by Martin Harris at $.66 each) for the printing of 5,000 copies of the Book of Mormon. Each copy sold for $1.25. Two ¼–inch holes were placed on the book. It was covered with sheep skin and glued onto the backing. It took seven months to print and two years to bind them all.

—*Grandin Printing Historical Summary; HC,* 1:71

The Book of Mormon has 268,163 words and 238 chapters, twenty of which cover the Savior's visit to the American continent. Four prophets wrote 98 percent of the book: 63 percent by Mormon, 22 percent by Nephi, 10 percent by Moroni, and 4 percent by Jacob.

—Internet

The translation of the Book of Mormon was a greater miracle than Moses leading the children of Israel across the Red Sea.

—Mark L. McConkie Tapes

The Book of Mormon has 3,925 references to Jesus Christ, with 101 different titles.

—Susan Easton Black, fireside

Between 1830 and 1987 (157 years), 39 million copies of the Book of Mormon were printed. In 1988, President Benson said, "The time is long overdue for a massive flooding of the earth with the Book of Mormon." In 2010, the 150 millionth copy of the Book of Mormon was printed (112 million in 32 years) with presses in the United States, Brazil, Germany, Japan, Taiwan, and Korea. Languages include 82 complete languages with selections in 25 more languages. Danish was the first foreign language printed in the Book of Mormon in 1851, followed by French, Italian, Welsh, and German in 1852.

—*Ensign,* March 2010, 74–75

Absence of modern words

Words that were used in Joseph Smith's period were not used in the Book of Mormon. Some examples are pants, vest, necktie, percale, gingham, muslin, calico, broadcloth, cathedral, gentlemen, barn, corral, reverend, and beer.

—George Edward Clark, *I Cry Joseph: Fifty–Four Evidences of the Divine Calling of Joseph Smith*, 120

Literary style

Critics have come forward with "half–baked" ideas to explain the origins of the Book of Mormon. One example presented was that Sidney Rigdon or Parley Pratt must have written it. (Sidney and Parley both met Joseph for the first time after the Book of Mormon was published.) There are 578 words in Nephi's writings that are exclusively Nephi's and not Mormon's. Alma's book contains 683 words not used by Nephi or Mormon. It is easy to believe that Joseph translated the book.

—George Edward Clark, *I Cry Joseph: Fifty–Four Evidences of the Divine Calling of Joseph Smith*, 123–24

Steel tools

Decades after Joseph Smith lived, scientists were able to verify that steel tools were used in the Americas. 2 Nephi 5:15 speaks of steel, iron, copper, and brass. All of these items have now been verified.

—George Edward Clark, *I Cry Joseph: Fifty–Four Evidences of the Divine Calling of Joseph Smith*, 117–18

Jaredites landed on western shores of North America

According to Elder James E. Talmage, the Jaredites landed on the western shore of North America between California and Panama.

—*Jesus the Christ*, 15

Literary evidences

Literary evidences that the Prophet was what he said he was are enormous. The Book of Mormon chiasmus, parallelisms of forms of different kinds, word pairs, and Hebrew idioms are a few examples.

—Matthew B. Brown, *All Things Restored: Evidences and Witnesses of the Restoration*, 205–7

Lost 116 manuscript pages

Joseph finally agreed that Martin Harris could take the Book of Lehi, as long as he showed it to only five individuals: his wife, Lucy, his brother, his parents, and his wife's sister. It was shown to more than those five people, and it was stolen and lost. Martin never returned to Joseph Smith's home in Harmony, Pennsylvania. The angel Moroni took the plates and did not return them until one year later, on September 22, 1828.

—Daniel H. Ludlow, ed., *Encyclopedia of Mormonism*, 855

The five individuals who were allowed to see the lost 116 manuscript pages were:

- Lucy Harris (1792–1837), wife of Martin Harris.
- Preserved Harris (1785–1867), brother of Martin Harris.
- Nathan Harris (1758–1869), father of Martin Harris.
- Rhoda Lapham Harris (1759–1849), mother of Martin Harris.
- Polly Harris Cobb (1794–?), sister of Lucy Harris.

—Proctor, *History of Joseph Smith by His Mother*; birth and death dates by compiler; Biographical Index of 1844

Solomon Spaulding theory

Solomon Spaulding wrote a brief story about people that came to America that had no valid similarities to the Book of Mormon, but it was promoted as the source of Joseph Smith's inspiration. Doctor Philastus Hurlburt (who was not a doctor; Doctor was his actual first given name) was instrumental in publicizing this lie. He had been baptized into the Church but, while on a mission, became immoral and then apostatized and boasted that he would destroy the Church. Joseph Smith took him to court and won the case, and the judge fined Hurlburt for libel.

—*My Life's Review*, 24–26; Ted Gibbons, *Sealing the Testimony*, 58

Non-LDS scholars of Ohio's Oberlin College, where the Solomon Spaulding manuscript was located in 1881, declared soberly, after examination, that there was no similarity. "The world will have to look elsewhere for the source of the Book of Mormon," stated the president of Oberlin College.

—Hartt Wixom, *Critiquing the Critics of Joseph Smith*, 104

Steel in the Americas

When Joseph translated the Book of Mormon, the idea of fine steel was used by enemies of Mormonism as evidence that the Book of Mormon was false. But with every passing year, more evidence is brought forward that steel, iron, bronze, and copper were all used in all parts of the Americas.

—*Wikipedia*; Compiler's note

Translation

Is it possible that the translation took place as Joseph used the Urim and Thummim, which worked by faith to allow the words to appear? David

Whitmer said, "Brother Joseph would read . . . to Oliver Cowdery . . . and when it was written down and repeated to Brother Joseph to see if it was correct, then it would disappear, and another character with the interpretation would appear."

—David Whitmer, *Kansas City Journal*, June 5, 1881; Hyrum L. Andrus, *Joseph Smith, the Man and the Seer*, 102

"Joseph Smith was twenty-three years old when he began to translate the Book of Mormon. He had only a superficial education. He dictated the manuscript within a period of about sixty days. There was no research, there was no cross-checking, there was no editing; it was a remarkable accomplishment."

—Dallin H. Oaks, *American Prophet: The Story of Joseph Smith*, Lee Groberg and Heidi S. Swinton, 58

Joseph and Oliver translated about twelve pages a day.

—Truman G. Madsen tapes

Joseph translated the Book of Mormon before the standardization of the English language.

—Mark L. McConkie tapes

Tumbaga

The gold used by early goldsmiths in ancient North, South, and Central America was called tumbaga. It was usually 8 karat gold, or about 75 percent copper and 25 percent gold. Citric acid was used to treat it and dissolve the copper on the surface to expose the gold.

—"Pre-Columbian Gold and metals of Gold, Silver, Bronze, and Iron," *Wikipedia*; "*Were the Gold Plates Made of Tumbaga?" Improvement Era*, vol. 69:9, 1966, 788

Writing

"We need not apologize at all for the language or structure or form of the Book of Mormon. It is among the great books of the world. . . . Joseph Smith did not produce it and could not have produced it."

—Truman G. Madsen, *Joseph Smith the Prophet*, 24

The Restored Church

Apostles

Joseph Smith became the first ordained apostle in over 1,700 years since John the Beloved.

—Compiler's note

As of 2011, there have been 110 apostles called since 1830, of which 98 served in the Quorum of the Twelve. Twelve others were ordained apostles but served as members of the First Presidency.

—Church Almanac 2009

Baptized before April 6, 1830

- Oliver Hervey Piney Cowdery (1806–1850) May 15, 1829

  HC, 1:41

- Joseph Smith (1805–1844) May 15, 1829

  HC, 1:41

- Samuel Harrison Smith (1808–1844) May 25, 1829

  HC, 1:44

- Christian Whitmer (1798–1835) June 6, 1829

  HC, 1:44

- John Whitmer (1802–1878) June 6, 1829

  HC, 1:44

- David Whitmer (1805–1888) June 6, 1829

  HC, 1:51

- Peter Whitmer Jr. (1809–1836) June 6, 1829

  LDSBE 1:277; *HC*, 1:51

- Hyrum Smith (1800–1844) June 1829

HC, 1:51

- Wheeler Baldwin (1793–1887) January 8, 1830

HC, 4:94

- Sylvester Hulet (1800–1883) March 1830

HC, 1:44

These individuals were later rebaptized on April 6 or after, as instructed by Doctrine and Covenants 22:1–4.

Church hymns

Three Church hymns mention Joseph Smith by name:

- #25 *Now We'll Sing with One Accord*
- #26 *Joseph Smith's First Prayer*
- #27 *Praise to the Man*

—Compiler's note

Church names

- April 6, 1830: Church of Jesus Christ.
- April 1834: Church of the Latter-day Saints.
- April 26, 1838: The Church of Jesus Christ of Latter-day Saints.
- Nicknames: Latter-day Saints, Mormons, Mormonites, Josephites.

—*HC*, 1–2

Converts arrive from England

Several ships brought Saints from Liverpool, England, to strengthen Nauvoo and the Prophet. Here is a listing of ships with the number of Saints onboard and the date:

- *Britannia*—41 Saints—June 6, 1840 (first ship)
- *North America*—200 Saints—September 8, 1840
- *Sheffield*—235 Saints—February 7, 1841
- *Echo*—109 Saints
- *Uleste*—54 Saints—March 17, 1841
- *Rochester*—130 Saints—April 21, 1841,
- *Chaos*—170 Saints—November 8, 1841
- *Tyrean*—204 Saints—November 24, 1841
- *Tremont*—143 Saints—January 12, 1842
- *Hope*—270 Saints—February 5, 1842
- *John Cummins*—200 Saints—January 5, 1842

- *Hanover*—200 Saints—March 12, 1842
- *Sidney*—180 Saints—September 12, 1842
- *Medford*—214 Saints—September 25, 1842
- *Henry*—157 Saints—September 29, 1842
- *Emerald—250 Saints*—October 29, 1843
- *Swanton*—212 Saints—January 16, 1843
- *Yorkshire*—82 Saints—March 8, 1843
- *Clayborne*—106 Saints—March 21, 1843
- *Mitoka*—280 Saints—September 5, 1843
- *Champion*—91 Saints—October 21, 1843
- *Fanny*—210 Saints—January 23, 1844
- *Isaac Allerson*—60 Saints—February 6, 1844
- *Swanton*—81 Saints—February 11, 1844
- *Glasgow*—150 Saints—March 5, 1844

—*LDSCC*, 21

Council of fifty

1. George J. Adams	1810–1880	
2. Almon Whiting Babbitt	1812–1856	
3. Alexander Badlam	1806–1894	
4. Samuel Bent	1778–1846	
5. John Milton Bernhisel	1799–1846	
6. Edward Bonney	1807–1864	(possible non-LDS)
7. Uriah Brown	1784–?	
8. Reynolds Cahoon	1790–1861	
9. William Clayton	1814–1879	
10. Joseph Coolidge	1814–1871	
11. Alpheus Cutler	1784–1864	
12. Marenus G. Eaton	1811– ?	(possible non-LDS)
13. James Emmett	1803–1852	
14. Amos Fielding	1792–1875	
15. Joseph Fielding	1797–1863	
16. David Fullmer	1803–1879	
17. Jedidiah Morgan Grant	1816–1856	
18. John Portineus Greene	1793–1844	
19. Peter Haws	1796–1862	
20. David Sprague Hollister	1808–1858	
21. Orson Hyde	1805–1878	
22. Samuel James	1814–1876	
23. Benjamin Franklin Johnson	1818–1905	

24. Heber Chase Kimball	1801–1868
25. John Doyle Lee	1812–1877
26. Cornelius Peter Lott	1798–1850
27. Amasa Mason Lyman	1813–1877
28. William Marks	1792–1872
29. George Miller	1794–1856
30. John Edward Page	1799–1867
31. John Davis Parker	1799–1891
32. William Wines Phelps	1792–1872
33. Orson Pratt	1811–1881
34. Parley Parker Pratt	1807–1857
35. Charles Coulsen Rich	1809–1883
36. Levi Richards	1799–1876
37. Willard Richards	1804–1854
38. Sidney Rigdon	1793–1876
39. Orrin Porter Rockwell	1815–1878
40. Elias Smith	1804–1888
41. George Albert Smith	1817–1875
42. Hyrum Smith	1800–1844
43. John Smith	1781–1854
44. Joseph Smith Jr.	1805–1844
45. William B. Smith	1811–1894
46. Erastus Snow	1818–1888
47. Orson Spencer	1802–1855
48. John Taylor	1808–1887
49. Ezra Thayer	1790–1856
50. Lorenzo D. Wasson	1819–1857
51. Newel Kimball Whitney	1795–1850
52. Lyman Wight	1796–1858
53. Wilford Woodruff	1807–1898
54. David Dutton Yearsley	1808–1849
55. Brigham Young	1801–1877

Some records say there were only forty-six called before Joseph Smith was murdered.

Note: All of the Twelve were, but the counselors in the First Presidency, Sidney Rigdon, and William Law were not.

—*HC,* 7: 231; Bejamin F. Johnson, *Friend of the Prophets*, 53; Michael Quinn, "The Mormon Hierarchy," Internet

Doctors and physicians who followed Joseph Smith

The following is a list of doctors and physicians, their birth and death dates, and the year they were baptized.

- Bennett, John Cook (1804–1867)—1840; Medical doctor in 1825.
  —*Revelations*, 253
- Bernhisel, John Milton (1799–1881)—1841; Physician, graduated from University of Pennsylvania in 1827.
  —*Prominent Characters,* xxxvi
- Cowdery, Warren A. (1788–1851)—1831; Physician, druggist. Apostatized and stayed in Kirtland.
  —*BR,* 538
- Foster, Robert D. (1811–1878)—1839; Medical doctor.
  —*Revelations*, 257
- Galland, Isaac (1791–1858)—1839; Medical doctor since 1821.
  —*Revelations*, 258
- Hovey, John Grafton (1820–1868)—1837; Doctor.
  —*GD,* 164
- Hullinger, Harvey Coe (1824–1926)—1842; Physician.
  —*GD,* 164
- Johnson, Luke (1807–1861)—1831; Doctor, teacher, and farmer.
  —*BD,* 418
- Marsh, Thomas Baldwin (1799–1866)—1830; Doctor. Apostatized but later returned to the Church and went to Utah.
  —*Revelations*, 42
- McCord, James (*est.*1806–?)—*est.*1836; Medical doctor at Far West. On High Council.
  —*BR,* 12
- McLellin, William E. (1806–1883)—1830; Medical doctor and teacher.
  —*LDSBE,* 1:83
- Morley, George (1803–1875)—*bef.*1840; Physician. Left the Church and joined RLDS.
  —*BR,* 502
- Nuebaur, Alexander (1808–1883)—1838; Surgeon and dentist. First Jewish convert.
  —*GD,* 252

- Page, Hiram (1800–1852)—1830; Medical doctor.

  —*Revelations*, 40

- Riggs, Burr (1811–1860)—*bef.* 1834; Physician.

  —*Revelations*, 155

- Richards, Levi (1799–1914)—1836; Brother of Willard. He was a doctor in Nauvoo.

  —*GD*, 293

- Richards, Willard (1804–1854)—1836; Medical doctor near Boston.

  —*LDSBE*, 1:53

- Whitlock, Harvey G. (1809–1874)—1831; Doctor. Excommunicated and rebaptized three times. Moved to California.

  —*Revelations*, 81; *BR*, 520

- Williams, Frederick Granger (1787–1842)—1830; Medical doctor.

  —*LDSBE*, 1:51

First 100 converts baptized into the Church

This list of the first 100 converts represents the best efforts of the compiler comprising thousands of hours of research, spanning several years, and involving hundreds of sources. It will never be 100 percent accurate because many early Church records were lost, and many sources contain conflicting data. For some individuals, including Joseph Smith's sisters Catherine and Sophronia, there is no baptismal date available from any known source. They were probably baptized within the first 100, but neither Church records nor any diary or book lays claim to that information. It is hoped that this list will facilitate continued research and refinement of the available data. See Appendix A for an expanded listing, as well as *Joseph Smith A–Z: Reference Encyclopedia, Volume 3 (Tribute)* by Wayne J. Lewis.

1. Cowdery, Oliver Hervey Piney (1806–1850)—May 15, 1829

   —*HC*, 2:374; *GD*, 75; *EPB*, 7; *Kirtland Sketch Book*, 3; *Profile*, 19; *Mormon Land*, 103

2. Smith, Joseph Jr. (1805–1844)—May 15, 1829

   —*HC*, 1; *ELDS*; *EPB*, 13, 51; *Mormon Land*, 150; *Affidavits*, 601

3. Smith, Samuel Harrison (1808–1844)—May 25, 1829

   —*HC*, 1:44; *GD*, 327 ; *ELDS*; D&C*WW*, 148; *Mormon Land*, 150; *Affidavits*, 597; *Revelations*, 19

4. Whitmer, Christian (1798–1835)—June 6, 1829

   —*HC*, 1:81; *LDSBE*, 1:276; *Mormon Land*, 161

5. Whitmer, David (1805–1888)—June 6, 1829

—*Profile,* 114; *Mormon Land,* 161; *RJ,* 452

6. Whitmer, John (1802–1878)—June 6, 1829

—*HC,* 2:126; D&C*WW,* 166; *Profile,* 76; *Mormon Land,* 161

7. Whitmer, Peter Jr. (1809–1836)—June 6, 1829

—*Biographical Appendix,* 19 ; *LDSBE,* 1:277; *Mormon Land,* 161; *ELDS*

8. Smith, Hyrum Sr. (1800–1844)—June 1829

—*GD,* 321; *HC,* 2:183–85; *Profile,* 112; *Mormon Land,* 150; *Affidavits,* 619–38; Jeffrey S. O'Driscoll, *Hyrum Smith,* 27

9. Hulet, Sylvester (1800–1824)—March 6, 1830

—*HC,* 2:139; *Biographical Appendix,* 10; *ELDS*; *Mormon Land,* 122

10. Harris, Martin (1783–1875)—April, 6, 1830

—D&C*WW,* 42; *Profile,* 33; *Mormon Land,* 118; *EPB,* 37; William G. Hartley, *Stand By My Servant Joseph,* 60

11. Rockwell, Orrin Porter (1813 or 1815–1878)—April 6, 1830

—*GD,* 300; *ELDS*; *Mormon Land,* 146

12. Rockwell, Sarah Witt (1785–?)—April 6, 1830

—*ELDS*; *Affidavits,* 529

13. Smith, Joseph Sr. (1777–1840)—April 6, 1830

—*BD,* 440; *HC,* 1; William G. Hartley, *Stand By My Servant Joseph,* 60

14. Smith, Lucy Mack (1775–1856)—April 6, 1830

—*BD,* 440; *GD,* 326; *RJ,* 73; *HC,* 1:2; *LDSBE* 1:590; *ELDS*; *Mormon Land,* 131; William G. Hartley, *Stand By My Servant Joseph,* 60

15. Page, Catherine Whitmer (1807–?)—April 11, 1830

—*HC,* 1:81; *ELDS*

16. Page, Hiram (Doctor) (1800–1852)—April, 11, 1830

—*HC,* 1:81; *Revelations,* 40; *Mormon Land,* 138; Lewis Missouri Land Index of 1979; *Missouri Mormon Burial,* 109

17. Whitmer, Anne Schott (1801–1866)—April, 11, 1830

—*BR*-2, 521; *HC,* 1:81; *LDSBE* 1:276

18. Whitmer, Elizabeth Anne Schott (1803–?)—April, 11, 1830; her middle name was Anne like her sister's first name.

—*BR*-2, 521

19. Whitmer, Jacob C. (1800–1856)—April 11, 1830

—*HC*, 1:81; *LDSBE* 1:276; *Profile*, 114; *Mormon Land*, 161

20. Whitmer, Mary (*est.*1802–?)—April 11, 1830

—*HC*, 1:81

21. Jolly, Elizabeth (*est.*1810–?)—April 18, 1830

—*HC*, 1:81

22. Jolly, Vincent (1809–1863)—April 18, 1830

—*HC*, 1:86; *BR*, 494

23. Jolly, William (1777–1863)—April 18, 1830

—*HC*, 1:86; *BR*, 494

24. Peterson, Richard B. Ziba (*est.* 1807–1849)—April 18, 1830

—*HC*, 1:367; D&C*WW*, 114 ; *Biographical Appendix*, 14, *Revelations*, 45

25. Whitmer, Elizabeth Ann (1815–1856)—April 18, 1830

—*BR*-2, 521

26. Whitmer, Mary Elsa Musselman (1778–1856)—April 18, 1830

—*HC*, 1:81; *BR*-1, 522; *ELDS*; *Missouri Mormon Burials*, 117

27. Whitmer, Peter Sr. (1773–1854)—April 18, 1830

—D&C*WW* 168; *Mormon Land*, 161

28. Dille, David Buel (1812–1887)—May 6, 1830

—*Jonathan Oldham Duke Journal*, 16; *ELDS*

29. Conover, Evaline Golden (1808–1847)—May 27, 1830

—*ELDS*

30. Knight, Newel Kimball (1800–1847)—May 1830

—*HC*, 1:84; *Profile*, 43, 107; *Biographical Appendix*, 10, *BR*-2, 487; *Mormon Land*, 128; Lewis Missouri Land Index of 1979; *Affidavits*, 580; *HC*, 1:77

31. Smith, Katherine (1813–1900)—June 9, 1830

—*HC*, 1:86; *BR*, 515; *The Joseph Smith Papers* 1:451

32. Smith, William B. (1811–1890)—June 9, 1830

—*GD*, 327; *Profile*, 112; *Mormon Land*, 151; D&C*WW*

33. Basset, Heman A. (1814–1876)—June 28, 1830

—D&C*WW*, 6; *Mormon Land*, 93

34. Colburn, Emily (*est.* 1800–?)—June 28, 1830

—*HC,* 1:87; William G. Hartley, *Stand by My Servant Joseph,* 75, 135

35. Crosby, Phebe (1800–?)—June 28, 1830

—*GD,* 198; D&C*WW,* 83; *Revelations,* 22; *ELDS*

36. Culver, Aaron (*est.*1766–1831)—June 28, 1830

—*BR* 482; *Missouri Mormon Burials,* 23

37. Culver, Esther Peck (1766–1836)—June 28, 1830

—*HC,* 1:88; *BR,* 482; *Mormon Land,* 104

38. DeMille, Anna Knight (1804–1878)—June 28, 1830

—William G. Hartley, *Stand by My Servant Joseph,* 98; *ELDS*

39. Godkin, Elizabeth (1821–?)—June 28, 1830

—*HC,* 1:117; *Mormon Land,* 113

40. Hale, Levi (*est.*1804–?)—June 28, 1830

—*HC,* 1:88; Gracia N. Jones, *Emma & Joseph, Their Divine Mission,* 15

41. Knight, Joseph Jr. (1818–1846)—June 28, 1830

—*GD,* 198; *Mormon Land,* 127; Lewis Missouri Land Index of 1979

42. Knight, Joseph Sr. (1772–1847)—June 28, 1830

—*GD,* 198; D&C*WW,* 83, *Revelations,* 22

43. Knight, Polly (1811–1844)—June 28, 1830

— *ELDS*; William G. Hartley, *Stand by My Servant Joseph,* 98

44. Knight, Polly Peck (1774–1831)—June 28, 1830

—*BR*-2, 497; *ELDS*; *Missouri Mormon Burials,* 24

45. Knight, Sarah Sally Colburn (1804–1834)—June 28, 1830

—William G. Hartley, *Stand by My Servant Joseph,* 75; *Profile,* 43; *Mormon Land,* 128; *Missouri Mormon Burials,* 69

46. Peck, Hezekiah (1782–1850)—June 28, 1830

—*HC,* 1:88; *BD,* 429; *Missouri Mormon Burials,* 194

47. Peck, Martha Long (1789–?)—June 28, 1830

—*BR*-2, 505, *HC,* 1:88

48. Smith, Emma Hale (1804–1879)—June 28, 1830

—*BD*–2, 438; *ELDS*; *EPB,* 30

49. Stringham, Esther Knight (1798–1831)—June 28, 1830

—*BR-2*, 517, *ELDS*; *Missouri Mormon Burials*, 26

50. Stringham, Julia Harriet (*est.*1810–?)—June 28, 1830

—William G. Hartley, *Stand by My Servant Joseph*, 75; *ELDS*

51. Stringham, William (1787–1865)—June 28, 1830

—*HC*, 1:88

52. Whiting, Sally Hulett (1786–1846)—June 28, 1830

—*ELDS*; Whiting family records; *Missouri Land*, 161

53. Curtis, Thomas (1799–1838)—June 29, 1830

—*ELDS; Missouri Mormon Burial*, 178

54. Dibble, Philo Sr. (1806–1895)—June 29, 1830

—*HC*, 1:431; *GD*, 89; *BR*, 431; *ELDS*; *Mormon Land*, 106; Alex Baugh, *Call to Arms*, 173; *Mormon Land*, 106; *Affidavits*, 593

55. DeMille, Freeborn (1795–1881)—June 30, 1830

—*ELDS*; *Mormon Land*, 106

56. Hulet, Charles (1790–1863)—June 30, 1830

—*Biographical Appendix*, 10; *Mormon Land*, 122; *ELDS*

57. Jolly, Harriet (1816–1865)—June 1830

—*HC*, 1:86

58. Jolly, John (*est.*1800–?)—June 1830

—*HC*, 1:86; *Mormon Land*, 125

59. Jolly, Julia Anne (1815–1889)—June 1830

—*HC*, 1:86; *BR*, 494

60. Poorman, John (*est.*1784–?)—June 1830

—*HC*, 1:86; *BR*, 506; *Mormon Land*, 142

61. Rockwell, Caroline (*est.* 1810–?)—June 1830

—*HC*, 1:86

62. Rockwell, Electa (1814–1900)—June 1830

—*HC*, 1:86; *Mormon Land*, 146

63. Rockwell, Peter (*est.* 1812–?)—June 1830

—*HC*, 1:86

64. Rollins, Mary Elizabeth (1818–1913)—June 1830

—*BR*, 486; *RJ*, 77; *GD*, 212; *ELDS*

65. Smith, Don Carlos (1816–1841)—June 1830

—*HC*, 1:86; *GD*, 592; *Revelations*, 275; *ELDS*; *Mormon Land*, 150

66. Smith, Jerusha Barden (1805–1837)—June 1830

—*HC*, 1:86; *BR*, 514; *Mormon Graves in Kirtland*, 33

67. Sweet, Northrup (1802–?)—June 1830

—D&C*WW*, 156

68. Williams, Frederick Granger (Doctor) (1787–1843)—June 1830

—*HC*, 1:125; *Mormon Land*, 162; *EPB*, 7

69. Porter, Arreta Warringer (1790–1864)—August 10, 1830; he baptized Morris Phelps in August 1831, evidence he had been a member for a while.

—Porter family records; *ELDS*

70. Porter, Chauncy Warringer (1812–1868)—August 10, 1830

—*Biographical Appendix*, 14; *Mormon Land*, 142; Porter family records

71. Porter, Malinda (1814–1870)—August 10, 1830

—*HC*, 3:211; *RJ*, 94; Porter family records

72. Porter, Nancy Warringer (1790–1864)—August 10, 1830

—Porter family records

73. Porter, Sanford Sr. (1790–1873)—August 10, 1830

—Porter family records; *LDSBE*, 4:622; *Mormon Land*, 142

74. Porter, Sarah (1816–1839)—August 10, 1830

—Porter family records

75. King, Thomas Jefferson (1806–1876)—September 1, 1830

—*LDSBE*, 2:81; *Mormon Land*, 127; *ELDS*

76. Pratt, Parley Parker Sr. (1807–1857)—September 1, 1830

—*HC*, 1:181; *GD*, 282; *HC*, 2:183–85; *Profile*, 55; Alex Baugh, *A Call to Arms*, 173; *Mormon Land*, 143; *Affidavits*, 580, 639–46; *Mormon Graves in Kirtland*, 9

77. Marsh, Thomas Baldwin (1799–1866)—September 3, 1830

—*GD*, 227; *ELDS*; *Mormon Land*, 132

78. Reed, John (1783–1846)—September 12, 1830

—*HC,* 2:206; *LDSBE,* 3:247; *ELDS*; *Profile,* 57

79. Pratt, Orson (1811–1881)—September 19, 1830

—*HC,* 1:127; D&C*WW,* 116–17; *GD,* 281; *Profile,* 10: *ELDS*; *A Call to Arms* by Alex Baugh, 173; *Mormon Land,* 143; *Affidavits,* 580

80. Johnson, Elizabeth Knight (1817–1883)—September 1830

—*ELDS*

81. Marsh, Elizabeth Godkin (*est.* 1801–1866)—October 1830

—*Profile,* 44; *ELDS*; *Mormon Land,* 132

82. Billings, Titus Sr. (1793–1866)—October 6, 1830

—*LDS Chronology,* xxiii; *Revelations,* 102; *Church Almanac 1910;* Alex Baugh, *A Call to Arms,* 173; *Revelations,* 102; *Wikipedia*; 2010 *Church Almanac,* 134

83. Murdock, John (1792–1871)—October 6, 1830

—*GD,* 250; *HC,* 2:183–185 ; *Profile,* 109; *LDSBE,* 2:364; *ELDS*; *Mormon Land,* 136; *FarWestHistory.com*

84. Whitney, Elizabeth Ann L. Smith (1800–1881)—October 6, 1830

—*HC,* 1:146; *Profile,* 76; *LDSBE,* 3:563, 4:200; *ELDS*

85. Whitney, Newel Kimball (1795–1850)—October 6, 1830

—Church Almanac 2010, 132; *Profile,* 76, 114; *Mormon Land,* 161; *Kirtland Sketch Book,* 14

86. Burk, John Mathias (1793–1853)—October 9, 1830

—*Profile,* 12; *ELDS*; *Mormon Land,* 98; Lewis Missouri land index 1979.

87. Hancock, Levi Ward (1803–1882)—October 9, 1830

—*GD,* 138; *Profile,* 32; *Revelations,* 77; *Mormon Land,* 115

88. Thayer, Ezra (1787–1856)—October 10, 1830

—*HC,* 3:39; *BR–3,* 517, 598; *Biographical Appendix,* 18; *Mormon Land,* 155

89. Cahoon, Reynolds (1790–1861)—October 11, 1830

—*BD,* 403; *BR-2,* 477; *Mormon Land,* 99

90. Cahoon, William Farrington (1813–1897)—October 16, 1830

—*BD,* 403; *Profile,* 13; *BR-2,* 480; *Mormon Land,* 99

91. Dibble, Celia Kent (1803–1840)—October 16, 1830

—*ELDS*

92. Murdock, Julia Clapp (1796–1831)—October 16, 1830

—*LDSBE,* 2:375; *Profile,* 49; *Mormon Graves in Kirtland,* 86

93. Cole, Barnet (1796–1857)—October 1830

—*HC,* 3:254; *Millenniel Star,* 730–31; *ELDS*; *Mormon Land,* 101; *Affidavits,* 577

94. Cole, Phebe Van Alstine (1803–1883)—October 1830

—*Mormon Land,* 101; *ELDS*; Internet

95. Williams, Rebecca Swain (1798–1861)—October 1830

—*RJ,* 502; *EPB,* 44; *ELDS*; *Ensign,* April 2011, 38–41

96. Hancock, Solomon Jr. (1793–1847)—November 3, 1830

—*HC,* 2:113; *BD,* 411; *BR,* 671; *ELDS*; *RJ,* 3; *Mormon Land,* 118; *Affidavits,* 607; *Missouri Mormon Burials,* 68

97. Stanton, Clinda Graves (1797–?)—November 3, 1830

—*ELDS*

98. Stanton, Daniel Sr. (1795–1872)—November 3, 1830

—*Biographical Appendix,* 17; *Mormon Land,* 152; *Affidavits,* 609

99. Cleveland, Henry Alanson (1809–1867)—November 5, 1830

—William G. Hartley, *Stand by My Servant Joseph,* 191; *ELDS*; *Mormon Land,* 101; *Far West History.com*

100. Beman, Alvah (1775–1837)—November 6, 1830

—*BD,* 399; *HC,* 2: *Mormon Land,* 93; *Profile,* 183–85; *BR,* 659

It's all over—the game's up

"At a dozen points it seems it's all over. The game's up. There's no way. And yet out of it comes a greater success and a growing movement that ultimately survives [Joseph]."

—Ronald Esplin, *American Prophet: The Story of Joseph Smith,* Lee Groberg and Heidi S. Swinton, 107

Key that will never rust

"I heard him say, 'I will give you a key that will never rust—if you will stay with the majority of the Twelve Apostles, and the records of the Church, you will never be led astray.' "

—William G. Nelson, *They Knew the Prophet,* Hyrum L. Andrus, 134

Keys of the Kingdom

Joseph Smith received *all the keys of all the prophets* who ever lived so that he could carry forth the final, greatest, and last dispensation of the fulness of times.

—Compiler's note

Given to the Twelve Apostles

On March 18, 1844, Joseph conferred the keys and responsibility for the kingdom to the Twelve Apostles.

—Wilford Woodruff, *RJ*, 373

Kirtland Camp members

This is the alphabetized list of the Saints who traveled as a group from Kirtland, Ohio, in March 1838 to Missouri. They signed a constitution to help, assist, and protect each other for this thousand mile journey. With Joseph Smith and others being in the Liberty Jail, the Missouri Saints were in the middle of leaving the state of Missouri. The Kirtland Camp had projected to settle in the Adam-ondi-Ahman area. Most of them, after arriving in Daviess and Caldwell Counties, just turned around and joined the fleeing Saints back to Quincy, Illinois.

Name and number in group

Allen, Daniel Jr. (4)
Angell, Thomas O. (4)
Baker, Baker (2)
Baker, Benjamin (6)
Baldwin, Amos (12)
Baldwin, Nathan B. (2)
Barnet, Samuel (5)
Bird, Charles (7)
Blanchard, Asaph (1)
Bliss, Daniel (2)
Blood, Justin (5)
Bond, Abram (3)
Boynton, Abram (7)
Bowen, Daniel (7)
Brasier, Richard (4)
Brewster, Zephaniah W. (9)
Brooks, George W. (4)
Brown, Alfred (2)
Brown, James (7)
Brunett, Jason (7)
Butterfield, Benjamin (7)
Butterfield, Josiah (4)
Butterfield, Thomas (3)
Byington, Hiram H. (8)
Call, Anson (3)
Campbell, Alexander (?)
Carey, William (?)
Carpenter, William (5)
Carter, John (2)
Carter, Dominicus (6)
Cheney, Amasa (6)
Cheney, Edwin (4)
Cheney, Elijah (2)
Cheney, Nathan (4)
Cheney, Orin (9)
Clark, Joseph C. (6)
Cooley, Adonijah (5)
Coon, Joseph (4)
Cowles, Austin W. (9)
Crosby, Jonathan (2)
Crosier, Munro (2)
Daniels, Rueben (7)
Dayton, Hiram (12)
Dewitt, Isaac (8)
Draper, Thomas (?)
Draper, William, Sr. (2
Draper, Zemira (6)
Drury, Joel (5)

Dunham, Jonathan (4)
Dustin, David K. (2)
Eager, Lewis (3)
Earl, William (11)
Field, Wiliam (5)
Fisher, Cyrus B. (6)
Fisher, Jonathan (5)
Folger, John R. (4)
Foster, James (6)
Fowler, Samuel (8)
Fuller, Amos B. (3)
Gaylord, E. B. (6)
Gilbert, Shearman A. (3)
Gray, David (8)
Greabble, John (8)
Gribble, William (3)
Griffiths, Hiram (3)
Griffith, Michael (6)
Hale, Jonathan H. (5)
Hale, Samuel (3)
Hamond, John (6)
Hampton, Jonathan (4)
Hanchet, Martin (5)
Harmon, Jesse (6)
Harvey, Joel (5)
Headlock, Stephen (2)
Healey, Arnold (3)
Hedlock, Rueben (8)
Harriman, Henry (2)
Holmer, Jonathan H. (7)
Holmon, James S. (7)
Holman, Joshua S. (8)
Hull, Benjamin K. (6)
Johnson, Aaron (4)
Johnson, Joel Hills (6)
Johnson, Julia (8)
Judd, Joel (3)
King, Eleaser (7)
King, Eleaser, Jr. (3)
King, John M. (4)
Knight, Nathan K. (9)
Lake, Jabez (5)
Lamereaux, Andrew (7)
Lamereaux, John (6)
Lethead, James (?)
McArthur, Duncan (9)
McCaseland, Joseph (4)
McDonald, Michael (5)
Merriam, Elijah (5)
Miller, Josiah (10)
Moore, Ethan A. (8)
Morris, Laban (2)
Mulliner, Samuel (5)
Munroe, Henry (3)
Nickerson, Amos (6)
Noble, Joseph Bates (7)
Nuptire, Daniel L. (3)
Olney, Oliver (9)
Osgood, Levi (5)
Packard, Noah (9)
Peck, Martin H. (6)
Parker, J. D. (3)
Parker, Mary (8)
Parker, Samuel (4)
Perry, William (4)
Pettingill, Alanson (5)
Pierce, Isaac W. (5)
Pine, Joseph (6)
Porter, Jared (3)
Pratt, William B. (4)
Pulsipher, Daniel (4)
Pulsipher, Elias (8)
Pulsipher, John
Pulsipher, Zerah (7)
Putnam, Jonas (6)
Redfield, David Harvey
Richardson, Stephen (8)
Rogers, Isaac (4)

Rowe, Oliver (6)
Rowe, Stephen (6)
Rulison, John (8)
Sanborn, Enoch S. (5
Scovil, Lucius N. (4)
Shumway, Otis (7)
Shumway, Stephen (3)
Shuman, William (7)
Smith, Elias (5)
Smith, Warren (7)
Snow, Gardner (3)
Starks, Stephen (6)
Staker, Nathan (6)
Stevens, Henry (3)
Stringham, George (6)
Strop, James (6)
Sweat, John (10)
Tanner, John (10)
Thompson, Charles (2)
Thornton, Ira (7)
Thorp, John (7)
Vanleuven, Cornelius (3)
Vanleuven, Frederick M. (6)
Vanleuven, John Jr. (9)
Whittle, Alba (6)
Wilbur, W. S. (2)
Wilson, William (3)
Wiley, Jeremiah (4)
Wood, Abraham (4)
Wright, Alexander (1)
Wright, Asa (10)
York, Aaron M. (4)
Young, Joseph (5)

—*HC*, 3:91–93

Millions shall know Brother Joseph again

The Church reached one million members in 1947.

—Church Almanac 2008, 599

Mission statement

"No unhallowed hand can stop the work from progressing; persecutions may rage, mobs may combine, armies may assemble, calumny may defame, but the truth of God will go forth boldly, nobly, and independent, till it has penetrated every continent, visited every clime, swept every country, and sounded in every ear, till the purposes of God shall be accomplished, and the Great Jehovah shall say the work is done."

—Joseph Smith, *Wentworth Letter*

Missionaries

There were 16 missionaries in 1830 and 586 in 1844. There was a total of 1,782 missionaries called during Joseph's lifetime. By 2003, a total of 1 million had been called to serve.

—*Church Almanac* 2008, 655

Under the Lord's direction, Joseph sent missionaries to

- New York.
- All the states of the Union and to others, states like Missouri.

- The Lamanites in present day Sandusky, Ohio, and other locations.
- England.
- The Pacific Islands (Noah Rogers and Addison Pratt).
- Jerusalem (Orson Hyde).

—*HC*, 5:405; Compiler's note

Missionary until the day of his death

Joseph Smith went on dozens of short missions, in duration from a few days to a few months.

—Compiler's Note

Mississippi baptisms for the dead

On Sunday, March 20, 1842, Joseph Smith performed 80 baptisms for the dead in the Mississippi River. The next Sunday, March 27, he performed 107 more.

—*LDSCC*, 21

Spark kindled in Palmyra

"The spark that was kindled in Palmyra will march boldly on."

—Gordon B. Hinckley, *No One Can Take Your Place,* Sheri Dew, 150

Stakes organized

Joseph organized a dozen stakes during his leadership of the Church:

- Kirtland Stake—February 17, 1834
- Clay/Caldwell, Missouri Stake—July 3, 1834
- Adam-ondi-Ahman Stake—January 28, 1838
- Nauvoo Stake—October 5, 1839
- Zarahemla, Iowa Stake—October 5, 1839
- Ramus, Illinois Stake—July 4, 1840
- Quincy, Illinois Stake—October 25, 1840
- Freedom, Illinois Stake—October 27, 1840
- Lima, Illinois Stake—October 22, 1840
- Mt. Hope, Illinois Stake—October 27, 1840
- Geneva, Illinois Stake—November 1, 1840
- Springfield, Illinois Stake—November 5, 1840

—*Church Almanac,* 2008

Wards in Nauvoo

By December 4, 1842, Nauvoo was divided into ten wards, with bishops in each.

—*LDSCC*, 21

Witnesses were predominately part of the Whitmer family

- Three Witnesses: David Whitmer was one of the Three Witnesses. His brother-in-law Oliver Cowdery (husband of Elizabeth Ann Whitmer) was also one of the Three Witnesses. Two of the Three Witnesses were from the Whitmer family.
- Eight Witnesses: Four Whitmer brothers, John, Christian, Jacob, and Peter Jr., were among the Eight Witnesses. Also, a Whitmer in-law, Hiram Page (husband of Catherine Whitmer), was one of Eight Witnesses. Five of the Eight Witnesses were from the Whitmer family.
- Additional Whitmer witness: Mother Mary Musselman Whitmer (1778–1856) saw Moroni and the gold plates and became the only woman to see them.

Three Witnesses saw eight things

Oliver Cowdery, David Whitmer, and Martin Harris saw eight things:

- A resurrected glorified celestial being, the angel Moroni.
- The Liahona (directors or interpreters given to Lehi).
- A table.
- The sword of Laban (this sword was supposed to be made by Joseph in Egypt, making it about 4,000 years old, and handed down by lineage to Laban).
- The extra large breastplate.
- Urim and Thummim (perhaps the same set that Mahonri Moriancumer, or the Brother of Jared, had 4,300 years before).
- The gold plates (they both saw and hefted them).
- The engravings on the gold plates as the sheets of gold were turned. They also heard the angel's voice and his serious commandants to them, which stuck with them for a lifetime.

—D&C 17:1

Eight Witnesses saw three things

The Eight Witnesses saw:

- A resurrected glorified celestial being, the angel Moroni.
- The gold plates (they both saw and hefted them).
- The engravings on the plates.

These witnesses included the four Whitmer brothers, their brother-in-law Hiram Page, and Joseph's father and his two brothers.

Note: Oliver Cowdery was also their brother-in-law (his wife was Elizabeth Ann Whitmer).

—D&C, preface testimony

The extra witness saw two things

Mary Whitmer, mother of a most wonderful family, saw:

- A resurrected glorified celestial being, the angel Moroni.
- The gold plates. She heard him speak with sympathy and kindness of her service in caring for a houseful of a dozen or more individuals.

Note: Five of her sons and two of her sons-in-law were allowed to see the gold plates. Counting herself, that is eight of the twelve witnesses who saw the plates.

—*The Twelfth Witness,* Church movie about Mary Whitmer's experience

Ten logical individuals who could have been witnesses if Joseph were choosing

Joseph was not in charge of who was to see the gold plates; it was the angel Moroni. If Joseph had been able to choose, certainly a few more would have been added to the list:

- Joseph's mother, Lucy Mack Smith.
- His wife, Emma Hale Smith (from tradition, we are told that she desired and asked Joseph for this privilege).
- Isaac Hale, his father-in-law (this could have saved Emma years of stress).
- Elizabeth Lewis Hale, his mother-in-law (every man wants to please his mother-in-law).
- Joseph Knight Sr. (provided hundreds of dollars of food and supplies so the translation could take place).
- His sister, Sophronia.
- Hyrum's wife, Jerusha.
- Lucy Harris (which would have quieted her nagging and eased Martin's burden).
- Peter Whitmer Sr. (furnished room and board for the translating team).
- Josiah Stowell (it was his carriage Emma and Joseph used to go to the Hill Cumorah, and Joseph and Emma spent their honeymoon at his house in Bainbridge, New York).

—Compiler's note

Zion's Camp

Joseph's group of Zion's Camp left Kirtland on May 5, 1834, arriving in Missouri on June 4th and in Clay County on June 24th. They arrived back in Kirtland on August 1, 1834. The trip took nearly three months.

—*HC*, 2:180–81

Zion's Camp Members List

A list of the 210 members of Zion's Camp, including women and children. Also the names of the fourteen individuals who died of cholera in the camp. The list of prominent Church members who did not go on Zion's Camp.

Name	Birth/ Death	Baptism	Miscellaneous and Source
Aldrich, Hazen	1797–1886	1832	Apostatized in 1837 and joined Brewsterites. Moved to California. —*HC,* 2:183–85
Allen, Joseph Stewart	1810–1889	*est.*1834	—*HC,* 2:183–85; *Profile,* 1
Allred, James	1784–1878	1832	—*Coneto Creek Taylors,* 17
Allred, Isaac	1813–1859	1832	—*HC,* 2:183–85; *Profile,* 2
Allred, Martin Carrol	1806–1840	*est.*1834	—*HC,* 2:183–85; *Profile,* 2
Allred, Reddick Newton	1822–1905	1833	Joined Zion's Camp at Salt River, Missouri. —*Reddick Newton Allred Journal*
Andrus, Milo	1814–1893	1833	Later a patriarch. —*HC,* 2:183–85; *Wikipedia; LDSBE,* 3:585
Angell, Solomon	1806–1881	1832	—*HC,* 2:183–85
Avery, Allen Aaron	1812–1877	*bef.*1834	—*HC,* 2:183–85; *BR,* 472
Babbitt, Almon Whiting	1812–1856	1835	—*HC,* 2:183–85; *BR,* 398
Backman, Hiram	*est.*1800–?	*bef.*1834	—*HC,* 2:183–85

Name	Birth/ Death	Baptism	Miscellaneous and Source
Badlam, Alexander Sr.	1818–1894	*bef.*1834	—*BR*, 398. *HC*, 2:183–85
Baker, Samuel	1755–	*bef.*1834	Was oldest member of Zion's Camp at seventy-nine years old. —*Wikipedia. HC*, 2:183–85
Baldwin, Nathan Bennett	1812–1891	1833	—*HC*, 2:183–85
Barber, Elam	*est.*1830–1840	*bef.*1834	Died in Missouri. —*HC*, 2:183–85
Barlow, Israel	1806–1883	*bef.*1834	—*HC*, 2:183–85
Barnes, Lorenzo D.	1812–1842	1833	—*HC*, 2:183–85. *GD*, 19
Barney, Edson	1805–1905 or 1906	1831	Saw Joseph Smith receive a revelation. Carpenter. —*HC*, 2:183–85
Barney, Royal Jr.	1808–1890	*bef.*1834	—*HC*, 2:183–85
Benner, Henry	1800–1880	1833	—*HC*, 2:183–85
Bent, Samuel	1778–1846	1833	—*HC*, 2:183–85
Booth, Lorenzo Dow	1807–1847	1833	—*HC*, 2:183–85
Brooks, George W.	1808–1889	*bef.*1834	—*HC*, 2:183–85
Brown, Albert	1807–1901	1832	—*HC*, 2:183–85
Brown, Harry	1808–1852	*bef.*1834	Died in Keokuk, Iowa. —*HC*, 2:183–85
Brown, Samuel Webster	1801–1882	*bef.*1834	—*HC*, 2:183–85
Brownell, John	*est.*1800–?	*bef.*1834	—*HC*, 2:183–85
Buchanan, Peter	1798–?	*bef.*1834	—*HC*, 2:183–85

Name	Birth/ Death	Baptism	Miscellaneous and Source
Bump, Jacob	1791–*bef.*1865	*bef.*1834	Left Church, started Church of Christ in Kirtland with William McLellin and Levi Richards in 1837. Later became a Strangite. Died in Iowa. —*BD,* 433; *BR,* 402; *HC,* 2:183–85
Burdick, Alden	1795–1845	1833	—*HC,* 2:183–85
Burgess, Harrison	1814–1883	1832	—*HC,* 2:183–85
Byur, David	*est.*1800–?	*bef.*1834	—*HC,* 2:183–85; *LDSBE*
Cahoon, William Farrington	1813–1893	1830	Carpenter, joiner. —*HC,* 2:183–85
Carpenter, John Button	1810–*est.*1880	*bef.*1834	—*HC,* 2:183–85
Carter, John Sims	1796–1834	1832	Died of Cholera in Clay County. —*HC,* 2:183–85
Cathcart, Daniel R.	1803–?	*bef.*1834	—*HC,* 2:183–85
Champlin, Alonzo	*est.*1800–?	*bef.*1834	—*HC,* 2:183–85
Chapman, Jacob Kimble	1803–?	*bef.*1834	—*HC,* 2:183–85
Cherry, William	*est.*1810	*bef.*1834	—*HC,* 2:183–85
Chidester, John Madison	1809–1893	1832	—*HC,* 2:183–85
Childs, Alden	*est.*1800–?	*bef.*1834	—*HC,* 2:183–85
Childs, Nathaniel	1789–?	*bef.*1834	—*HC,* 2:183–85
Childs, Stephen	*est.*1800–?	*bef.*1834	—*HC,* 2:183–85
Clements, Albert	1801–1883	*bef.*1834	—*HC,* 2:183–85
Colborn, Thomas	1801–1887	*bef.*1834	—*HC,* 2:183–85

Name	Birth/ Death	Baptism	Miscellaneous and Source
Colby, Alanson	1813–1875	*bef.*1834	—*HC,* 2:183–85
Cole, Zera Smith	1805–1886	1834	Baptized February 9, 1834, a couple of months before Zions Camp. —*HC,* 2:183–85
Coltrin, Zebedee	1804–1887	1831	Patriarch —*BR,* 404; *HC,* 2:183–85
Coon, Libeus Thadeus, Dr.	1811–1872	1832	—*HC,* 2:183–85
Cowan, Horace	*est.*1810–?	*bef.*1834	—*HC,* 2:183–85
Curtis, Lyman	1812–1898	1833	—*HC,* 2:183–85
Curtis, Mecham	1817–1887	1833	—*HC,* 2:183–85
Dailey, James (or Dayley)	*est.*1810–?	*bef.*1834	Brother-in-law to Milo Andrus. Joined Zions Camp in Florence, Ohio. —*Milo Andrus Autobiography,* 3
Denton, Solomon Wilber	1814–?	*bef.*1834	—*HC,* 2:183–85
Doff, Peter	*est.*1800–?	*bef.*1834	—*HC,* 2:183–85
Dort, David D.	1793–1841	1831	—*BR,* 407; *HC,* 2:183–85
Duncan, John	1780–1872	1832	—*HC,* 2:183–85
Dunn, James	1793– *est.*1841	*bef.*1834	—*HC,* 2:183–85
Duzette, Philemon	1782–1834	*bef.*1834	—*HC,* 2:183–85
Elliott, Bradford White	1824–1852	1831	—*HC,* 2:183–85
Elliott, David	1799–1855	1831	—*BR* 407; *HC,* 2:183–85
Ettleman, Philip	1791–1854	*bef.*1834	—*HC,* 2:183–85
Evans, David	1804–1883	1833	—*HC,* 2:183–85
Field, Asa	1794–1869	*bef.*1834	—*HC,* 2:183–85
Fish, Alfred	1806–1834	*bef.*1834	Died of cholera in Clay County, Missouri. —*HC,* 2:183–85

Name	Birth/ Death	Baptism	Miscellaneous and Source
Fish, Hezekiah	1775–1839	*bef.*1834	Died in Nauvoo, Illinois —*Wikipedia. HC,* 2:183–85
Fisher, Edmund	1803–1872	*bef.*1834	—*HC,* 2:183–85
Fordham, Elijah	1798–1844	*bef.*1834	—*BR* 408; *HC,* 2:183–85
Fordham, George Fisher	1825–1922	*bef.*1834	—*HC,* 2:183–85
Forney, Frederick	1813–?	*bef.*1834	—*HC,* 2:183–85
Fossett, John McKee	1804–1874	*bef.*1834	—*HC,* 2:183–85
Foster, James	1775–1841	*est.*1833	—*HC,* 2:183–85
Foster, Solon	1811–1896	1833	—*HC,* 2:183–85
Gates, Jacob	1811–1892	1833	—*GD,* 119
Gifford, Benjamin	*est.*1802–?	1831	—*HC,* 2:183–85
Gifford, Levi	1789–1860	1831	—*HC,* 2:183–85
Gilbert, Sherman A.	*est.*1810–?	*bef.*1834	—*HC,* 2:183–85
Glidden, True	1782–?	*bef.*1834	—*HC,* 2:183–85
Gould, Dean C.	*est.*1810–after 1840	*bef.*1834	—*HC,* 2:183–85
Grant, Jedediah Morgan	1816–1856	1833	—*HC,* 2:183–85
Green, Addison	1819–1892	*bef.*1834	—*HC,* 2:183–85
Griffith, Michael	1816–1892	*bef.*1834	—*HC,* 2:183–85
Griswold, Michael	*est.*1800–?	*bef.*1834	—*HC,* 2:183–85
Groves, Elisha Hurd	1797–1867	1832	—*HC,* 2:183–85; *GD,* 132
Hancock, Joseph	1799–1893	1830	Contracted cholera but recovered. —*HC,* 2:183–85
Hancock, Levi Ward	1803–1882	1830	—*BD,* 41; *GD,* 138; *HC,* 2:183–85

Name	Birth/ Death	Baptism	Miscellaneous and Source
Harmon, Jesse Perse (Joseph)	1795–1877	*bef.*1834	Also called Joseph, Jesse, or Jesse D. —*HC,* 2:183–85; *Profile,* 33
Harriman, Henry	1804–1891	1832	—*BD,* 411; *HC,* 2:183–85
Harris, Martin	1783–1875	1830	—*BD,* 412; *HC,* 2:183–85
Hartshorn, Joseph	1765–1850	*bef.*1834	—*HC,* 2:183–85
Hayes, Thomas	*est.*1800–1834	1834	Baptized and died in Missouri —*HC,* 2:183–85
Higgins, Nelson	1806–1890	*bef.*1834	—*HC,* 2:183–85
Hitchcock, Seth	1781–1834	*bef.*1834	Died of cholera in Clay County, Missouri. He lasted 30 minutes after he took sick. —*HC,* 2:183–85
Hogers, Amos	*est.*1810–?	*bef.*1834	—*HC,* 2:183–85
Holbrook, Chandler	1807–1889	1833	Baptized January 14, 1833. —*HC,* 2:183–85
Holbrook, Joseph	1806–1885	1833	Baptized January 6, 1833. Miner, farmer. —*GD,* 161; *HC,* 2:183–85
Holmes, Milton	1811–1881	1831	Later in Mormon Battalion. —*BD,* 414; *HC,* 2:183–85
Houghton, Ornan	1806–1847	*bef.*1834	—*HC,* 2:183–85
Hubbard, Marshall Moore	1805–1838	1833	Baptized June 1833. Had cholera and was sick last three years of his life; died in Michigan. —*HC,* 2:183–85; *LDSBE,* 4:689
Humphrey, Solomon	1775–1834	1830	Baptized in fall of 1830 by Joseph Smith. Died in Clay County, Missouri, September 1834. —*BD,* 415; *HC,* 2:183–85
Huntsman, Joseph Jesse	1804–1861	*bef.*1834	—*HC,* 2:183–85

Name	Birth/ Death	Baptism	Miscellaneous and Source
Hustin, John	*est.*1810–?	*bef.*1834	—*HC,* 2:183–85
Hutchins, Elias	1784–1845	*bef.*1834	—*HC,* 2:183–85
Hyde, Heman T.	1788–1867	1834	Baptized April 7, 1834. —*HC,* 2:183–85
Hyde, Orson	1805–1878	1834	—*BD,* 416; *HC,* 2:183–85
Ingalls, Warren S.	*est.*1805–1834	*bef.*1834	Died of cholera June 30, 1834, Clay County, Missouri. —*HC,* 2:183–85
Ivie, Edward	*est.*1810–1834	*bef.*1834	Died of cholera in Clay County, Missouri. —*HC,* 2:183–85
Ivie, James Russell	1802–1866	1832	—*HC,* 2:183–85
Ivie, John Anderson	*est.*1800–?	*bef.*1834	—*HC,* 2:183–85
Ivie, William Shelton	1811–1882	*bef.*1834	—*HC,* 2:183–85
Jessop, William	*est.*1822–?	*bef.*1834	—*HC,* 2:183–85
Johnson, Luke	1807–1861	1831	—*BD,* 418
Johnson, Lyman Eugene	1811–1856	1831	Died in Wisconsin. —*BD,* 41; *HC,* 2:183–85
Johnson, Noah	1763–1834	*bef.*1834	Died of cholera June 2, 1834, Clay County, Missouri. —*HC,* 2:183–85
Johnson, Seth	1805–1835	1832	—*HC,* 2:183–85
Jones, Isaac	*est.*1806–?	*bef.*1834	—*HC,* 2:183–85
Jones, Levi	*est.*1810–?	*bef.*1834	—*HC,* 2:183–85
Kelly, Charles	1810–?	*bef.*1834	—*LDSBE,* 1:389; *HC,* 2:183–85
Kimball, Heber Chase	1811–1897	1832	—*HC,* 2:183–85
Kingsley, Samuel	*est.*1816–?	*bef.*1834	—*HC,* 2:183–85
Lake, Dennis	*est.*1810–?	*bef.*1834	—*HC,* 2:183–85

Name	Birth/ Death	Baptism	Miscellaneous and Source
Lawson, Jesse B.	1798–1834	*bef.*1834	Died of cholera June 30, 1834, in Clay County, Missouri. —*HC,* 2:183–85
Lewis, L. S.	*est.*1810–?	*bef.*1834	—*HC,* 2:183–85
Littlefield, Josiah	*est.*1780–?	*bef.*1834	Fought in War of 1812. Grandfather of Lyman and Waldo Littlefield. —*HC,* 2:183–85
Littlefield, Lyman Omer	1819–1893	1834	—*HC,* 2:183–85
Littlefield, Waldo	1797–1879	1832	—*HC,* 2:183–85
Lyman, Amasa Mason	1813–1877	1832	—*HC,* 2:183–85
Martin, Moses	1812–1900	*bef.*1834	—*HC,* 2:183–85
Marvin, Edward W.	*est.*1810–?	*bef.*1834	—*HC,* 2:183–85
McBride, Rueben	1803–1891	1834	Baptized in March 4, 1834. —*BR,* 500; *HC,* 2:183–85
McCord, Robert	1810–1834	*bef.*1834	Died of cholera in Zion's Camp, Clay County, Missouri. —*HC,* 2:183–85
Miller, Eleazer	1795–1876	1831	—*HC,* 2:183–85
Miller, John	1810–?	*bef.*1834	—*HC,* 2:183–85
Morse, Justin Justus (Justice)	1809–1887	1833	—*HC,* 2:183–85
Murdock, John	1792–1871	1830	—*GD,* 250; *HC,* 2:183–85
Nicholas, Joseph	*est.*1810–?	*bef.*1834	—*HC,* 2:183–85
Nickerson, Freeman	1799–1847	1833	—*Joseph Smith Papers,* vol. 2; *HC,* 2:183–85
Nickerson, Levi Stillman	1814–1853	1833	Baptized in June 1833. Son of Freeman. —*Joseph Smith Papers,* vol. 2; *HC,* 2:183–85

Name	Birth/ Death	Baptism	Miscellaneous and Source
Nickerson, Uriah Chittendon Hatch	1810–1888	1833	Son of Freeman. Died in Wisconsin. —*Joseph Smith Papers,* vol. 2; *HC,* 2:183–85
Noble, Joseph Bates	1810–1900	1832	Baptized by Brigham Young. —*HC,* 2:183–85
North, Ur	*est.*1800–?	*bef.*1834	—*HC,* 2:183–85
Orton, Roger	1795–1851	1833.	Captain in Zion's Camp. —*Wikipedia; HC,* 2:183–85
Parker, John Davis	1799–1890	1832	—*HC,* 2:183–85
Parrish, Warren Farr	1803–1887	1833	Clerk in 1835. Took $25,000 from Kirtland Safety Society. Excommunicated and formed a Baptist church and took over Kirtland Temple. Died in Kansas. —*BD,* 428*; HC,* 2:183–85
Pratt, Orson	1811–1881	1830	—*LDSBE, 1; HC,* 2:183–85
Pratt, Parley Parker	1807–1857	1830	Numerous missions—at least ten in Joseph Smith's lifetime. Murdered in Arkansas. —*GD,* 282; *HC,* 2:183–85
Pratt, William Dickerson	1802–1870	1831	—*HC,* 2:183–85
Rich, Charles Coulson	1809–1883	1832	—*HC,* 2:183–85
Rich, Leonard	1800–1856	*bef.*1834	Apostatized. Formed church with William McLellin and Jacob Bump in Kirtland. —*BD,* 432*; LDSBE,* 1:189; *HC,* 2:183–85
Richardson, Darwin Charles	1812–1860	1833	Utah. —*HC,* 2:183–85
Riggs, Burr	1811–1860	*bef.*1834	—*HC,* 2:183–85
Riggs, Harpin	1809–1865	*bef.*1834	—*HC,* 2:183–85

Name	Birth/ Death	Baptism	Miscellaneous and Source
Riggs, Nathaniel	1798–1869	*bef.*1834	—*HC,* 2:183–85
Riley, Alanson	1798–?	*bef.*1834	—*HC,* 2:183–85
Riley, Milcher	*est.*1800–?	*bef.*1834	—*HC,* 2:183–85
Robbins, Lewis	1811–1864	1832	—*HC,* 2:183–85
Rollins, James Henry	1816–1899	1832	In Zion's Camp. Note: Not in *History of the Church* list. —*GD,* 302
Rudd, Erastus Harper	1787–1834	1833	Died of cholera June 27, 1834, Rush Creek, Clay County, Missouri —*Profile,* 60
Rudd, John	*est.*1800–?	*bef.*1834	—*HC, 2: 327*
Sagers, William Henry Harrison	1814–1886	1833	Colonized in Idaho. —*HC,* 2:183–85
Salisbury, Wilkins Jenkins	1809–1853	*bef.*1834	—*BR,* 511*; HC,* 2:183–85
Sherman, Alman	*est.*1800–?	*bef.*1834	—*HC, 2:149*
Sherman, Lyman Royal	1804–1839	1832	Called to be an Apostle but died at Far West, Missouri, before he could be ordained. —*BR,* 513*; HC,* 2:183–85
Sherwood, Henry Garlie	1785–1867	1832	Died in California. —*HC,* 2:183–85
Shibley, Henry	1800–?	*bef.*1834	—*HC,* 2:183–85
Smalling, Cyrus	*est.*1810–?	*bef.*1834	—*HC,* 2:183–85
Smith, Avery	*est.*1810–?	*bef.*1834	—*HC,* 2:183–85
Smith, George Albert	1817–1875	1832	Was armor-bearer of Zion's Camp. —*BR,* 593*; Wikipedia; HC,* 2:183–85
Smith, Hyrum	1800–1844	1829 and 1830	Was a captain in camp. —*HC,* 2:183–85

Name	Birth/ Death	Baptism	Miscellaneous and Source
Smith, Jackson Osborn	1815–1880	*bef.*1834	—*HC,* 2:183–85
Smith, Jesse J.	1808–1834	*bef.*1834	Died of cholera in Clay County, Missouri, July 1, 1834. Cousin to Joseph Smith. —*HC,* 2:183–85
Smith, Joseph Jr.	1805–1844	1829 and 1830	Prophet, leader, and commander of Zion's Camp. —*HC,* 2:183–85
Smith, Lyman	*est.*1817–1837	*bef.*1834	—*HC,* 2:183–85
Smith, Sylvester	*est.*1805–?	1831	—*BR,* 516; *HC,* 2:183–85
Smith, William B.	1811–1893	1830	—*HC,* 2:183–85
Smith, Zechariah	1782–?	*bef.*1834	—*HC,* 2:183–85
Snow, Willard Trowbridge	1811–1854	1833	Baptized June 1833 by Parley Pratt. Died at sea. —*HC,* 2:183–85
Snow, Zerubbabel	1809–1888	1832	Brother to Lorenzo Snow. Lawyer. —*BR,* 516; *HC,* 2:183–85
Stanley, Harvey	1811–1862	1834	Stone cutter. Dairyman. Migrated to California. —*BR,* 597; *HC,* 2:183–85
Stephens, Daniel	1819–1899	*bef.*1834	—*HC,* 2:183–85
Strong, Elias (Elial)	*est.*1810–1834	1832	Died of cholera in Clay County, Missouri. —HC, 2:183–85
Tanner, John Joshua	1811–1893	1832	—*HC,* 2:183–85
Tanner, Nathan	1815–1910	1832	—*HC,* 2:183–85
Taylor, John	1812–?	*est.*1833	—*Coneto Creek Taylors,* 17

Name	Birth/ Death	Baptism	Miscellaneous and Source
Taylor, William	1823–1910	1834	Baptized in Zion's Camp in Clay County. —*Coneto Creek Taylors,* 17
Thayer, Ezra	1791–?	1830	—*HC,* 2:183–85
Thomas, Tinney	*est.*1800–?	*bef.*1834	—*HC,* 2:183–85
Thompson, James Lewis	1818–1891	*bef.*1834	—*HC,* 2:183–85
Thompson, Samuel	1813–1892	1833	—*HC,* 2:183–85
Tippetts, William	1812–1877	*bef.*1834	—*HC,* 2:183–85
Tribbs, Nelson	*est.*1800–?	*bef.*1834	—*HC,* 2:183–85
Vaughn, Joel	*est.*1810–?	*bef.*1834	—*HC,* 2:183–85
Warner, Salmon Jr.	1798–1870	1833	—*LDSBE,* 3:139
Weden, Salmon	*est.*1798–?	*bef.*1834	—*HC,* 2:183–85
Wells, Elias	*est.*1810–?	*bef.*1834	—*HC,* 2:183–85
White-sides, (John) Alexander	1805–1865	*bef.*1834	—*HC,* 2:183–85
Whitlock, Andrew W. (Hiram)	1805–1865	1831	—*HC,* 2:183–85
Wight, Lyman	1796–1858	1830	Apostatized after Joseph Smith died, and died in Texas choking on some meat. —*HC,* 2:183–85
Wilcox, Eber	1806–1834	*bef.*1834	Died of cholera June 26, 1834, Clay County, Missouri —*HC,* 2:183–85
Wilkinson, Sylvester B.	*est.*1800–1834	*bef.*1834	Died of cholera Clay County, Missouri. —*HC,* 2:183–85
Williams, Frederick Granger	1787–1842	1830	—*HC,* 2:183–85

Name	Birth/ Death	Baptism	Miscellaneous and Source
Winchester, Alonzo	1814–*est.*1845	1833	—*HC,* 2:183–85
Winchester, Benjamin	1817–1901	1833	—*HC,* 2:183–85
Winchester, Steven Sr.	1795–1873	1833	—*LDSBE,* 4:692
Winegar, Alvin	1816–1874	1832	—*HC,* 2:183–85
Wingar, Samuel Thomas	1782–1874	1833	—*HC,* 2:183–85
Winter, Hiram	1805–1889	*bef.*1834	—*HC,* 2:183–85
Wissmiller, Henry	*est.*1790–?	*bef.*1834	A captain in camp. —*Wikipedia; HC,* 2:183–85
Woodruff, Wilford	1807–1898	1833	—*HC,* 2:183–85
Young, Brigham	1801–1877	1832	Utah. —*HC,* 2:183–85
Young, Joseph	1797–1882	1832	—*Biographical Register,* 607; *HC,* 2:183–85
Young, Lorenzo Dow	1807–1895	1832	Note: not in list of History of the Church. —*Biographical Register,* 607

Women in camp

- Alvord, Charlotte
- Chidester, Mary
- Curtis, Sophronia
- Clements, Ada
- Drake, Diana
- Gates, Mary Snow
- Holbrook, Eunice
- Holbrook, Nancy Lambson
- Houghton, Aurelia Curtis
- Parrish, Betsy Patten (wife of Warren Parish; died of cholera)
- Ripley, Sister ______
- Taylor, Elizabeth Patrick (wife of William)

Children in camp

- Holbrook, Diana (daughter of Chandler Holbrook)
- Chidester, Eunice (daughter of John M. Chidester)
- Chidester, John (son of John M. Chidester)
- Holbrook, Sarah Lucretia (daughter of Joseph Holbrook)
- Holbrook, Charlotte and ________ (daughters of Joseph Holbrook)
- Pulsipher, Sarah (daughter of Zera Pulsipher)
- Winegar, ____ (daughter of Alvin Winegar)

Between June 25 and July 1, 1834, Zion's Camp came down with cholera while at Algernon Sidney Gilbert's home in Clay County. Sixty-eight got sick, and among those who died were one woman, Betsy Parrish, and thirteen men.

—*HC*, 2:114–21

Those who died of cholera

- Carter, John Sims (1796–1834)
- Fish, Albert (1806–1834)
- Hitchcock, Seth (1781–1834)
- Ingalls, Warren (*est.*1805–1834)
- Ives, Edward (*est.*1810–1834)
- Johnson, Noah (1763–1834)
- Lawson, Jesse B. (1798–1834)
- McCord, Robert (1810–1834)
- Parrish, Betsy, (1797–1834)—Wife of Warren Parrish.
- Rudd, Erastus Harper (1787–1834)
- Strong, Elial (*est.*1810–1834)
- Smith, Jesse J. (1808–1834
- Wilcox, Eber (1806–1834)

Other deaths associated with Zion's Camp cholera

- Gilbert, Algernon Sidney (1789–1834)—He already lived in Missouri and was not in camp, but they camped at his home.

—*HC, 3*

- Murdock, Phebe (1828–1834)—This six-year-old girl of John Murdock lived with the Gilbert family in Clay County and died of cholera on July 6, 1834.

—*James Rollin Autobiography*, BYU, 4

- Weeden, William (*est.*1810–1834)—Died at Gilbert home in early July, 1834.

—*James Rollin Autobiography*, BYU, 4

Note: Rueben McBride Sr. (1803–1891) quoted Joseph Smith saying that "all the members of Zion's Camp were sealed up to eternal life before leaving on Zion's Camp march." After arriving in Missouri, these were sealed up a second time.

—*GD*, 231

Divine Calling

Accomplishments of Joseph Smith—a short list

1. Gave us more pages of scripture than any other prophet.
2. Translated the Book of Mormon, a second witness of Jesus Christ.
3. Saw God the Father and the Savior, Jesus Christ.
4. Was visited, instructed, and tutored by several dozen angels.
5. Showed the world the heavens were not closed, that God had not forgotten mankind.
6. Was foreordained to open the seventh and final dispensation.
7. Was called by God to be a prophet.
8. Became a seer, with power to see the past, present, and future.
9. Was chosen to restore the Aaronic and Melchizedek Priesthoods.
10. Restored the true Church of Jesus Christ.
11. Set up an unpaid lay clergy to lead the Church, where millions serve without pay.
12. Initiated work for the dead, the Spirit of Elijah flooding the earth.
13. Established credibility of the gospel with teachings of the spirit world and work for the dead, without which the world would be destroyed at the Second Coming of the Savior.
14. Revealed the endowment and the purposes of temples.
15. Helped reduce much of the Bible's confusion when he was commanded by God to make corrections, and thus we have the Joseph Smith Translation of the King James Bible.
16. Was a general of what was once the largest army in United States, except for the regular US army.
17. Was a spiritual leader of Christ's true Church with 45,000 to 50,000 members by 1844.

18. Was a political leader of his people.
19. Revealed new doctrine unknown to the world.
20. Clarified doctrine of the Old and New Testament of the Bible.
21. Revealed the doctrine of celestial marriage and eternal families, giving true meaning to eternal life.
22. Built two temples and planned many others.
23. Was the city planner of Kirtland, Independence, Far West, Adam–ondi–Ahman, and Nauvoo.
24. Was mayor of Nauvoo.
25. Was a store proprietor but usually gave most of the profits away to the poor and canceled their debts.
26. Was a powerful inspirational speaker.
27. Was a strong supporter of the United States Constitution.
28. Worked hard to learn Hebrew, German, Latin, and other languages.
29. Set up an effective welfare system.
30. Healed many and even raised one person who was dead.
31. Became a candidate for the United States presidency.
32. Gave many prophecies that have come true.
33. Was a loving husband and provider.
34. Was a devoted father who spent time with his children, playing with and nurturing them.
35. He died to seal his testimony of the work God assigned him to do.

—Compiler's note

Columbus egg illustration

Joseph said, "I lead the way like Columbus when he was invited to a banquet where he was assigned the most honorable place at the table, and served with the ceremonials which were observed towards sovereigns. A shallow courtier present, who was meanly jealous of him, abruptly asked him whether he thought that in case he had not discovered the Indies, there were not other men in Spain who would have been capable of the enterprise? Columbus made no reply, but took an egg and invited the company to make it stand on end. They all attempted it, but in vain; whereupon he struck it upon the table so as to break one end, and left it standing on the broken part, illustrating that when he had once shown the way to the new world nothing was easier than to follow it."

—Joseph Fielding Smith, *Teachings of the Prophet Joseph Smith*, 304

Fools deride him

"Just as prophesied, fools deride him, hell rages against him, and his name is 'both good and evil spoken of.'"

—Neal A. Maxwell, "How Choice a Seer!" *Ensign,* November 2003

Hundreds of gallons of ink

"Since 1830 hundreds of gallons of printer's ink have filled thousands of reams of paper with millions of words on the relationship between Joseph Smith and the development of religion in America."

—Thomas G. Alexander, *The Prophet Puzzle: Interpretive Essays on Joseph Smith,* Brian Waterman, 2

Joseph's name

What is the likelihood of a fourth son being named after his father? Joseph was the fourth son but was still named after his father as prophesied.

—Compiler's note

Known for good and evil

Moroni prophesied correctly when he said, "His name would be known by every nation, kindred, tongue and people." Almost 200 years later, his name has been known exactly to that extent. The Book of Mormon is published in over 100 languages, and the Church is organized in 168 nations. The song "Praise to the Man" could to be updated to "billions" instead of "millions shall know Brother Joseph again."

—Compiler's note

Penetrated the vistas of unborn years

Early Church leader Preston Nibley described that Joseph's mission "penetrated the vistas of unborn years, and placed the view of the future before men of today."

—Preston Nibley, *Inspirational Talks For Youth*

Preparation of Joseph

"Joseph was the most spiritually able soul since Jesus. He had the largest spiritual reach and was prepared from the eternities."

—Mark L. McConkie tapes

Presiding patriarch

Joseph was the priest and king over the presiding patriarchal order of the last days.

—Hyrum L. Andrus, *Doctrines of the Kingdom,* 556, 558

Puzzle pieces of religion

In 1820, the gospel had about 100 pieces of the puzzle of religious understanding in place. Joseph Smith, in the Latter-day Restoration, put the other 900 pieces of the puzzle in place.

—Tad Callister, "Joseph Smith—Prophet of the Restoration," *Ensign*, November 2009

Religious chains broken

"He burst asunder the chains which for ages past had held in bondage the nations of the earth."

—Gilbert Belnap, *They Knew the Prophet*, Hyrum L. Andrus, 203

Restorationist

"Joseph Smith on the other hand was a restorationist, in contrast with a reformist. He restored that which was on the earth anciently—the teachings, the doctrines, the practices of the Savior."

—Gordon B. Hinckley, *American Prophet: The Story of Joseph Smith*, Lee Groberg and Heidi S. Swinton, 68

Restored a nation of prophets and priests

Said Joseph Fielding McConkie, "The Lord [through Joseph] has established the kingdom that he sought to establish in the days of Moses—a nation of prophets and priests."

—*Prophets and Prophecy*, 100

Senses were attuned

"All of his senses—physical, mental and spiritual—were so attuned that little was missed."

—Leon R. Hartshorn, *Joseph Smith: Prophet of the Restoration*, 73

Joseph was as familiar with the spirit world

"He seemed to be just as familiar with the spirit world, and as well acquainted with the other side, as he was with this world."

—William Taylor, *They Knew the Prophet*, Hyrum L. Andrus, 182

Spiritual generator set up by Restoration

The Restoration, brought about by the Prophet Joseph Smith, provided the gift of the Holy Ghost to allow members to generate spiritual light and to keep that light by their efforts to light their own path.

—Compiler's note

His teachings made him tower above all other men.

— John A Widtsoe, *Fate of the Persecutors of the Prophet Joseph Smith*, N. B. Lundwall, 22

Took heaven and brought it down to earth

"He took heaven . . . and brought it down to earth; and he took the earth, brought it up, and opened up, in plainness and simplicity, the things of God."

—Brigham Young, *They Knew the Prophet,* Hyrum L. Andrus, 39

Translating

Just how the Prophet translated is not known. He never told anyone that we know of. "It is certain, however, that it required great mental as well as spiritual powers." He did have the gift of seership.

—Hyrum L. Andrus, *Joseph Smith, the Man and the Seer,* 101

Divine Tutoring

Education

If you consider by whom he was tutored, Joseph Smith had the equivalent to hundreds of PhDs, as he was taught by God, Christ, and scores of angels.

—Compiler's note

Joseph had three years of formal education.

—Truman G. Madsen tapes

The fact that young Joseph Smith was unschooled is powerful additional evidence that he was a prophet called of God. All that he accomplished in translating the Book of Mormon, the writings of Abraham from the papyrus of the Egyptian mummies, and dozens of other things are evidence that God wanted to acquaint mankind with his called-young prophet. As revelation and visions were crowned upon Joseph's head, he became learned and schooled from the "University of God Almighty" and received his heavenly AA, BA, and PhDs by the dozens.

—Compiler's note; see Abraham 1 and *HC,* 1

Egyptian hieroglyphics

At the age of twenty-three, Joseph made a list of approximately 144 Egyptian hieroglyphics for Martin Harris to take to New York for Egyptian scholars to examine. Some may wonder what library he went to in Harmony, Pennsylvania, to find such characters, of which Harris was told were correct. His critics have worked for over 180 years to try to explain it and can't.

—Compiler's note

Key of Knowledge

"I heard him say that God had given him the key of knowledge by which he could trace any subject through all its ramifications."

—Howard Coray, *They Knew the Prophet*, Hyrum L. Andrus, 151

Knew more than all the world put together

Said Joseph Smith, "I am learned, and know more than all the world put together. The Holy Ghost does, anyhow, and He is within me, and comprehends more than all the world: and I will associate myself with Him."

—Hyrum L. Andrus, *Joseph Smith the Man and the Seer*, 134

Learned and most intelligent

"Joseph Smith was ignorant of letters as the world has it, but he was the most profoundly learned and intelligent man that I ever met in my life, and I have traveled hundreds of thousands of miles, been on different continents and mingled among all classes and creeds of people. Yet I have never met a man so intelligent as he was. Where did he get his intelligence from? Not from books, not from the logic or science or philosophy of the day, but he obtained it through the revelation of God."

—John Taylor, *They Knew the Prophet,* Hyrum L. Andrus, 212

Plural principles and covenants

It is interesting that Joseph used words that an attorney would use but used the plural. Examples are "all covenants, contracts, bonds, obligations, oaths, vows, performances, connections, associations, or expectations." Joseph was "simplicity-minded" not "simpleminded," having the ability to reduce elaborate ideas to a core center or essence. Note: He had the help of Almighty God.

—Truman G. Madsen, *Joseph Smith the Prophet*, 23

"The Prophet's voice was like the thunders of heaven, yet his language was meek. . . . He truly had been educated pertaining to the kingdom of God."

—Joseph Lee Robinson, *The Prophecies of Joseph Smith*, Duane S. Crowther, 33; Hyrum L. Andrus, *They Knew the Prophet*, 185

Six-year finishing school

Moroni spent four years teaching Joseph about the importance of the Nephite record before Joseph received the plates, and then two more years after, while he was translating them. He visited Joseph at least *twenty-three times over a period of six years* in order to help the young Prophet bring forth this powerful record.

—Compiler's note

Vast learning

He received revelation and open visions on hundreds of subjects.

—Compiler's note

Power

No one could call him an imposter if they listened to him

"Who could listen to these words of inspiration and honestly say Joseph Smith is an imposter? No one, not even his bitter enemies. . . . [He] turned the key, and the door of knowledge sprang wide open, disclosing precious principles, both old and new."

—Wandle Mace, *They Knew the Prophet,* Hyrum L. Andrus, 131–32

Leader

All of Joseph's associates soon found out that Joseph was in charge.

—*Improvement Era,* vol. 4, November 4, 1901, 258

Lion of the tribe of Judah

"Joseph then arose and like the lion of the Tribe of Judah poured out his soul in the midst of the congregation of Saints."

—Wilford Woodruff, *Joseph Smith, the Man and the Seer,* Hyrum L. Andrus, 63

Mouthpiece of the Almighty

"Joseph Smith . . . was the mouthpiece of the Almighty, and was always ready to rebuke them when requisite. . . . He had a word of comfort and consolation to the humble and faithful, and a word of rebuke to the froward and disobedient."

—Brigham Young, *JD,* 8:189

Noble face lit up

"I often had the privilege of seeing his noble face lit up by the Spirit and power of God."

—James Leech, *They Knew the Prophet,* Hyrum L. Andrus, 161

Power of Joseph

Hyrum Smith said, "Joseph Smith possessed the power of all the Prophets."

—Truman G. Madsen tapes

Rose like a lion

In Philadelphia, with about three thousand present, "Brother Joseph arose like a lion about to roar; and being full of the Holy Ghost, spoke in great power."

—Parley Pratt, *RJ*, 203

Spirit of God flowed from him like heat from a stove

"You knew he was a true prophet of God because you could not be in his presence without feeling the influence and Spirit of God, which seemed to flow from him almost as heat does from a stove."

—William Henrie, *RJ*, 358

Spirited young horse

"It might have been easier if [Moroni] had 'broken' and trained Joseph the way one might break and train a spirited young horse. But if Joseph were to be trusted with the powers of priesthood, he must also be trusted to exercise those powers in the full strength of his own personality."

—LeGrand L. Baker, *Joseph and Moroni: The 7 Principles Moroni Taught Joseph Smith*, 3

Thunder of heaven

"The Prophet's voice was like the thunders of heaven, yet his language was meek."

—Joseph L. Robinson, *RJ*, 204

Bared his chest

"[William] Law came staggering [drunk] out of the house shouting out what he intended to do. . . . Calmly the Prophet unbuttoned his shirt and bared his chest [and] then said, 'I'm ready now, Mr. Law.' . . . [Law] aimed, and pressed the trigger [on his pistol]. There was complete silence (nothing happened)." Law then shot at a can on a fence post and hit the target dead center. "The Prophet buttoned up his shirt . . . then said, 'If you are finished with me now, Mr. Law, I have other things needing to be done.' "

—Sarah Stoddard, *Joseph Smith: The Man, the Mission, the Message,* Matthew B. Brown, 82

Constable risked his life to help

"[The constable] lodged Joseph in an upper room of a tavern [in South Bainbridge, New York]; and in order that all might be safe for himself and

Joseph, he slept during the night with his feet against the door, and kept a loaded gun by him (Joseph occupied a bed in the same room), and declared that if they were unlawfully molested he would fight for Joseph and defend him to the utmost of his ability."

—Newel Knight, *They Knew the Prophet,* Hyrum L. Andrus, 9

Gun misfired six times

Apostate William Law attempted to kill Joseph and fired a pistol at him six times at close range. It misfired six times, and he then pointed it at a post and all six shots discharged properly.

—Charles H. Stoddard, *RJ*, 74

Spirit left his body

"On one occasion, at a meeting held near the Temple in Nauvoo, [Joseph made a few remarks regarding the incident in Ohio when he was tarred and feathered]. His spirit he said, left his body, and hovered over it in the air, and returned after it was over. They supposed they had killed him, but he had come back [to] take his body."

—Frederick Kesler, *Jesus and Joseph: Parallel Lives,* Rodney Turner, 144

Three witnesses saved Joseph's life

According to Doctrine and Covenants 12:1–4, the Three Witnesses saved Joseph Smith's life by seeing and bearing witness of what they saw.

—D&C 17:4

Spiritual Standing

Assignment—second most important on earth

"With the exception of Jesus Christ, Joseph Smith had the most important assignment upon the earth."

—*Leon R. Hartshorn, Joseph Smith: Prophet of the Restoration*, 121

Consent of Joseph

"No man or woman in this dispensation will ever enter into the celestial kingdom of God without the consent of Joseph Smith."

—Brigham Young, *Images of the Prophet Joseph Smith,* Davis Bitton, 134

Distant second to the Savior

"Joseph Smith was a man—a distant second, but second [to the Savior], which places him in a remarkable position."

—Leon R. Hartshorn, *Joseph Smith: Prophet of the Restoration*, 121

Identity

Joseph said, "They know [not] who I am, and I dare not tell. They will not know until they see me at the bar of God."

—Mary Elizabeth Rollins Lightner, *RJ*, 150

Joseph of Egypt compared to Joseph Smith

Joseph of Egypt saved the house of Israel from starving from a famine. Joseph Smith helped to save a world from a spiritual famine of hearing the word of the Lord, as prophesied by the Old Testament Prophet Amos (Amos 3:7). Both were very forgiving. Both had visions in their youth.

—Calvin R. Stephens, BYU Education Week, 2009, speech

Parallels of Joseph Smith Jr. with the Savior

"Unmistakable similarities are there. Both Jesus and Joseph were born in lowly surroundings. Both had rather short lives. Both were prophets. Both founded churches (both of which were Christ's Church)." Both went through great persecution. And both had traitors.

—Joseph Fielding McConkie, *Images of the Prophet Joseph Smith*, Davis Bitton, 76–77

Parallels of Joseph Smith Jr. with Abraham

"Parallels between the lives of Abraham and Joseph Smith are . . . noticeable." Writes E. Douglass Clark, "[Joseph Smith's prayer leading to the First Vision at age fourteen] echoes young Abraham's prayer at the same age. . . . Both men had been foreordained; both received the priesthood, preached the gospel, and encountered formidable opposition; both spoke face to face with divine messengers and God Himself; both possessed a Urim and Thummim, translated ancient records, and wrote scripture; and both founded an influential community of believers.' "

—Davis Bitten, *Images of the Prophet Joseph Smith*, 70

Parallels of Joseph Smith Jr. with Joseph of Egypt

"Both had 'inauspicious beginnings'; both had visions when young; both were hated; . . . both were 'falsely accused'; both were 'generous to those who betrayed them'; both were jailed and knew what it was to be in a 'pit'; both prophesied; both knew separation from family and friends; both were 'amazingly resilient in the midst of adversity."

—Neal A. Maxwell, *A Choice Seer*, 6–15; Davis Bitton, *Images of the Prophet Joseph Smith*, 71

Parallels of Joseph Smith Jr. with Paul

"Both had a 'first vision.' Both delayed giving a description of the event. Both had revelations of the resurrected Lord. Both put forth insightful doctrinal instruction but did not claim to know all the answers. . . . Both were 'considered blasphemers by their contemporaries.' Both had visions of the degrees of glory. . . . Both anticipated martyrdom," noted Richard L. Anderson. It could also be said that only these two prophets taught clearly about baptism for the dead.

—Davis Bitton, *Images of the Prophet Joseph Smith*, 75–76; 1 Corinthians 15:29 (baptism)

Ranks with Adam and Abraham in premortal life

"As a [premortal] spirit he had ranked with Adam and Abraham; he was one of the noble and great ones of whom Abraham wrote." (See Abraham 3:22–23.)

—Bruce R. McConkie, *Mormon Doctrine*, 285

Rod and root of Jesse

Joseph Smith is both the rod and the root of Jesse as spelled out in Doctrine and Covenants 113:3–6. He is the rod, as shown in verses 3–4, "What is the rod spoken of in the first verse of the 11th chapter of Isaiah, that should come of the Stem of Jesse? Behold, thus saith the Lord: It is a servant in the hands of Christ, who is partly a descendant of Jesse as well as of Ephraim, or of the house of Joseph, on whom there is laid much power." He is also the root, as shown in verses 5–6, "What is the root of Jesse spoken of in the 10th verse of the 11th chapter? Behold, thus saith the Lord, it is a descendant of Jesse, as well as of Joseph, unto whom rightly belongs the priesthood, and the keys of the kingdom, for an ensign, and for the gathering of my people in the last days." This is referenced in Isaiah 11:1–5.

—D&C 113:1–6; Hyrum L. Andrus, *Doctrines of the Kingdom*, 539

Second best man who ever lived

"I am bold to say that, Jesus Christ excepted, no better man ever lived or does live upon this earth [than Joseph Smith]."

—Brigham Young, *They Knew the Prophet*, Hyrum L. Andrus, 40

Simile of God

Edward Stevenson said, "I have never heard or seen a man so filled with inspiration as the Prophet. He was full of light. I began to believe that he possessed an infinity of knowledge. I looked upon him as upon no other man. I have often heard him speak under divine influence, and I have felt as though I have been lifted in spirit beyond mortality, and that I was looking upon a simile of God, and at times I found myself in tears of joy. "

—Hyrum L. Andrus, *They Knew the Prophet*, 98

Spiritual ability helped like binoculars

Joseph's spiritual gifts made him like a pair of binoculars, like a telescope, or like a microscope where he could see things beyond the natural eye.

—Compiler's note

Spiritual capacity

"He had developed an amazing spiritual capacity . . . a keen mind."

—Leon R. Hartshorn, *Joseph Smith, Prophet of the Restoration*, 73

Spiritual eyes

The Prophet saw things with his spiritual eyes that no other man has seen.

—Compiler's note

Spiritual light

The Prophet became the greatest revealer of spiritual light since the Savior.

—Compiler's note

Statesman and philosopher

"He was a great statesman, philosopher and philanthropist, logician, and last, but not least, the greatest prophet, seer and revelator that ever lived, save Jesus Christ only."

—Daniel Tyler, *They Knew the Prophet,* Hyrum L. Andrus, 55

Joseph was mighty

Joseph was a mighty prophet, seer, revelator, and translator.

—Mark L. McConkie tapes

Truth revealed

"Joseph revealed more truth than any other prophet in the history of the world."

—LeGrande Richards

Joseph Smith's power of revelation grew to the point that he became like unto a Urim and Thummim.

—John A. Widtsoe, *Joseph Smith: Seeker After Truth: Prophet of God*, 109; Truman Madsen tapes

"Joseph Smith became a kind of Urim and Thummim."

—Truman Madsen tapes

Walked a godly walk

"Joseph walked a more godly walk than any person since Jesus."

—Mark L. McConkie tapes

Walked large on the stage of history

"Joseph [Smith] was an incredible man. For someone to walk large on the stage of history, and accomplish incredible things, without a remarkable invention, or an inherited fortune, or a stroke of luck or discovering something is incredible."

—Dallin H. Oaks, *American Prophet: The Story of Joseph Smith,* Lee Groberg and Heidi S. Swinton, 21

Divine influence in his presence

"What I remember best is that I always felt a divine influence whenever I was in his presence."

—Sarah A. Johnson Workman (daughter of Joel Hills Johnson), *They Knew the Prophet,* Hyrum L. Andrus, 112

Electrified me when I shook his hand

"When he took my hand, I was simply electrified—thrilled through and through to the tips of my fingers, and every part of my body, as if some magic elixir had given me new life and vitality. . . . I was overwhelmed by indefinable emotion."

—Emmeline Blanche Wells, *They Knew the Prophet,* Hyrum L. Andrus, 177

Familiar—Like I had always known him

"A carriage containing a number of persons was meeting us. As we neared it, the appearance of a large man sitting in front driving seemed to be familiar to me, as if I had always known him. Suddenly the thought burst on my mind that it was none other than the Prophet Joseph Smith."

—George Miller, *They Knew the Prophet,* Hyrum L. Andrus, 129

Fire went through me

"On . . . the 6th of May, 1844, the Prophet Joseph came up to the Temple and clasping his arms around me, lifted me off my feet, then said, 'The Lord bless thee, and I bless thee, and I bless thee in the name of the Lord Jesus Christ.'

"It went through my whole system like fire.

"Then he turned to those around and said, 'The Lord bless the whole of you, and peace be with you.' "

—Charles Lambert, *They Knew the Prophet*, Hyrum L. Andrus, 194

Greatness of soul never seen in another man

Wilford Woodruff said, "I have felt to rejoice exceedingly in what I saw of Brother Joseph, for in his public and private career he carried with him the Spirit of the Almighty, and he manifested a greatness of soul which I had never seen in any other man."

—Hyrum L. Andrus, *They Knew the Prophet*, 91

Like a heavenly being

"When I was but a child, I had a positive testimony that Joseph was a prophet of God, and as I looked at him he seemed to me like a heavenly being."

—Susan E. Johnson Martineau, *They Knew the Prophet*, Hyrum L. Andrus, 112

Mighty Prophet of God

"We listened to the words of instruction and counsel which fell from the inspired lips of Joseph Smith, each word carrying to our hearts deeper and stronger convictions that we were listening to a mighty prophet of God."

—Mercy R. Thompson, *They Knew the Prophet*, Hyrum L. Andrus, 134

Nonmember's impressions

"Joseph Smith was much more than an ordinary man. He . . . deemed himself born to command, and he did command. . . . He had great influence over others . . . (conversed) freely with everyone." Smith possessed a "native intellect" and he "looked like a God," said Peter H. Burnett.

—Hyrum Andrus, *They Knew the Prophet*, 112; Nels Anderson, *Desert Saints*, 5

"He was full six feet high, strongly built, and uncommonly well muscled . . . [he had] a superiority of his physical vigor," said Governor Thomas Ford.

—*RJ*, 29, 30

"I am absolutely convinced that he described a vision. And when visions are described, it is not up to outsiders to say that couldn't have happened."

—Jan Shipps, *American Prophet: The Story of Joseph Smith*, Lee Groberg and Heidi S. Swinton, 44

Nonmembers' praise

"Joseph Smith Jr., is unquestionably the *most important reformer and innovator in American religious history*. . . . [He] is the religious figure in United States history who has had the largest following."

—Robert V. Remini, *Joseph Smith*, IX, X

"There was a kind, familiar look about him that pleased you. . . . He had the capacity for discussing a subject in different aspects and for proposing many original views."

—Peter Hardeman Burnett, *They Knew the Prophet*, Hyrum L. Andrus, 126

"Joseph Smith is obviously the most successful American prophet that we've ever had. He established a religion that has not only lasted but flourished and grown to become the most powerful, uniquely American religion that we've ever had."

—Gordon Wood, *American Prophet: The Story of Joseph Smith*, Lee Groberg and Heidi S. Swinton, 21

Nonmembers' reasoning

"Look what he did. Is one human being capable of doing this? Without divine help and intervention?"

—Robert Remini, *American Prophet: The Story of Joseph Smith,* Lee Groberg and Heidi S. Swinton, 46

"There have been any number of such people, I think, who do feel that they have been divinely inspired, that they are directed to fulfill their mission. That gives them, I think, the determination by which I think they can do extraordinary things. And Joseph Smith did."

—Robert Remini, *American Prophet: The Story of Joseph Smith,* Lee Groberg and Heidi S. Swinton, 124

Non-Mormon feelings about Joseph

After an arrest in Missouri, three officers discussed their feelings while being around the prisoner Joseph.

The first officer said, "Did you not feel strangely when Smith took you by the hand? I never felt so in my life."

The second officer replied, "I could not move. I would not harm a hair of that man's head for the whole world."

The third officer said, "This is the last time you will catch me coming to kill Joe Smith."

—Hyrum L. Andrus, *Joseph Smith, the Man and the Seer*, 7; *History of the Life of Joseph Smith by His Mother Lucy Mack Smith*, 254–56

Not a "stuffed shirt"

A nonmember, George W. Taggart, who met Joseph in 1843, said of him, "Neither is he puffed up in his greatness as many suppose but on the contrary is familiar with any decent man. . . . And I assure you it would make you wonder to hear him talk and see the information which comes out of his mouth and it is not in big words either but that which anyone can understand."

—*RJ*, 37

Remember most about him

The things that early Saints remember most about Joseph are:

- His healings of the blind and the deaf and raising the dead.
- His revelations.

—Mark McConkie tapes

Shaking his hand

"[Joseph] put out his hand and shook hands with my father first, then grasped my hand, inviting us to come in. I cannot describe the feelings I had when he grasped my hand."

—John F. Bellows, *They Knew the Prophet*, Hyrum L. Andrus, 190

Striking hands with him

"I then had the opportunity of striking glad hands with him and my heart leaped in me for joy, for I had greater affection towards him than for any person on earth."

—George Laub, *Joseph Smith, the Man and the Seer*, Hyrum L. Andrus, 42

Superior spirit

"I felt there was a superior spirit in him. He was different from anyone I had ever met before; and I said in my heart, he is truly a prophet of the Most High God."

—James Leech, *They Knew the Prophet*, Hyrum L. Andrus, 160

Supernatural glow

"After emerging from a revelatory experience, his face glowed in an unforgettable manner."

—Davis Bitton, *Images of the Prophet Joseph Smith*, 86

Trick played on Joseph

Martin Harris found a stone that looked like the seer stone and he replaced it with the stone Joseph used some in the translation. When

Joseph tried to use it, he could see nothing. "Martin, what is wrong?" Finally Martin confessed what he had done. When Joseph asked why he had done this, he said, "Well, people were saying you were just making this up." Martin then said, "Now I know that you were not."

—Royal Skousen, *KBYU discussion of the Joseph Smith Papers,* May 18, 2009

Truth of heaven

"Never did I hear preaching sound so glorious to me. . . . I realized it was the truth of heaven, for I had a testimony of it myself."

—Mary A. Noble, *They Knew the Prophet,* Hyrum L. Andrus, 18

Words penetrated the heart

"[His] words were spoken with such power that they penetrated the heart of every soul that believed on him."

—Mary Elizabeth Rollins Lightner, *They Knew the Prophet,* Hyrum L. Andrus, 30

Would have known him among 10,000

"[I] knew him instantly. [I] would have known him among 10,000. There was that about him, which . . . distinguished him from all the men [I] had ever seen."

—George Q. Cannon, *RJ,* 105

Fencing and sword practice

Joseph, with fifteen of the brethren, practiced fencing with Colonel Brewer.

—*HC,* 5:84

Golden stream of words

"The Prophet then arose and poured forth a golden stream of words, many of which were verily pearls without price."

—Lydia Bailey Knight, *They Knew the Prophet,* Hyrum L. Andrus, 49

Ice sliding

Joseph exercised with little Frederick by sliding on the ice on February 8, 1843.

—*HC, 5:265*

Infinity of knowledge

Edward Stevenson said that he "began to believe that [Joseph] possessed an infinity of knowledge."

—Hyrum L. Andrus, *Joseph Smith, the Man and the Seer,* 98

Kicked Warren Waste

At the incident of the tar and feathering in Kirtland, Warren Waste, reputedly the strongest man in the Western Reserve, bragged that he alone could take the Prophet out of the house. About fifty men worked together to take him out of the house. Mr. Waste had hold of one foot and "the Prophet gave him a kick that sent him sprawling off the steps. The imprint made in the ground by his head and shoulders could still be seen the next morning. With his boastful spirit cooled, Waste recovered himself and cried, 'Do not let him touch the ground, or he will run over the whole of us.' He afterwards said that the Prophet was 'the most powerful man' he had ever had hold of in his life."

—Hyrum L. Andrus, *Joseph Smith, the Man and the Seer*, 20

Memory

It has been stated that "Joseph has a wonderful memory. He remembers the names and faces of everyone that stops at the hotel if it's only for a night."

—Mabel A. Sanford, *Joseph's City Beautiful*, 95

Mind as broad as eternity

"Joseph Smith had a mind as broad as eternity."

—Hugh Nibley, *His Life*, September 28, 2009

Opened the door of understanding

The Prophet Joseph Smith opened the door to understanding the workings of God and heaven. "He gave me a complete understanding of who I am."

—John Tanner, *Treasures in Heaven: The John Tanner Story, 2009,* DVD

Poems written

In 1843, Joseph wrote a long poem called "I Will Go," or "The Vision." This nine-page poem, 78 stanzas, was sent to W. W. Phelps as a poetic version of section 76 of the *Doctrine and Covenants,* the vision of the glories.

—*The Vision*, a letter to W. W. Phelps

Powerful speaker

"As he addressed the Saints, his words sometimes so affected me that I would rise upon my feet in the agitation that would take hold of my mind."

—Agnus M. Cannon, *They Knew the Prophet*, Hyrum L. Andrus, 184; —
Duane S. Crowther *The Prophecies of Joseph Smith*, 33

Preaching

"Joseph was the greatest preacher of substance since Jesus."

—Mark L. McConkie tapes

Parley Pratt said, "I have known him to retain a congregation of willing and anxious listeners for many hours together, in the midst of cold or sunshine, rain or wind, while they were laughing at one moment and weeping the next. Even his most bitter enemies were generally overcome, if he could once get their ears."

—Autobiography of Parley Parker Pratt , 47

"It was his custom in addition to his arm gesture to walk the stand from one end to the other (it was 20–30 feet long), and sometimes call upon the audience for an expression of approval which was usually answered by a loud 'Aye' from the congregation. I have never but once since heard a preacher or lecturer exercise the mental power and earnestness manifested by that great man."

—Job F. Smith, *RJ*, 205

Pulling sticks

Joseph pulled sticks and beat Justice A. Morse, the strongest man in Ramus, with one hand. Another time he pulled sticks and won against the two men who tried to kidnap him and take him back to Missouri.

—Hyrum L. Andrus, *Joseph Smith, the Man and the Seer*, 15–16

Sports

"In all his boyish sports and amusements, I never knew any one to gain advantage over him, and yet he was always kind and kept the good will of his playmates."

—Newel Knight, *They Knew the Prophet*, Hyrum L. Andrus, 7

"I've seen the Prophet wrestle, and run, and jump, but have never seen him beaten."

—Lucy Diantha Morley Allen, *They Knew the Prophet*, Hyrum L. Andrus, 7

"There was a bully, from LaHarpe . . . [that] was eager to have a tussle with the Prophet, so Joseph stepped forward and took hold of the man . . . whirled him around and took him by the collar and seat of his trousers and walked out to a ditch and threw him in it. Then, taking him by the arm, he helped him up and patted him on the back and said, "You must not mind this. When I am with the boys I make all the fun I can for them."

—Calvin W. Moore, *They Knew the Prophet*, Hyrum L. Andrus 90

"Joseph Smith was a very stout, athletic man, and was a skillful wrestler."

—Peter Hardiman Burnett, *They Knew the Prophet*, Hyrum L. Andrus, 127

"I have seen him on the playground . . . ball playing, wrestling [and] jumping."

—James W. Phippen, *RJ*, 82

Other sports he participated in:

- Horseback riding
- Playing ball with children
- Stick pulling, of which he was the champion
- Duck hunting
- Log sawing contests
- Running foot races

Squirrel hunting

"The Prophet and I spent most of our time during the day in the woods . . . shooting squirrels."

—William Taylor, *They Knew the Prophet*, Hyrum L. Andrus, 181

Surpassed Sidney and Orson in Greek and Hebrew

"In his later studies of Hebrew and Greek he outstripped his fellows, including Sidney Rigdon and Orson Pratt."

—Hyrum L. Andrus, *Joseph Smith, the Man and the Seer*, 54

Talented to handle any emergency

"Joseph had a talent for meeting every emergency as it came up with promptness and effectiveness."

—John Henry Evans, *Joseph Smith, an American Prophet*, 83

"He could reduce heavenly things to the understanding of the finite," said Brigham Young.

—Hyrum L. Andrus, *They Knew the Prophet*, 39

Teachings made plain

"He reduced his teachings to the capacity of every man, woman, and child, making them as plain as a well-defined pathway."

—Brigham Young, *They Knew the Prophet*, Hyrum L. Andrus, 39

Truth and error

"He possessed a keen ability to draw the line between truth and error, sincerity and hypocrisy; and against the latter he spoke out without fear."

—Hyrum L. Andrus, *Joseph Smith, the Man and the Seer*, 45

Wrestling

According to the internet, baseball started in 1845 (Alexander Cartright), soccer started in 1862, football started in 1876 (Walter Camp), and basketball started in 1891 (James Naismith). Joseph wrestled, ran races, jumped, stick pulled, and played ball with the kids. However, there were a few bat-the-ball type of games in early America.

—Internet

"In the sports of the day, such as wrestling, etc., he was over an average. Very few of the Saints had the strength needed to throw the Prophet in a fair tussle; in every gathering he was a welcome guest, and always added to the amusement of the people. . . . [On one occasion, while camping, the men were cold and] feeling out of sorts and quite cast down. The Prophet came up . . . and caught first one and then another and shook them up, and said, 'Get out of here, and wrestle, jump, run, do anything but mope around . . . this inactivity will not do for soldiers.' The words of the Prophet put life and energy into the men. A ring was soon formed. . . . The Prophet stepped into the ring, ready for a tussel. . . . Several went into the ring to try their strength, but each one was thrown by the Prophet. . . . Then he stepped out of the ring and took a man . . . to take his place. . . . A man would keep the ring so long as he threw his adversary."

—John D. Lee, *RJ*, 225

"He was a skillful wrestler . . . he would not bet anything; . . . it was nothing but a friendly trial of skill and manhood for the satisfaction of others."

—Peter Hardeman Burnett, *Recollections of an Old Pioneer*, 40–42; Hyrum L. Andrus, *They Knew the Prophet*, 127

Joseph's Personality Traits

Axe always sharp

"[Joseph Smith's] ax was stolen from his woodyard, and I contrived to loan him my ax because of the unfailing habit of the Prophet to always sharpen the ax he had been using before it left his hand," relates Jesse W. Crosby.

—Hyrum L. Andrus, *They Knew the Prophet*, 162

Cheerful

"He was cheerful and comforting," said Edward Stevenson.

—Hyrum L. Andrus, *They Knew the Prophet*, 99

"He always had a smile on his face and was cheerful," said Mosiah L. Hancock.

—Hyrum L. Andrus, *They Knew the Prophet*, 115

"He was always cheerful," said Rachel Ridgeway Grant.

—Hyrum L. Andrus, *They Knew the Prophet*, 142

"He spoke kind and cheering words to us and sent us on our way to school rejoicing," said Margarette McIntire Burgess.

—Hyrum L. Andrus, *They Knew the Prophet*, 143

Children

"Joseph was noted for his child–like love and familiarity with children, and he never seemed to feel that he was losing any of his honor or dignity in doing so."

—Helen Mar Whitney, *They Knew the Prophet*, Hyrum L. Andrus, 197: *Woman's Exponent*, December 1, 1881, 146

"[He] would talk to children and they loved him."

—Elam Cheney, *RJ*, 29

"He would go out of his way to talk to a little one."

—*Improvement Era,* December 1917, 167

"He was a great lover of children."

—Sarah A. Johnson Workman, *They Knew the Prophet,* Hyrum L. Andrus, 112

Corrected with kindness

"Those that spoke in his presence, no matter on what subject, allowed themselves to be corrected if needed, which he did in a kind and Christianlike manner."

—James Palmer, *They Knew the Prophet,* Hyrum L. Andrus, 174

Courteous

"He was very courteous in discussion. . . but had due deference to your feelings," said nonmember lawyer Peter Hardeman Burnett.

—Hyrum L. Andrus, *They Knew the Prophet,* 126

Cry of a child

"If he heard the cry of a child, he would rush out of the house to see if it was harmed."

—Helen Mar Whitney, *They Knew the Prophet,* Hyrum L. Andrus, 197

Cultivated intellectual

"He possessed. . . the innate refinement that one finds in the born poet, or in the most highly cultivated intellectual and poetical nature."

—Emmaline Blanche Wells, *They Knew the Prophet,* Hyrum L. Andrus, 177

Debts forgiven

Joseph ran a store and sold things with IOUs. Joseph F. Smith remembers that Joseph, Hyrum Smith, Brigham Young, Sidney Rigdon, Willard Richards, and others were discussing what they should do with all of the notes that were overdue. " 'What shall we do with them?' they said. 'They are impoverished.' By and by, I saw the Prophet gather them up one after another; . . . he opened the door of the stove and stuck them in, and I saw them burn."

—*RJ*, 58

Defended the character of others

"He always took up for the brethren, when their characters were assailed, sooner than for himself, no matter how unpopular it was to speak in their favor."

—Alexander McRae, *They Knew the Prophet,* Hyrum L. Andrus, 126

Denied himself luxuries

He didn't travel to Europe like nine of the Twelve did or travel to Jerusalem like Orson Hyde. He didn't build himself a palace. His so–called mansion in Nauvoo was a modest L–shaped frame home, not constructed of brick or marble.

—Compiler's note

Die for a Presbyterian or Baptist

"If it has been demonstrated that I have been willing to die for a 'Mormon,' I am bold to declare before Heaven that I am just as ready to die in defending the rights of a Presbyterian, a Baptist, or a good man of any other denomination."

—Joseph Smith, *HC,* 5:498; Matthew B. Brown, *Joseph Smith: The Man, the Mission, the Message,* 44

Discuss any subject with ease

Wandle Mace said that members would come up to Joseph Smith in Nauvoo and say, "Brother Joseph talk to us. He would say, "What do you want me to talk about, start something.'" Brother Mace would then lean back and listen. "Ah, what pleasure this gave me; he would unravel the scriptures and explain doctrine as no other man could. What had been mystery he made so plain it was no longer mystery."

—*RJ,* 63

Down to earth

Joseph proved you could be "down to earth" and still reach the heavens. He did not accept the "backward" collar of the ministers of his day.

—Compiler's note

Easy manner

"He had a free and easy manner, not the least affectation."

—Wandle Mace, *They Knew the Prophet,* Hyrum L. Andrus, 130

Eloquent speaker

"He was . . . very interesting and eloquent in speech."

—Wandle Mace, *They Knew the Prophet,* Hyrum L. Andrus, 38

Energy

"[Joseph] is possessed of much energy and decision of character."

—John M. Bernhisel, *They Knew the Prophet*, Hyrum L. Andrus, 199

Enlarged views

"He is a man of . . . enlarged views."

—John M. Bernhisel, *They Knew the Prophet*, Hyrum L. Andrus, 199

False traditions

"He boldly and bravely confronted the false traditions, superstitions, religious bigotry, and ignorance of the world—proved himself true to every heaven–revealed principle—true to his brethren and true to God, then sealed his testimony with his blood."

—Eliza R. Snow, *They Knew the Prophet*, Hyrum L. Andrus, 64

Favorites

- Angel—Moroni
- Attire—A scarf tied at his neck
- Attorney—Alexander W. Doniphan (He named a son after this attorney—Alexander Hale Smith, 1838–1909)
- Bible—German
- Book—Book of Mormon
- Defender—Orrin Porter Rockwell
- Hairstyle—Combed forward on the sides
- Horse—Charlie
- Judge—Nathaniel Pope of Springfield, Illinois
- Person—Emma
- Secretary—Willard Richards, Howard Coray, John Bernhisel, William Clayton, and Benjamin F. Johnson
- Shirt—A white one with ruffles in the front
- Sport—Wrestling
- Suit color—White
- Title—Although the Prophet held almost a dozen titles such as Prophet, Seer, Revelator, General, Supreme Justice of the Nauvoo Court, and Mayor, his favorite title was Brother Joseph.

—Compiler's notes

- Hymns—"I Know That My Redeemer Lives," "The Spirit of God," "When Joseph, His Brethren First Beheld" (referring to Joseph of Egypt), "Redeemer of Israel," and "A Poor Wayfaring Man."

—James Palmer, Truman Madsen Tapes; *They Knew the Prophet* by Hyrum L. Andrus, 172

- Songs—"Wives, Children and Friends," "Battle of River Russon," "Soldier's Tear," "Soldier's Dream," and "Last Rose of Summer."

—Benjamin F. Johnson, *Joseph Smith, the Man and the Seer,* Hyrum L. Andrus, 36

Fearless

"His faith was so strong that he knew no fear."

—Christopher Layton, *They Knew the Prophet,* Hyrum L. Andrus, 196

"As Seer and Revelator he was fearless and outspoken, yet humble, never considering that he was more than the mouthpiece through whom God spoke."

—Jane Snyder, *They Knew the Prophet,* Hyrum L. Andrus, 186; *New York Herald,* February 19, 1842; Preston Nibley, *Joseph Smith the American Prophet,* 562; Emerson R. West, *Profiles of the Presidents,* 45

First in motion

"In the midst of difficulties he was always the first in motion."

—John Taylor, *They Knew the Prophet,* Hyrum L. Andrus, 218

Flowers for a little orphan girl

"I can never forget the tender sympathy and brotherly kindness he ever showed toward me and my fatherless child. When riding with him and his wife Emma in their carriage, I have known him to alight and gather prairie flowers for my little girl."

—Mercy R. Thompson, *They Knew the Prophet,* Hyrum L. Andrus, 136

Force of character

Daniel D. McArthur said, "To me, Joseph Smith seemed to possess more power and force of character than any ordinary man. I would look upon him when he was with hundreds of other men, and he would appear greater than ever. The more I heard his sayings and saw his doings, the more I was convinced that he had of a truth seen God the Father and His Son Jesus Christ, and also the holy angels of God. If I know anything on this earth, I surely know that he was a prophet."

—Hyrum L. Andrus, *They Knew the Prophet,* 82

Forgives W. W. Phelps

W. W. Phelps was excommunicated twice and was a large part of the reason that Joseph Smith was imprisoned in Missouri. But Joseph forgave him and invited him back.

—Compiler's note

Friend

Joseph used the words *my friends* a lot. "Oh, how glad I was that he was my friend!" said Benjamin F. Johnson.

—Hyrum L. Andrus, *They Knew the Prophet,* 110

"Joseph was a prophet of God, and a friend of man."

—Emily D. Partridge Young, *They Knew the Prophet,* Hyrum L. Andrus, 195

"Joseph Smith is the best friend you will ever have outside of Deity because of what he has done for you."

—Mark L. McConkie tapes

Joseph was a "warm and sympathizing friend."

—John M. Bernhisel, *They Knew the Prophet,* Hyrum L. Andrus, 199

Friendly

A nonmember, George Taggard, on September 10, 1843, said of Joseph, "[He] is ready to talk on any subject. . . . He is a man that you could not help liking as a man."

—*RJ,* 37

"[He] never passed me without shaking hands with me"

—Jane James, *They Knew the Prophet,* Hyrum L. Andrus, 178

General's wife loved him almost instantly

Nonmember General Moses Wilson said of Joseph, "He was a very remarkable man. I carried him into my house, a prisoner in chains, and in less than two hours my wife loved him better than she did me."

—*JD,* 17:92; Hyrum L. Andrus, *Joseph Smith, the Man and the Seer,* 5

Generous and benevolent

"He is kind and obliging, generous and benevolent."

—John M. Bernhisel, *They Knew the Prophet,* Hyrum L. Andrus, 199; *My Life's Review,* unpublished letter from Benjamin F. Johnson to Gates, 1903

Brilliant

Truman Madsen calls Joseph brilliant and a genius. Although he was not trained in school, he was trained by a host of tutors and visions, perhaps on many subjects he would know more than all the text books in all the libraries of the world and more than all the sum total of all the knowledge of all the current experts on earth. Joseph was a secret keeper and said that he could not tell even a small part of what was revealed to him.

—Truman G. Madsen tapes; Compiler's note

Inspired

For the critics of Joseph Smith, there is a "Catch 22." If they say he was inspired of God, then they must accept him as a prophet. If they say instead that he was a genius, they acknowledge that all of his thoughts are his thoughts and not God's. Truman Madsen, PhD in philosophy, noted, "Take section 93 of the Doctrine and Covenants. In my considered judgement (and I have read a little in the philosophers of the world) this section is superior in content to Plato's Timaeus. Plato may or may not deserve the reputation of being the greatest philosopher of the Western world. . . . But I say that Joseph Smith, as an instrument for receiving and transmitting God's word, was more profound than Plato. He had the added advantage of the Holy Ghost."

—Truman G. Madsen, *Joseph Smith the Prophet*, 24

Gentleman

"He was all the word *gentleman* would imply—pure in heart, always striving for right, upholding innocence, and battling for the good of all."

—Emily D. Partridge Young, *They Knew the Prophet*, Hyrum L. Andrus, 195

Cheerful

Instead of being a gloom-and-doom prophet, Joseph was positive and cheerful during tough times.

—Randy Bott, *KBYU Discussions on the Doctrine and Covenants,* November 18, 2009

Godlike man

"The Prophet was incomparably the most godlike man I ever saw. I know by his nature he was incapable of lying and deceitfulness,"

—Jesse N. Smith, *Juvenile Instructor* 27:23

"[He was] noble and godlike."

—John F. Bellows, *They Knew the Prophet*, Hyrum L. Andrus, 191

Good Samaritan caregiver

In May of 1832, while traveling back from Independence, Missouri, Joseph Smith and Newel K. Whitney were involved in an incident with a runaway stagecoach near Greenville, Indiana. Newel got his foot caught in a wagon wheel while trying to jump, breaking it in several places. Joseph stayed with him for four weeks instead of going on home and getting someone else to care for him. After this delay, Joseph prophesied that if they took a wagon to the river, there would be a ferry-boat waiting. And then they would take a hack to the landing, where they would find a boat and have a prosperous trip home. They found everything exactly like he had predicted and arrived back in Kirtland in June.

—*HC*, 1:272

Grandest of manhood

"He was one of the grandest samples of manhood that I ever saw walk or ride at the head of a legion of men."

—Agnus M. Cannon, *They Knew the Prophet*, Hyrum L. Andrus, 184

Gratitude immediately answered

John L. Smith was eating at the Joseph Smith home when he heard Joseph offer a blessing: "Lord, we thank Thee for this Johnny cake, and ask Thee to send us something better. Amen."

Before the corn bread was all eaten, a man came to the door and brought some flour and a ham.

"Joseph arose and took the gift, and blessed the man in the name of the Lord. Turning to his wife, Emma, he said, 'I knew the Lord would answer my prayer.' "

—*RJ*, 115–16

Handling contention

"None who saw him administer righteousness under such trying circumstances, could doubt that the Lord was with him, as he acted—not with the wisdom of man, but with the wisdom of God."

—Newel Knight, *Joseph Smith, the Man and the Seer*, Hyrum L. Andrus, 60

Happy person

"He was always jolly and happy. He would play with the people, and he was always cheerful and happy."

—Rachel Ridgeway Grant, *They Knew the Prophet*, Hyrum L. Andrus, 142: George Q. Cannon, *The Life of Joseph Smith*, XXXVI

Hater of sham

Said George Q. Cannon, "He was a great hater of sham. He disliked long–faced hypocrisy."

—Hyrum L Andrus, *Joseph Smith, the Man and the Seer*, 45

Heart

"His heart is felt to be keenly alive to the kindest and softest emotions of which human nature is susceptible."

—John M. Bernhisel, *They Knew the Prophet*, Hyrum L. Andrus, 199

When Joseph received a letter from W. W. Phelps, he wrote back and said, "Truly our hearts were melted into tenderness and compassion. . . . I shall be happy once again to give you the right hand of fellowship."

—Leon Hartshorn, *Joseph Smith: Prophet of the Restoration*, 95

Holy Ghost was his constant companion

"He was highly charged with the Holy Ghost, which was his constant companion."

—Joseph Lee Robinson, *They Knew the Prophet,* Hyrum L. Andrus, 185

Honest completely, and trustworthy

"He is honest, frank [and] fearless," said John M. Bernhisel.

—Leon Hartshorn, *Joseph Smith Prophet of the Restoration*, 73;
Hyrum L. Andrus, *They Knew the Prophet*, 199

Joseph told the truth and did not exaggerate the details. He was an honest storyteller.

—Joseph Fielding McConkie, *KBYU Discussions on the Doctrine and Covenants*, November 23, 2009

Hospitable

Eight negro converts walked 1,000 miles from Connecticut to Nauvoo and showed up barefoot at Joseph's door. Jane James, one of the eight, relates,"Sister Emma she come to the door first, and she says, 'Walk in, come in all of you.' " Joseph soon came in. Jane continued, "I knew it was Brother Joseph, because I had seen him in a dream." They stayed with the Smiths while homes were found for them. However, Jane could not find a place. When Joseph found this out, he said to Emma, "Here's a girl who says she's got no home. Don't you think she's got a home here?" Emma said, "[She does] if she wants to stay here." Joseph replied, "Go . . . to the store and clothe her up."

—Jane James, *They Knew the Prophet*, Hyrum L. Andrus, 178–79

Humble

"In his devotion he was as humble as a little child."

—Eliza R. Snow, *They Knew the Prophet*, Hyrum L. Andrus, 63

When Joseph said, "I am a rough stone rolling," he was merely giving a statement of humility. Long before this day and statement, he had become "a polished shaft in the hands of the Almighty," as stated by President Joseph F. Smith.

—Sharon, Vermont, Birthplace Memorial, 1905

The Prophet's humility was astonishing.

—Leon R. Hartshorn, *Joseph Smith: Prophet of the Restoration*, 75

"He was kind and considerate . . . considering every one his equal."

—Jane S. Richards, *RJ*, 35

Humor

"[Aunt Clarissa] was a very fleshy woman. One day the Prophet came to this house and said he believed he weighed as much as Aunt Clarissa but when they were weighed [on the scales] she weighed the most. He went in the house and got a piece of bread and butter in each hand, then he got on the scales and said, 'Come down, come down' (urging the scale's hand to come down so he would weigh more than Clarissa)."

—Caroline S. Callister, *RJ*, 85

Joseph said, "Sister Horne, if I had a wife as small as you, when trouble came I would put her in my pocket and run."

—Mary I. Horne, *RJ*, 85

Integrity

"His integrity was as firm as the pillars of heaven. He knew that God had called him to the work, and all the powers of earth and hell combined failed either to deter or divert him from his purpose," recalled Eliza R. Snow.

—Hyrum L. Andrus, *They Knew the Prophet*, 63–64

Jokes he told

Joseph loved to tell jokes about mobocrats and other things.

—Benjamin F. Johnson, *My Life's Review*, 82

"I saw him rejoicing with the people . . . occasionally uttering jokes for their amusement."

—Mercy R. Thompson, *They Knew the Prophet*, Hyrum L. Andrus, 135

Jovial manner

"[He] was always jovial and could crack a joke," said Jacob Jones.

—*RJ*, 31

"When [he was] with us there was no lack of amusement, for with jokes, games, etc., he was always ready to provoke merriment," said Benjamin F. Johnson

—Hyrum L. Andrus, *Joseph Smith, the Man and the Seer*, 29; *My Life's Review*, 82

Kindness

"[Joseph's] lips ever flowed with instruction and kindness; . . . very forgiving, indulgent, and affectionate in his temperament," recalled Eliza R. Snow.

—Hyrum L. Andrus, *They Knew the Prophet*, 63

"[He was] possessing the greatest kindness and nobility of character," said Jesse N. Smith.

—Hyrum L. Andrus, *They Knew the Prophet*, 111

Samuel Miles reflected on Joseph's "kind manner and gentle words."

—Hyrum L. Andrus, *They Knew the Prophet*, 110

"Oh how kind he was to the old folks, as well as to little children. He always had a smile for his friends, and was always cheerful."

—Mosiah L. Hancock, *They Knew the Prophet*, Hyrum L. Andrus, 116

"He was very kind and sociable with both young and old."

—Orange L. Wight, *They Knew the Prophet*, Hyrum L. Andrus, 118

A noted panel of lawyers who researched the life of Joseph Smith through his legal documents said Joseph was a kind judge.

—*KBYU Joseph Smith Paper*, September 8, 2009

Lovable

"He was always the most companionable and lovable of men—cheerful and jovial!"

—William Taylor, *They Knew the Prophet*, Hyrum L. Andrus, 181

Magnetic personality

"Much has been said of his geniality and personal magnetism. I was witness of this—people, old or young, loved him and trusted him instinctively."

—William Taylor, *They Knew the Prophet*, Hyrum L. Andrus, 182;
Emerson R. West, *Profiles of the Presidents*, 41

Manners

"[His] manners [were] at once majestic yet gentle, dignified yet exceedingly pleasant."

—Lydia Bailey Knight, *RJ*, 31

Napoleon (Joseph Smith was bigger)

W. W. Phelps told Joseph, "You should have a small table like

Bonaparte, just enough for the victuals you want yourself." Emma replied, "Mr. Smith is a bigger man than Bonaparte; he can never eat without his friends." Joseph remarked, "That is the wisest thing I ever heard you say."

—*HC*, 6:165–66

No strangers to him

"To him there were no strangers. . . . I saw him rejoicing with the people, perfectly sociable and without reserve, occasionally uttering jokes for their amusement and moving upon the same plane with the humblest and poorest of his friends."

—Mercy R. Thompson, *They Knew the Prophet*, 135

Noble

Benjamin F. Johnson said, "[Joseph] was nobility itself, in love and honor of his parents. As a brother he was loving and true even unto death. As a husband and father, his devotion . . . stopped only at idolatry."

—*Doctrine of the Priesthood: Unpublished letter 1903—Patriarch Benjamin F. Johnson's Letter to Elder George F. Gibbs*, 4; Richard I. Winwood, *Take Heed That You Be Not Deceived*, 40

Sarah M. Pomeroy remembers that in the spring of 1843, they moved to Nauvoo. "A gentleman rode up. . . . [O]f course I didn't know who it was, but there was something so noble and dignified in his appearance that it struck me forcibly. My father soon came out . . . and called him Brother Joseph. I knew then it was the Prophet."

Said Samuel Miles, "His noble deportment when before the people . . . his firm dislike of that which was degrading—all these combined to give me a very favorable opinion of this noble man."

—Hyrum L. Andrus, *They Knew the Prophet*, 110, 193

"His was a noble character. All who knew him can testify to that assertion."

—Emily D. Partridge Young, *RJ*, 81

Nothing unbecoming

"I have lived with him in his family; was with him morning, noon, and night, early and late. I saw him in most trying situations, with friends and enemies; . . . I never saw the slightest act, nor heard one word, unbecoming a man of God."

—Curtis E. Bolton, *Joseph Smith: The Man, The Mission, The Message*, Matthew B. Brown, 41

One direction—forward

Joseph knew only one direction—forward. At his death, he was still building Nauvoo into a major city of the West.

—Leon R. Harshorn, *Joseph Smith: Prophet of the Restoration*, 72

Opposition

"Opposition dogged him all his days, yet he was driven by what he said was a 'work that God and angels have contemplated with delight.' "

—Lee Groberg and Heidi S. Swinton, *American Prophet: The Story of Joseph Smith*, 24

Joseph actually thrived on opposition he was so used to it.

—John Henry Evans, *Joseph Smith an American Prophet*, 9

Optimistic

Joseph was an optimistic man.

—Leon R. Hartshorn, *Joseph Smith: Prophet of the Restoration*, 81

Outspoken yet humble

"He was fearless and outspoken, yet humble, . . . modest and considerate."

—Jane Snyder Richards, *They Knew the Prophet*, Hyrum L. Andrus, 186

Patriotism

A nonmember, George W. Taggart, said of Joseph on September 10, 1843, "He is one of the warmest patriots and friends to his country and laws that you ever heard speak on the subject."

—*RJ*, 37

Said Joseph Smith on July 3, 1841, "I would ask no greater boon, than to lay down my life for my country."

—*HC*, 4:382; John W. Welch, ed., *A Chronology of the Life of Joseph Smith*, BYU Studies, 120

"He is a true lover of his country and is a bright and shining example of integrity and moral excellence in all the relations of life."

—John M. Bernhisel, *They Knew the Prophet*, Hyrum L. Andrus, 199

Perfect witness

Joseph simply told the truth: "I saw two Personages whose brightness and glory defy all description." Others like Oliver Cowdery and Sidney Rigdon would go on and on to eloquently describe the event while Joseph would understate or under tell.

—Joseph Fielding McConkie, KBYU roundtable discussion replay, July 17, 2009; Mark L. McConkie tapes

Personality Profile: a fun-loving yellow

If Joseph Smith were to be assigned a personality profile, he would likely be a fun-loving yellow (as opposed to red, blue, or white): "[He] was a hail-fellow-well-met, easily inclined to laughter, sociable, animated, the life of the party, and colorful in his use of language."

—Truman G. Madsen, *Joseph Smith the Prophet*, 25; Hartman Personality Profile; Wikipedia

Philanthropist

"As a philanthropist, his soul was broad as eternity," said Eliza R. Snow.

—Hyrum L. Andrus, *They Knew the Prophet*, 63

Phrase

Heber C. Kimball said that Joseph used to encourage people to get to work on something by saying, "Yankee doodle do it."

—*RJ*, 83

Played marbles with the boys

"I have known him . . . to stop as he passed the playgrounds, when we were out of school, and shake hands with the girls, and play a game of marbles with the boys."

—Mary Jane Lytle Little, *Joseph Smith, the Man and the Seer,* Hyrum L. Andrus, 38

Playful and cheerful

Joseph publicly declared that he was "playful and cheerful."

—*HC*, 5:411

Prayed

About February 7, 1844, Joseph prayed for the Saints to be delivered from the harassment of Missouri governor Thomas Reynolds. Within two days, Joseph learned that he had committed suicide.

—*JD*, 24:55

Joseph had compassion and love even as he prayed for the Lord's mercy to be on the wicked mobs.

—See D&C 109:50

"I heard [Joseph] . . . address his Maker as though He was present listening as a kind father would listen to the sorrows of a dutiful child. . . . [I] partook of the learning and eloquence of heaven. There was no ostentation, no raising of the voice as by enthusiasm, but a plain conversational tone, as a man would address a present friend."

—Daniel Tyler, *Joseph Smith, the Man and the Seer*, Hyrum L. Andrus, 61

Remarkable courage

Joseph had remarkable courage. He asked the people to do nothing he would not do himself.

—Leon R. Hartshorn, *Joseph Smith: Prophet of the Restoration*, 1–14

Riches of the world he did not seek or realize

Ministers and preachers of today like Billy Graham and Robert Schuller are all millionaires. Billy Graham spent 72 million dollars on just his museum. Joseph Smith was not interested in money or he would have set up a different system. He sure would not have sacrificed over and over for a temple until he had built a grand palace for himself. Even the kings of Israel built larger palaces for themselves than the temple they erected.

—Compiler's note

Shared his last dollar

A destitute sister had an offer to go back home and be cared for. "Brother Joseph asked her what she would rather do. She said she would rather stay with the Saints if she was not too burdensome. He said, 'Then stay, sister, and God bless you.' He put his hand in his pocket and gave her his last dollar."

—Christopher Merkley, *Biography of Christopher Merkley*, pp. 9–11;
They Knew the Prophet by Hyrum L. Andrus, 137–138

Singing songs

Joseph loved to call for the singing of one or more of his favorite songs. "Of those, 'Wives, Children and Friends,' 'Battle of River Russen,' 'Soldier's Tear,' 'Soldier's Dream,' and 'Last Rose of Summer' were most common."

—Hyrum L. Andrus, *They Knew the Prophet*, 100

Single sentence statements of truth

"Joseph . . . gave his views in a series of short pronouncements. The aphorism—the oracular, single sentence utterance containing a truth, a principle, or . . . fact," was characteristic of his preaching stye.

—Davis Bitton, *Images of the Prophet Joseph Smith*, 91–92

Smile for his friends

"He always had a smile for his friends."

—*Life Story of Mosiah Lyman Hancock*, 3

Sociable

"He was as free and sociable as though we had all been his own brothers and sisters," recorded Mercy R. Thompson.

—Hyrum L. Andrus, *They Knew the Prophet*, 135

Said John M. Bernhisel, "He is kind and obliging, generous and benevolent, sociable and cheerful."

—Hyrum L. Andrus, *They Knew the Prophet*, 135, 199

Stage fright

Heber C. Kimball often heard Joseph say that many times his legs "trembled like Belshazzar's when he got up to speak before the world, and before the Saints."

—*JD*, 2:220; *RJ*, 68

Strength of personality

"It was impossible to meet him and not be impressed by the strength of his personality and influence."

—Mary Alice Cannon Lambert, *They Knew the Prophet*, Hyrum L. Andrus, 189

Strong mental powers

"General Joseph Smith is . . . a man of strong mental powers, and is possessed of much energy and decision of character, great penetration and a profound knowledge of human nature.

—John M. Bernhisel, *They Knew the Prophet*, Hyrum L. Andrus, 199

Sympathies: affectionate toward others

Leonard Arrington said that Joseph Smith's affectionate sympathies toward others was what people loved about him.

—Lee Groberg and Heidi S. Swinton, *American Prophet: The Story of Joseph Smith*, 130

"Joseph Smith, the very teacher of gentleness and long suffering."

—Leon Hartshorn, *Joseph Smith: Prophet of the Restoration*, 97

Tears trickling down his cheeks

"I perceived sadness in his countenance and tears trickling down his cheeks. . . . [He] said he often wondered why it was that he should have so much trouble in the house of his friends, and he wept as though his heart would break."

—Daniel Tyler, *RJ*, 224

Tell me to my face

Joseph said, "Brethren and friends if any of you have anything against me, come and tell me, and I will make it right. Do not be backward. Come publicly or privately and see if I do not satisfy you."

—William A. Hickman, *RJ*, 80

Tender feelings

Leonard Arrington said, "The quality that most of his followers saw in him was his . . . tender and affectionate sympathies towards people."

—Lee Groberg and Heidi S. Swinton, *American Prophet: The Story of Joseph Smith*, 130

Joseph was a "tender and affectionate husband and parent."

—John M. Bernhisel, *They Knew the Prophet*, Hyrum L. Andrus, 199

Heber C. Kimball told a story of Joseph Smith's tenderness: "My (Heber's) daughter had broken a saucer; her mother promised her a whipping, when she returned from a visit on which she was just starting; she went out under an apple tree and prayed that her mother's heart might be softened, and . . . she might not whip her; although her mother was very punctual when she made a promise to her children to fulfill it, yet when she returned she had no disposition to chastise her child. Afterwards the child told her mother that she had prayed to God that she might not whip her. Joseph wept like a child on hearing this simple narrative and its application."

—*RJ*, 115

Tore his pants while wrestling

"He was cheerful—often wrestling with Sidney Rigdon. One time he had his pants torn badly, but had a good laugh over it."

—Edward Stevenson, *RJ*, 83*; Hyrum L. Andrus, They Knew the Prophet*, 96

Trusted friends

"Those who knew Joseph best, trusted him the most."

—Steve Harper, *KBYU Joseph Smith Papers*, October 26, 2009

"Such were the social and religious elements of his unselfish nature that those who knew him best loved him most," wrote Benjamin F. Johnson. He continued, "To me . . . he was the embodiment and perfection of all that I could comprehend in perfect manhood."

—Hyrum L. Andrus, *They Knew the Prophet*, 100–101

Unassuming

"He was as unassuming as a child."

—Mercy R. Thompson, *They Knew the Prophet*, Hyrum S. Andrus, 135

Unswerving course

The Prophet Joseph Smith had an amazing capacity to not be overcome by the world.

—Leon Hartshorn, *Joseph Smith: Prophet of the Restoration*, 112

Voice of music to my ears

"I loved his company, the sound of his voice was music to my ears," said Gilbert Belnap (1821–1899) about Joseph Smith.

—*GD*, 24

Women's rights advocate

"[Joseph] was an advocate of women's rights, and his organization (on March 1, 1842) of the Female Relief Society of Nauvoo was an act which far preceded other movements for the betterment of womankind in the United States."

—Duane S. Crowther, *The Prophecies of Joseph Smith*, 37

Wood pile was neat and organized

"He was orderly. His woodyard was an example of order. Logs were neatly piled and all trash cleared away. If he did not finish the log on which he was chopping, the remnant was laid back on the pile and not left on the ground for a stumbling block. The chips he made he picked up himself into a basket."

—Jesse W. Crosby, *They Knew the Prophet,* Hyrum L. Andrus, 162

Worker—best he ever found

"At one point [a local] minister criticized [one girl's] father for hiring Joseph Smith. The minister . . . thought he might be a bad influence on others. The girl's father disagreed. He said that Joseph was the best worker he'd ever found. He said that when the boys of the neighborhood worked by themselves, they'd waste a lot of time arguing, quarreling, and fist fighting. But when Joseph Smith worked with them the work went steadily forward, and he got the full worth of the wages he paid.

—Glen S. Hopkinson, *A Faithful Life: The Story of Joseph Smith in Pictures*, 14

Joseph's Physical Appearance

Commanding figure and appearance

"His commanding presence could be discerned above all others, and all eyes were centered on him."

—Mary Ann Winters, *They Knew the Prophet,* Hyrum L. Andrus, 188

Description of Joseph Smith

Elam Cheney said, "Brother Joseph was a man weighing about two hundred pounds, fair complexion, light brown hair. He was about six feet tall, sound bodied, very strong and quick."

—*RJ,* 29

John D. Lee says, "He was rather large in stature, some six feet two inches in height, . . . light chestnut hair, upper lip full, . . . and [an] eagle eye."

—*RJ,* 32

James Palmer said, "He was . . . over six feet in height, . . . his hair was of a flaxen color, he wore no whiskers, his chin was a little tipped, his nose was long and straight, his mouth was rather massive, and his upper lip rather long and a little inclined to be thick. He had a large full chest and intelligent eyes and fine limbs."

—Hyrum L. Andrus, They Knew the Prophet, 174; *RJ,* 33

Jane James said, "Brother Joseph was tall, over six feet; he was a fine big, noble, beautiful man! He had blue eyes and light hair, and very fine, white skin."

—Hyrum L. Andrus, They Knew the Prophet, 180; *RJ,* 31

Engaging smile

Young Joseph had a bright, engaging smile.

—Robert V. Remini, *Joseph Smith*, 31

Face of Joseph Smith

Joseph had striking and penetrating blue eyes: "Handsome blue eyes, which seemed to dive down to the innermost thoughts with their sharp, penetrating gaze; a striking countenance."

—Lydia B. Knight, *They Knew the Prophet,* Hyrum L. Andrus, 47

Joseph had "the longest, thickest light [eye]lashes you ever saw belonging to a man." "He had . . . extended eyelashes and bushy eyebrows."

—*St. Louis Weekly Gazette,* June 1844; Robert V. Remini, *Joseph Smith*, 42

Face shone like Moses's

"I had before seen him in a vision, and now saw his countenance change to white; not the deadly white of a bloodless face, but a living, brilliant white."

—Anson Call, *They Knew the Prophet,* Hyrum L. Andrus, 120

"A halo of brightness hovered about him . . . he was full of light."

—Edward Stevenson, *They Knew the Prophet,* Hyrum L. Andrus, 97–98

"I saw his face become white and a shining glow seemed to beam from every feature."

—Lydia Bailey Knight, *They Knew the Prophet,* Hyrum L. Andrus, 47

"Joseph got up to speak. . . . All at once his countenance changed and he stood mute. He turned so white he seemed perfectly transparent. Those who looked at him that night said he looked like he had a searchlight within him. . . . I never saw anything like it on earth. . . . He got so white that anyone who saw him would have thought he was transparent. I remember I thought we could almost see the bones through the flesh of his face. . . . [He then said,] 'Brothers and Sisters, the Savior has been in your midst this night.' "

—Mary Elizabeth Rollins Lightner, *They Knew the Prophet,* Hyrum L. Andrus, 26; Hyrum L Andrus, *Joseph Smith the Man and the Seer,* 131

"His face was clear as amber."

—Wilford Woodruff, *RJ,* 373

"I stood close by the Prophet while he was preaching to the Indians in the grove by the temple. The Holy Spirit lighted up his countenance till it glowed like a halo around him."

—Mary Ann Winters, *RJ,* 208

"[Joseph] seemed to be dressed in an element of glorious white, and his face shone as if it were transparent."

—Philo Dibble, *They Knew the Prophet,* Hyrum L. Andrus, 76

"At such times there was a peculiar clearness and transparency in his face."

—Brigham Young, *They Knew the Prophet,* Hyrum L. Andrus, 39

"At times he was filled with the Holy Ghost, speaking as with the voice of an archangel and filled with the power of God. His whole person shone, and his face was lightened until it appeared as the whiteness of the driven snow."

—Lorenzo Snow, *They Knew the Prophet,* Hyrum L. Andrus, 37

"All the time he was delivering the word of the Lord his face shone as if there was a light within him and his flesh was transparent."

—Oliver B. Huntington, *RJ,* 138

Gentlemanly bearing

James Palmer said, "[Joseph] presented a very formidable appearance, being a man of gentlemanly bearing."

—*RJ,* 33; Hyrum L Andrus, *They Knew the Prophet,* 174

Glory of his countenance

"The glory of his countenance was beyond description."

—Emmaline Blanch Wells, *They Knew the Prophet,* Hyrum L. Andrus, 178

Good looking

"He was a fine looking man, tall and well proportioned."

—Wandle Mace, *They Knew the Prophet,* Hyrum L. Andrus, 130,

Hair color

In 1830, the term *blonde* hadn't been invented yet; instead, it was called "light brown."

—Compiler's note

His prominent frontals were covered with a heavy growth of light hair.

—John Henry Evans, Joseph Smith an American Prophet, 37

Handsome

"The Prophet was a handsome man—splendid looking, a large man, tall and fair," records Bathsheba W. Smith. Men, women, and enemies described him as being good looking.

—Hyrum L. Andrus, They Knew the Prophet, 138

On September 10, 1843, nonmember George W. Taggart described Joseph: "He is . . . one of the finest looking men there is in the country."

—*RJ*, 37

Heavenly appearance

"[He] had the most heavenly countenance; was genial, affable and kind; and looked the soul of honor and integrity."

—Bathsheba W. Smith, *They Knew the Prophet,* Hyrum L. Andrus, 138

"He had the appearance of one that was heaven–born."

—James Palmer, *They Knew the Prophet,* Hyrum L. Andrus, 174

"I never saw another man like Joseph. There was something heavenly and angelic in his looks that I never witnessed in the countenance of any other person. . . . [I] learned to love him more dearly than any other person I ever met, my father and mother not excepted."

—John W. Hess, *They Knew the Prophet,* Hyrum L. Andrus, 114

"As I looked at him he seemed to me like a heavenly being."

—Susan E. Johnson Martineau, *They Knew the Prophet,* Hyrum L. Andrus, 112

"He possessed. . . innate refinement. . .this extraordinary temperament and force combined is something of a miracle and scarcely be accounted for except as a 'heavenly mystery' of a higher sort."

—Emmeline B. Wells, *Joseph Smith, the Man and the Seer,* Hyrum L. Andrus, 37

"His countenance seemed to assume a heavenly whiteness."

—Edward Stevenson, *They Knew the Prophet,* Hyrum L. Andrus, 96

Height

It was recorded by various accounts that Joseph was either six feet, six feet and one inch, or six feet and two inches. Alvin was six feet and six inches tall. From calculations made from the actual sword of Joseph, which was forty-two inches long, Howard Carlos Smith calculated he was six feet three inches tall.

—*John Henry Evans, Joseph Smith an American Prophet*, 8 (6'0"); Howard Carlos Smith, *Keeper of the Prophet's Sword*, 15 (6'3")

Height compared to others

- President Joseph Smith 6'2" (there are numerous versions of his height from 6' to 6'3")
- James E. Talmage 5'2"
- Oliver Cowdery 5'5'

- Spencer W. Kimball 5'5"
- Sidney Rigdon 5'7"
- Martin Harris 5'8½"
- Frederick G. Williams 5'9"
- Gordon B. Hinckley 5'9"
- Brigham Young 5'9" (another source says 5'10")
- Hyrum Smith 5'11½"
- David O. McKay 6'1"
- William Smith 6'3" (another source says 6'6")
- Thomas S. Monson 6'4" (another source says 6'3")
- Alexander McCrae 6'6" (was in Liberty Jail for four months and ten days, and the jail ceiling was 6')
- Joseph Bates Noble 5'8"
- Elder James E. Talmage 5'2"
- Rebecca Williams 6' (Frederick G. Williams's wife. Joseph Smith wore one of her dresses to disguise himself so that he could escape from Kirtland undetected.)
- Elder William E. McLellin 6'4"

—*Welch and Morris, Oliver Cowdery, Scribe, Elder, Witness*, BYU Studies; Scot Facer Proctor and Maurine Proctor, *History of Joseph Smith by His Mother*; Nancy C. Williams, *After 100 years*

Light complexion

"He [had] . . . a light complexion, blue eyes, and light hair," records Wandle Mace.

—*Hyrum L. Andrus, They Knew the Prophet*, 130

Lofty appearance

"I made my way through the crowd. Then I saw this man whom I had noticed, because of his lofty appearance, shaking hands with all the people, men, women and children."

—Emmeline Blanche Wells, *They Knew the Prophet*, Hyrum L. Andrus, 176–77

Long legs and large feet

"He had long legs . . . and large feet."

—Robert V. Remini, *Joseph Smith*, 42

Looked good even in death

In the coffin, "his face was mild and pleasant; even in death [he] looked good."

—Emily S. Hoyt, *RJ*, 416

Majestic bearing

"His majestic bearing, so entirely different from anyone I had ever seen . . . was more than a surprise. It was as if I had seen a vision; I seemed to be lifted off my feet."

—Emmeline Blanche Wells, *Young Women's Journal,* vol. 16, 555; Hyrum L. Andrus, *They Knew the Prophet*, 176

"There was a power and majesty that attended his words and preaching that we never beheld in any man before."

—Joseph Lee Robinson, *Young Women's Journal,* vol. 16, 555; Hyrum L. Andrus, *They Knew the Prophet*, 185

Manly and almost godlike

"In all that he did he was manly and almost god–like. The only words that express his looks and actions are: 'Surely he was a man of God.' "

—Lucy Diantha Morley Allen, *They Knew the Prophet,* Hyrum L. Andrus, 35

Muscles

"He was . . . uncommonly well muscled."

—Governor Thomas Ford, *RJ*, 30

Nose

Joseph's nose was slightly prominent. It probably wasn't as big as the young actor who played Joseph in *Joseph Smith and the Restoration* and other LDS and non–LDS films, or even that of Liz Lemon Swindle's model for her paintings. "He had an aquiline nose."

—Robert V. Remini, *Joseph Smith*, 42; death mask of Joseph and Hyrum owned by the compiler

Physical descriptions

"He was nimble as a cat."

—Jacob Jones, *RJ*, 31

"He was standing with his youngest boy in his arms and he was the most beautifully formed man, and was laughing pleasantly [with] the brethren on board the steam boat and I never in this life shall look upon his like again."

—Curtis Edwin Brown, *GD,* 35

Physically strong

"He was well built, athletic, fond of many sports, and had physical courage of the highest order."

—Edwin F. Parry, *Glad Tidings Near Cumorah,* Bruce E. Dana, 70

"I saw a tall, well–built form, with the carriage of an Apollo."

—Lydia B. Knight, *RJ*, 31

Very little beard

"He was a fine looking man . . . [with] very little beard."

—Wandle Mace, *They Knew the Prophet,* Hyrum L. Andrus, 130

Weight

Most accounts say he weighed 200–212 pounds.

—Compiler's note

Extraordinary man

"Joseph Smith was a most extraordinary man; he was rather large in stature, some six feet two inches in height, . . . and all who saw were forced to admire him."

—John D. Lee, *RJ*, 32

Grand leader

"I saw him on parade at the head of the Nauvoo Legion, looking noble and grand as a leader could do."

—Mary Ann Winters, *They Knew the Prophet,* Hyrum L. Andrus, 188

Mild and penetrating glance

"I was introduced to the Prophet, whose mild and penetrating glance denoted great depth of thought and extensive forethought. While I was standing before his penetrating gaze, he seemed to read the very recesses of my heart. . . . I gazed with wonder at his person and listened with delight to the sound of his voice. My very destiny seemed to be interwoven with his."

—Gilbert Belnap, *They Knew the Prophet,* Hyrum L. Andrus, 202

Physical injuries of Joseph Smith

Leg surgery at age seven left him with a limp (1812).

Dislocated his thumb when he hit an attacker while taking home the plates from the Hill Cumorah (1827).

Chipped his tooth when he was tarred and feathered in Hiram, Ohio, causing a slight whistle when he spoke for the rest of his life (1834).

Received a lasting back injury from the tar and feathering (1834).

Lost 45 pounds in Liberty Jail (winter 1838–1839).

—Compiler's note

Physical strength

Brigham Young told of a time in 1838 that Joseph Smith sprung a wagon axletree back in place after a blacksmith told him it wasn't possible.

—*RJ*, 117

Silk scarf

"He (Joseph) most always wore a silk stock, and was smooth faced."

—Elam Cheney, *RJ*, 29

Adam-ondi-Ahman

Adam's alter was shown to Chapman Duncan and a few others by the Prophet Joseph. "He went about forty rods north of my house and placed the shovel with care and placed his foot on it. When he took out the shovelful of dirt it bared the stone, on the side of [the] upper edge nearly a foot deep. The dirt was two inches deep on the stone, I reckon. About four feet or more were disclosed. He did not dig to the bottom of the wall—three layers of good masonry wall put up, were unearthed. The stone looked liked dressed stone, nice joints, ten inches thick, eighteen inches or more long. . . . The Prophet. . . remarked, 'This . . . is the place where Adam gathered his posterity and blessed them, and predicted what should come to pass to later generations.' "

—Chapman Duncan, *RJ*, 350.

Note: The compiler has seen the name Adam-ondi-Ahman spelled eighteen different ways by various accounts of early Church history while researching for his master's thesis on Missouri.

Adam-ondi-Ahman's Altar Location

"He led us a short distance to a place where were the ruins of three altars built of stone, one above the other, and one standing a little back of the other, like unto the pulpits in the Kirtland Temple, representing the order of the three grades of priesthood; 'There,' said Joseph, 'is the place where Adam offered up sacrifice after he was cast out of the garden [of Eden].' The altar stood at the highest point of the bluff."

—Heber C. Kimball, *RJ*, 350

Adam-ondi-Ahman's Tower Hill of the Nephites

Joseph saw this pyramid-shaped hill when he went to Lyman Wight's place in 1838. He went to the top of the hill and gave it the name Tower Hill, "in consequence of the remains of an old Nephite altar or tower that stood there." Wilford Wood purchased thirty–eight acres of this hill on June 27, 1944, the one hundredth anniversary of the martyrdom of the Prophet Joseph Smith, from Eugene Johnson for $100 an acre.

—*HC*, 3:35; Lamar C. Berrett, *Sacred Places: Missouri*, 380–83

Cities and towns started through Joseph's instruction

Missouri

- Jackson County: Brush Creek, Big Blue, Ambrosia
- Clay County: Morley Settlement
- Ray County: Tenney's Grove
- Caldwell County: Far West, Plum Creek, Haun's Mill
- Daviess County: Adam–ondi–Ahman, Seth, Marrowbone Creek

Illinois

- Hancock County: Nauvoo, sixteen other little communities

Iowa

- Lee County: Zarahemla, Nashville, Montrose

—*Sacred Places*, volumes 1–4

Erie Canal travel

The Erie Canal became a miracle of the Restoration. One could travel about 20 miles a day. The Erie Canal was started July 4, 1817, and completed on October 26, 1825, and it cost 8.5 million dollars. Thousands of men worked on it for 80 cents a day. It became a 363 mile, 4-foot-deep ditch and had a 10-foot path for animals to pull the canal boats along. There were 83 locks and 300 bridges constructed. When Lucy Smith traveled on it, she sat down to sing a hymn, which was so beautiful it melted every heart that heard it. In 1825, 40,000 people traveled on 13,110 boats on the Erie Canal. It connected New York City with the Great Lakes.

—*The U.S. From Coast to Coast: 1785–1860,* Internet; Scot Facer Proctor and Maurine Jensen Proctor, eds., *The Revised and Enhanced History of Joseph Smith by His Mother, Lucy Mack Smith*; Madge Harris Tuckett and Beth Harris Wilson, *Martin Harris, Special Witness to the Book of Mormon*, 15; Robert V. Remini, *Joseph Smith*, 30

Farms

Joseph had a 140-acre hay farm in Kirtland, according to Joseph Bates Noble. The Prophet also owned a 160-acre farm outside of Nauvoo, south of Far West, that he stopped to look at while en route to Carthage. He commented, "If some of you had such a farm and knew you would not see it anymore, you would want to take a good look at it for the last time."

—Howard Carlos Smith, *Keeper of the Prophet's Sword*, 7, 72; Missouri Caldwell County Records

First MTC

The first missionary training center was the School of the Prophets in an upstairs room of the Newell K. Whitney store in Kirtland, Ohio.

—Milton Backman, *KBYU Joseph Smith Discussion*, January 3, 2010

Garden of Eden once located in Independence, Missouri

As revealed through Joseph Smith the Prophet, "The Temple Block in Jackson County, Missouri, stands on the identical spot where once stood the Garden of Eden."

—Alvin R. Dyer, *The Refiner's Fire*, 110

Hill Cumorah

Oliver Cowdery described the Hill Cumorah "forming a promontory without timber, but covered with grass." Later, trees were planted.

—Scot Facer Proctor and Maurine Jensen Proctor, eds., *The Revised and Enhanced History of Joseph Smith by His Mother*, 113n3

"Oliver Cowdery went with the Prophet Joseph when he deposited these plates; . . . the hill opened and they walked into a cave, in which there was a large and spacious room. He says he did not think, at that time, whether they had the light of the sun or artificial light; but that it was just as light as day. They laid the plates on a table; it was a large table that stood in the room. Under this table there was a pile of plates as much as two feet high, and there were all together in this room more plates than probably many wagon loads; they were piled up in the corners and along the walls. The first time they went there the sword of Laban hung upon the wall; but when they went again it had been taken down and laid upon the table across the gold plates; it was unsheathed, and on it was written these words: "This sword will never be sheathed again until the kingdoms of this world become the kingdom of our God and his Christ." Others were witnesses to this, including Don Carlos Smith, Samuel Smith, and Hyrum Smith.

—*RJ*, 250–51; Brigham Young, *JD*, 19:38

The Hill Cumorah is the largest drumlin in the Palmyra, New York area. However, there are over twenty drumlins in the Palmyra area similar to the Hill Cumorah. (The word *drumlin* comes from the Irish word *droimnin*, "little ridge." First recorded in 1833, it is an elongated hill in the shape of an inverted spoon or half–buried egg formed by glacial ice acting on underlying unconsolidated glacial debris.)

—Dale L. Berg, *Archaeology at the Boyhood Home of Joseph Smith, Jr., Palmyra, New York*, 5; *Wikipedia*

Jackson County land to be purchased

The Lord instructed Joseph that the Church was to collect money and purchase all the land they could in Jackson County and the surrounding areas. They were to buy up the whole region. Contrary to what is shown in Church History maps today, Jackson County at the time was 25 miles wide by 75 miles long. Since the Saints were there in 1831–1833 two counties have been split off from Jackson County, reducing it at present to about 25 miles wide and 25 miles long.

—See D&C 58:49–52, 63

Missouri

Joseph owned 1,120 acres in Daviess County, Missouri, of which 160 of these were co-owned with Isaac Beebe and Reed Peck. Most of this land was in section 27, township 56 north, range 29 west with 80 acres in section 2 of the same area. He owned 320 acres in Daviess County. Note: This acreage was in his name, but he often held Church land in his name.

—Compiler's note

Nauvoo

Joseph owned about 200 acres in Illinois, including:

- 160-acre farm toward Carthage
- Old Mound acreage toward LaHarpe
- 15 acres due north of the Mansion Home on the south bank of the Mississippi River
- The Mansion Home
- Red Brick Store
- Joseph Smith homestead
- Original old home next to the river

—Compiler's note

Kirtland

In Kirtland Joseph owned about ten acres: three acres east of the temple, four acres across the street south of the temple, two acres southwest of the temple, and one acre west of the temple.

—Compiler's note

Harmony

Joseph owned 13½ acres in Harmony, Pennsylvania, that he bought from Emma's father. This land dissected current Highway 171.

—Compiler's note

Lived in eight states

Joseph lived in

- Vermont (1805–1811, 1814–1816)
- New Hampshire (1811–1814)
- Massachusetts (1813)
- New York (1816–1827, 1829–1830)
- Pennsylvania (1827–1828)
- Ohio (1831–1838)
- Missouri (1838–1839)
- Illinois (1839–1844)

His time in Missouri was among the least in time of stays—only about eight months—but over half of that time was in jails. No wonder he made up his mind never to go back to Missouri.

—John W. Welch, ed., *A Chronology of the Life of Joseph Smith,* BYU Studies

Log cabin in Vermont

"[Joseph] could claim to have been born in a log cabin in Sharon, Vermont. He didn't stay there—heroes never do."

—Davis Bitton, *Images of the Prophet Joseph Smith*, 39

Love for Nauvoo

Just before leaving for Carthage on June 24, 1844, Joseph said, "I love the city of Nauvoo too well to save my life at your expense. . . . I fear not death; my work is done. Keep the faith and I will die for Nauvoo."

—Ted Gibbons, *Sealing the Testimony*, 32

Moves

Joseph moved at least twenty-six times in his life. His family moved at least eight times before his marriage. He and Emma moved at least eighteen times:

- To Joseph's parents' home in Farmington Township, south of Palmyra.
- To Harmony.
- To the Whitmers.
- To Newel K. Whitney store in Kirtland.
- To Hiram, Ohio, to live with the John Johnson family.
- To a home near the temple in Kirtland.
- Escaping to Far West, Missouri (left Kirtland on January 12, 1838, arrived in Missouri on March 14, 1838—57 days en route).
- To six different Missouri jails.

- To Quincy, Illinois.
- To a small log home in Commerce, Illinois.
- To a frame home in Nauvoo.
- To the Mansion Home.
- Into hiding at various homes, on an island in the middle of the Mississippi River, and so on.

—John W. Welch, ed., *A Chronology of the Life of Joseph Smith, BYU Studies,* 25, 32, 93, 107; Richard E. Turley and Lael Littke, *Stories From the Life of Joseph Smith*, 97, 109; Scot Facer Proctor and Maurine Jensen Proctor, eds., *History of Joseph Smith by His Mother,* 254

Mileage and travel time

The distance from where Emma's parents lived in Harmony, Pennsylvania, to Joseph's parents' home in Manchester Township was 128 miles and took four days by wagon.

—J. Christopher Conkling, *A Joseph Smith Chronology*, 6

Vermont: Sharon Township to

- Hanover, New Hampshire (Doctors of Dartmouth College)—35 miles SE
- West Lebanon, New Hampshire—30 miles SE
- Tonbridge, Vermont (Joseph Smith Sr. and Lucy met, and Hyrum born)—11 miles N
- Palmyra, New York (to Hill Cumorah)—400 miles SW
- Kirtland, Ohio—675 miles SW
- Nauvoo, Illinois—1,340 miles SW
- Harmony, Pennsylvania—365 miles S
- Carthage, Illinois—1,360 miles SW

New York: Palmyra to

- Harmony, Pennsylvania (Emma's home)—130 miles SE
- Fayette, New York (Church organized)—45 miles SE
- Colesville, New York (First large group of converts)—130 miles SE
- Kirtland, Ohio—275 miles W
- Independence, Missouri—1,203 miles SW

Note: Cleveland is 20 miles from Kirtland

Pennsylvania: Harmony to

- Bainbridge, New York—30 miles N
- Colesville, New York (First large group of converts)—35 miles N
- Fayette, New York—45 miles NW

Ohio: Kirtland to

- Hiram, Ohio (Joseph tarred and feathered at the Johnson home)—35 miles S
- Painesville, Ohio (Edward Partridge's home)—11 miles NE
- Amherst, Ohio (Brigham Young's home)—50 miles NE
- Mentor, Ohio (Sidney Rigdon's home)—4 miles N
- Independence, Missouri (took 24 days by riverboat for Joseph Smith in 1832)—928 miles SW
- Nauvoo, Illinois—690 miles SW
- Toronto (Kingston), Canada—190 miles N
- Salem, Massachusetts—627 miles E
- Boston, Massachusetts—607 miles N
- Washington, DC—326 miles SE

Missouri: Far West to

- Liberty, Missouri—35 miles S
- Independence, Missouri—50 miles S
- Richmond, Missouri—28 miles SE
- Adam-ondi-Ahman—25 miles N (70 miles from Independence, Missouri)
- Fairview, Missouri (Haun's Mill)—13 miles E
- Quincy, Illinois—175 miles E
- Colesville, New York—1,250 miles E (1,300 from Independence, Missouri)
- Nauvoo, Illinois—220 miles East

Illinois: Nauvoo to

- Far West, Missouri—200 miles W
- Carthage, Illinois—23 miles SE
- Quincy , Illinois—45 miles S
- Macedonia, Illinois (also called Ramah)—20 miles E
- Montrose, Iowa (across Mississippi River)—5 miles W
- Zarahemla, Iowa (D&C 125)—10 miles W
- Washington, DC (to visit President Van Buren)—956 miles E
- Philadelphia, Pennsylvania—1,035 miles NE
- Boston, Massachusetts—1,391 miles NE
- Liverpool, England (the first converts left in 1837)—3,400 miles E
- Salt Lake Valley, Utah—1,350 miles W

Vermont: Joseph's birthplace to where others were born

- Brigham Young (1801)—Whittingham, Vermont—114 miles S
- Oliver Cowdery (1806)—Well, Vermont—80 miles SW
- Sidney Rigdon (1793)—Allegany County, Pennsylvania—700 miles SE
- Heber C. Kimball (1801)—Shelton, Vermont—118 miles N
- Wilford Woodruff (1807)—Farmington, Connecticut—210 miles SE
- Edward Partridge (1793)—Pittsfield, Massachusetts—180 miles SE
- Parley Pratt (1807)—Burlington, New York—255 miles SW
- Orson Pratt (1811)—Hatford, New York—215 miles SW
- Erastus Snow (1818)—St. Anthony, Vermont—87 miles N
- Newel Knight (1800)—Marlboro, Vermont—105 miles S
- Joseph Knight (1772)—Oakham, Massachusetts—160 miles SE
- Orson Hyde (1805)—Oxford, Connecticut—270 miles SE
- Emma Hale (1804)—Harmony, Pennsylvania—365 miles SE
- Frederick G. Williams (1787)—Suffield, Connecticut—190 miles SE
- Willard Richards (1804)—Hopkinton, Massachusetts—210 miles S
- Lorenzo Snow (1814)—Mantua, Ohio—725 miles SW
- Eliza Roxey Snow (1804)—Beckett, Massachusetts—175 miles S

Travel time (miles per day)

- Walking: 15 miles (15 miles average, 20 miles on a good day, 30 miles pushing it).
- Horse: 20 miles on a good day, 30–40 miles pushing it on flat roads. (Joseph Smith raced with his favorite black horse, Charlie, 60 miles in one day to escape a mob.)
- Light buggy: 20–30 miles per day, up and down hills going slow, to save the horse.
- Covered wagon: 8 miles per day, loaded with 2,500 lbs. (Covered wagons traveled 2 miles per hour, 3–5 miles per day in mountains, ¼ mile in Iowa mud, 10–15 miles on a good day, and 20 on exceptional days on a flat road. Traveling up and down hills was slow. Cost was $400, equipped with $1,000 in supplies.)
- Canal boat: 20 miles per day (some accounts say 11, pulled by mules).
- Stage: 25–40 miles with change of horses (there were few stage lines).
- Train: 50–100 miles per day (there were only 1,300 miles of track in 1830 with speeds of 10–15 mph common in early days. Trains

existed only along the most populous areas of New York and Boston, which was 1–2 days travel).

Note: These figures include time for stops to rest, drink, and eat as well as to rest the animals.

Mileage from Nauvoo area to

- Carthage—13 miles SE (23 by present highway 96 and 136)
- Ramas—23 miles
- Ramus—18 miles E
- Yelrome (Morley's)—25 miles S (424 members)
- Plymouth—40 miles SE
- Bear Creek (present Basco)—21 miles SE
- String Town—3 miles E on LaHarpe Road
- LaHarpe—25 miles E
- Davis Mound—5 miles E
- Pontoosuc—13 miles NW
- Lima—28 miles S
- Green Plains—20 miles SE
- Warsaw—16 miles S

—Donald Q. Cannon, *Joseph Smith: Exploring the Life and Ministry of the Prophet*, Susan Easton Black and Andrew C. Skinner, 320–25; LaMar Berrett, *Sacred Places: Illinois*

Missouri: Flowing with milk and honey

David Osborn (1807–1893) moved to Caldwell County, Missouri, in 1838, and "[collected] five barrels of beautiful honey in six weeks."

—*GD*, 264

Nauvoo

Joseph envisioned eighteen communities with Nauvoo being the hub. "The Saints settled in 31 townships and villages, 18 in Hancock County, and at least 13 in Iowa, one of which—Brigham's barracks at Ft. Des Moines was already settled when the Saints moved there."

—Richard Lloyd Dewey, *Joseph Smith: A Biography*, 295–98

The Nauvoo Mansion was an L-shaped home containing twenty-two rooms. It was Joseph and Emma's first real home, which they moved into on August 31, 1843, after almost seventeen years of marriage. However, Joseph had a habit of inviting any homeless person into his house and it became somewhat of a hotel for visitors to Nauvoo.

—J. Christopher Conkling, *A Joseph Smith Chronology*, 199; *AJSC*, 199

A tabernacle was planned to be built in front of the Nauvoo Temple. It was to be a grand oval building made of canvas material and was almost the exact size of the Tabernacle that was eventually built in Salt Lake City. It was to house 8,000–12,000 people. They bought the canvas for the tabernacle, and when Joseph was killed and they had to leave Nauvoo, they used it to make covers for their wagons.

—*The Joseph Smith Papers*, KBYU, August 31, 2009

Nauvoo was often called "The Holy City," and the competition was fierce with neighboring towns for the economy of the region. Warsaw, farther down the Mississippi, as well as Carthage, competed for economics with Nauvoo.

—Robert S. Wicks and Fred R. Foister, *Junius and Joseph: Presidential Politics and the Assassination of the First Mormon Prophet*, 20; Compiler's note

There were 10,000 to 12,000 people who lived in Nauvoo and 30,000 beyond its limits.

—Howard Carlos Smith, *Keeper of the Prophet's Sword*, 50

Newel K. Whitney store—the building with the most revelations

More revelations were received by Joseph Smith in an upper room of the Newel K. Whitney store than any other building or room.

—Milton Backman, *KBYU Joseph Smith Discussion*, January 3, 2010

Offices in varied locations

Joseph Smith's office space while President of the Church, mayor, and so on were usually wherever he could find a little place to work out of. Some of his offices included

1. His bedroom
2. His home
3. The Kirtland printing office
4. The third floor of the Kirtland Temple
5. The smokehouse in Nauvoo
6. A small upper room in the Red Brick Store

—John W. Welch, ed., *A Chronology of the Life of Joseph Smith, BYU Studies*, 146; *HC*, 5:316; *Church News*, June 27, 2009, 5

Palmyra log home

After the Smith family moved to the town of Palmyra in 1816, they bought a hundred acres two miles south of Palmyra in Manchester Township, in 1818–1819, and built a log house. In a grove of trees just west of this house, Joseph was visited by God and Christ in 1820. On September 21, 1823, the angel Moroni appeared to Joseph Smith in an upstairs room. In 1825, the Smiths moved into a larger frame home just northeast of this old log cabin. In the spring of 1829, the Smiths moved back into the log home. In 1997–1998, the log house was reconstructed and then dedicated on March 27, 1998. The Palmyra Temple, which was dedicated on April 6, 2000, is on part of the original hundred acres.

—*Significant Events of the Smith Family Farm,* 2005 Church tour handout

Pioneer towns of the western United States named for Joseph

Pioneer towns in the western United States that honored Joseph:

- Joseph City in central Utah.
- Joseph City in Northern Arizona, originally named St. Joseph.

—Compiler's note

Preaching locations

Joseph spoke from various situations:

- From the back of a wagon.
- In a grove of trees.
- In a house.
- In a barn.
- In a borrowed church.
- In the Kirtland Temple.
- In the unfinished Nauvoo Temple.
- In structures that were temporarily built.
- Before the U.S. Congress.
- On the flats.
- In an unfinished temple basement.
- At a well.

—*RJ*, 205–6; *Teachings of the Prophet Joseph Smith*, 493; Matthew B. Brown, *Joseph Smith: The Man, The Mission, The Message*, 82

Proving ground

Kirtland, Missouri, and Nauvoo were all a proving ground for the Prophet and the Saints.

—Glenn Rawson, *KBYU Joseph Smith Papers*, September 28, 2009

Real estate revealed

God revealed to Joseph special places of real estate that were choice to Him. Some of these places include

- The Garden of Eden—to be the New Jerusalem (Independence, Missouri).
- Adam-ondi-Ahman (Spring Hill, Daviess County, Missouri).

- Location where Cain killed Abel (Far West, Missouri).
- Hill Cumorah—where the plates were hidden (Hill Cumorah in Ontario County, New York).

—Compiler's note

Sacred and holy places on earth

The Lord has chosen various places of real estate as His choice and sacred places.

- Jerusalem of old would be at the top of the list. Where the temple stood was where Abraham was supposed to have been willing to sacrifice Isaac.
- Independence, Missouri, where the Garden of Eden was and the New Jerusalem or Zion is to be built. He actually likes all of Jackson County and the surrounding area, which He commanded early Saints to buy.
- Adam-ondi-Ahman, where Adam blessed his children, and a future sacred event will take place. A holy city was to be built there.
- Far West was sanctified by Abel's blood as the place where he was murdered by Cain. The Lord told Joseph that the very ground was holy.
- The Hill Cumorah housed the gold plates.
- The Sacred Grove, where God the Father and Jesus Christ visited Joseph Smith in person.

—Compiler's note

Sacred Grove

About 150,000 people per year visit the Sacred Grove. In 1907, the Church bought 100 acres, with the grove being about 7 acres. After the Church purchased the Hyrum Smith farm to the north, the grove was expanded to 13 acres. In 1998, the Church acquired additional acres and the grove was expanded to about 150 acres, with the original grove in the middle of this wooded property. In 1962, the USDA dated about thirty trees in the grove, including several that were possibly old enough to have been there in 1820. Nonmember caretaker of the grove is Bob Parrott, and he believes it all happened just as Joseph said it did.

—Michael De Groote, *Mormon Times*, December 19, 2009, 1, 11

According to a recent author, there are three sacred gardens on earth: the Garden of Gethsemane, the Garden of Eden (the Lord's personally designed garden), and the Sacred Grove. The latter is a 15-acre garden of trees and plants that God the Father and His Son sanctified and made holy by Their presence.

—Bruce E. Dana, *Glad Tidings Near Cumorah*, 2–6

The trees in the Sacred Grove are 300–400 years old, and are made up of various hardwood varieties, including maple, ash, oak, hickory, beech, cherry, elm, and hophornbeam. Many of them are 100-feet tall with a diameter of 9–10 feet.

—Scot Facer Proctor and Maurine Jensen Proctor, eds., *Revised and Enhanced History of Joseph Smith by His Mother*, 92

South Bainbridge, New York

South Bainbridge (now Afton), New York, was where Joseph worked for Josiah Stowell. He and Emma also spent their honeymoon there at Stowell's home.

—Robert V. Remini, *Joseph Smith*, 49

Speculation where Saints would go

There was some speculation that the Saints would go to the Great American Desert. Some talked of Oregon, others talked of Vancouver Island. Some mentioned upper California and even Texas. However, the Prophet had clearly stated for years that the Saints would go beyond the Rocky Mountains.

—*Patriarch Benjamin F. Johnson to Elder George F. Gibbs: Johnson Tells of His Closest Association with the Prophet Joseph Smith*, 27–28

Storekeeper

On December 14, 1841, Joseph began efforts to start a new store in Nauvoo. On January 5, 1842, he began operating the Nauvoo mercantile store known as the Red Brick Store—not Joseph's Mercantile or anything like it. Most of the goods were sold on credit, which he forgave most of the time.

—Susan Easton Black, *Setting the Record Straight: Joseph Smith the Mormon Prophet*, 13; Compiler's note

Top places of early conversion

- Coleville, New York
- Kirtland, Ohio
- Liverpool, England

—Compiler's note

Township or town?

Joseph was not born in the town of Sharon but the *township* of Sharon. The Smith family did not live in the town of Manchester but the *township* of Manchester. The Church was not organized in the town of Fayette but in the *township* of Fayette, New York. In a township, there could be five to ten towns within its designation.

—Compiler's note

1805 (Joseph's birth)

Population estimate in the state of New York was 750,000. The United States population estimate was 6,258,000. The US President was Thomas Jefferson. The Vermont governor was Isaac Tichenor (1797–1807).

—*World Book Encyclopedia, Internet*

There were only two national holidays at the time of Joseph's birth: Washington's Birthday and Independence Day (July 4th). Violence was very common. There was no dominate religion in America. It was a time of an explosion of ideas. Farmers made up 95 percent of the employment. It was a time of survival.

—*KBYU Joseph Smith Papers*, October 12, 2009

1820 (First Vision)

- World population: 850,000,000
- US population: 9,638,400
- US President: James Monroe
- New York governors: John Taylor (1817); DeWitt Clinton (1817–1822 and 1825–1825); Joseph C. Yates (1823–1825); Nathaniel Pitcher (1828); Martin Van Buren (1829); Enos T. Throop (1829–1832)
- Illinois became a state in 1818

—Internet

1830 (Organization of the Church)

- World population: 1,000,000,000
- US population: 12,866,000
- US President: Andrew Jackson

—Internet

Nauvoo (1840)

- US President: Martin Van Buren (1837–1841); William H. Harrison (1841); John Tyler (1841–1845)
- Governors of Illinois: Joseph Duncan (1834–1838); Thomas Carlin (1838–1842); Thomas Ford (1842–1846); Augustus C. French (1846–1853)

—*World Book Encyclopedia, Internet*

Missouri

Church membership grew from 1,200 in 1833 to over 15,000 in 1839. In 1830 when missionaries first went to Missouri, the population was estimated at 100,000. The governors were John Miller (1826–1832), Daniel Duncan (1832–1836), Lilburn W. Boggs (1836–1840), and Thomas Reynolds (1840–1844). The US Presidents were Andrew Jackson (1829–1837), Martin Van Buren (1837–1841), William H. Harrison (1841), and John Tyler (1841–1845).

—World Book Encyclopedia, Internet

Burial Locations

Burial locations of the 12 witnesses to the Book of Mormon

- Oliver Cowdery—Richmond, Missouri: Old Mormon Pioneer Cemetery just north of downtown on Highway 13.
- David Whitmer—Richmond, Missouri: Richmond Cemetery, west of downtown on Highway 10.
- Martin Harris—Clarkston, Utah.
- John Whitmer—Kingston, Missouri.
- Christian Whitmer—Liberty (about two miles southwest), Missouri. November 27, 1835.
- Peter Whitmer—Liberty, Missouri (next to Christian). September 22, 1836.
- Jacob Whitmer—Richmond, Missouri: Mormon Pioneer Cemetery. April 21, 1856.
- Hiram Page—Ray County, Missouri (near Excelsior Springs).
- Joseph Smith Jr.—Nauvoo, Illinois: Smith family cemetery.
- Hyrum Smith—Nauvoo, Illinois: Smith family cemetery.
- Samuel Smith—Nauvoo, Illinois: Smith family cemetery.
- Mary Musselman Whitmer—Richmond, Missouri: Mormon Pioneer Cemetery.

—LaMar C. Berrett, Sacred Places: Missouri, 177, 263, 270–71

Joseph and Emma's children's burial locations

- Julia Murdock Smith—1880; Nauvoo, Illinois.
- Frederick Grainger Williams Smith—April 13, 1862; Lamoni, Iowa (president of RLDS Church).
- David Hyrum Smith—August 29, 1904; Lamoni, Iowa.
- Alexander H. Doniphan Smith—August 12, 1909; Mound Grove

Cemetary, Independence, Missouri (in First Presidency of RLDS Church).

- Joseph Smith III—December 10, 1914; Mound Grove Cemetary, Independence, Missouri (President of RLDS Church).

—Scot Facer Proctor and Maurine Jensen Proctor, eds., *The Revised and Enhanced History of Joseph Smith by His Mother by Lucy Mack Smith*

Nauvoo Smith Family cemetery

This cemetery in Nauvoo was located at the foot of Main Street. Many of the Smith Family were buried here, including:

- Joseph Smith Jr.
- Emma Hale Smith
- Hyrum Smith
- Hyrum Smith Jr.
- Joseph Smith Sr.
- Lucy Mack Smith
- Samuel Smith
- Don Carlos Smith
- Frederick G. W. Smith
- Stillborn son of Joseph and Emma
- Mary Bailey Smith (wife of Samuel)
- Lucy B. Smith (daughter of Samuel)
- Sophronia C. Smith
- Caroline Grant Smith (wife of William)

Others:

- Robert B. Thompson
- Lewis Crum Bidamon
- Wilber W. Gifford
- Celeste Gifford
- Edwin James Gifford
- Maude A. Gifford

—LaMar C. Barrett, *Sacred Places: Ohio and Illinois*, 139; Kyle R. Walker, *United by Faith*, 233

Apocrypha

"I was present when the books, writings, etc., were deposited in the southeast cornerstone of the Nauvoo Temple. . . . When a Bible was presented for deposit it was thought necessary that it should be complete—containing the Apocrypha. As there seemed to be none within reach, . . . Brother Reynolds Cahoon volunteered to go to his home, which was nearby, and cut out the Apocrypha from his large family Bible, which was accepted, and the Bible thus made complete."

Note: This is interesting because Joseph Smith had received a revelation against the need of studying the Apocrypha.

—Samuel Miles, *RJ*, 369.

Hosanna shout reinstated

"The [Kirtland Temple] dedication concluded with the entire congregation standing and rendering the sacred 'Hosanna Shout': Hosanna, hosanna, hosanna to God and the Lamb, amen, amen, and amen."

—Richard O. Cowan (BYU Historian), *Joseph Smith and the Doctrinal Restoration: 34th Annual,* Sidney B. Sperry Symposium BYU Religious Studies, 113

Kirtland Temple

March 27, 1836: "The number of official members present on this occasion was four hundred and sixteen, being a greater number than ever assembled on any former occasion."

—*HC*, 2:427–28

The Kirtland Temple measures 80 x 59 feet and is more than 60 feet high. The tower is 110 feet and faces east. The walls are two feet thick and made of sandstone quarried two miles south of the temple. It has a partial basement, two completed floors, and the third floor, an attic, consists of five offices with the presidency room. Translation was done here, as well as the display of the Egyptian mummies and papyrus. Several revelations were received here.

—LaMar C. Berrett, *Sacred Places: Ohio and Illinois: A Comprehensive Guide to Early LDS Sites*, 25–26; D&C 94

It took two years and eight months to build the Kirtland Temple, from July 7, 1833, (cornerstone—July 27) to March 27, 1836. The four-tiered priesthood pulpits were named:

- MPC: Melchizedek Presiding Council (First Presidency)
- PMH: Presiding Melchizedek High Priesthood (Quorum of Twelve)
- BPA: Bishop Presiding Aaronic (Presiding Bishopric)
- MHP: Melchizedek High Priesthood (High Priests)
- PEM: Presidency Elders
- PAP: Presidency Aaronic Priests
- PTA: Presidency of Teachers Aaronic
- PDA: Presidency of Deacons Aaronic

—Scott H. Faulring, ed., *An American Prophet's Record: The Diaries and Journals of Joseph Smith*, 17–78; *Mormon Apologetics*, Internet

Missouri: 27 temples proposed

Independence: A 24-temple complex was proposed for the New Jerusalem on August 30, 1831.

In Far West, the cornerstone was laid for a temple in Caldwell County, July 4, 1838.

A temple was planned for Adam-ondi-Ahman in Daviess County.

Another temple was proposed for Seth, another city of Zion, at Marrowbone Creek, about July 10, 1838.

—John W. Welch, ed., *A Chronology of the Life of Joseph Smith*, BYU Studies, 30, 95, 97

Nauvoo Temple

Measured 128 x 88 feet and was 66 feet high. The belfry tower was 158½ feet in height. The temple was made of local gray limestone and timber from Wisconsin and had three stories and a basement. The cornerstone was laid April 6, 1841. Joseph had seen it in a vision. William Weeks was the architect, and it took five years to build. It was privately dedicated by Joseph Young on April 30, 1846. The first and second floors had offices and an assembly room. The third floor had endowment rooms. The west end was used for endowments, and the east end for eternal marriages, a garden room, a terrestrial room, and a celestial room. Brigham Young had his office in the attic in the southeast corner. In the basement was a 12 x 16-foot limestone baptismal font mounted on the backs of twelve oxen. Wood for the temple was floated down the Mississippi River from Wisconsin. It cost one million dollars to build it. The temple was set on fire in October of 1848 and later suffered a tornado that knocked down its walls.

—LaMar C. Barrett, *Sacred Places: Ohio and Illinois*, 179–80; Richard E. Turley and Lael Littke, *Stories From the Life of Joseph Smith*, 155; *A Chronology of the Life of Joseph Smith*, BYU Studies, 160; *HC*, 6:196–97; Robert V. Remini, *Joseph Smith*, 158

Architect William Weeks argued with Joseph about the round windows in the Nauvoo Temple design. Joseph relates, "I told him I would have circles, if he had to make a temple 10 feet higher than it was originally calculated; and that one light in the center of the circular window would be sufficient to light the whole room; that when the whole building was thus illuminated, the effect would be remarkably grand. 'I wish you to carry out my designs. I have seen in vision the splendid appearance of that building illuminated.' "

—J. Christopher Conkling, *A Joseph Smith Chronology*, 213; *HC*, 6:196–97

Sacred Hosanna Shout

Almost a thousand people were in attendance at the Kirtland Temple dedication on March 27, 1836, and performed the first Hosanna Shout of this dispensation. The shout was given "with such power as seemed almost sufficient to raise the roof from the building."

—Eliza R Snow, *Joseph Smith: Exploring the Life and Ministry of the Prophet*, Susan Easton Black and Andrew C. Skinner, 261

Temple at Far West

"In the summer of 1837, preparations were begun for the building of a Temple. . . . [T]he excavation for the cellar under the prospective structure, 120 x 80 feet in area, and 5 feet in depth was made in about a half a day, more than 500 men being employed in the work." A cornerstone was laid July 4, 1838. And the Apostles came back from Illinois April 26, 1839, to meet prior to their leaving on their missions to England.

—Alvin R. Dyer, *The Refiner's Fire*, 153

Temple at Independence, Missouri

There was to be a 24-temple complex built at Independence, Missouri, and the temple for the Presidency was to be 97 feet long and 61 feet wide.

—Alvin R. Dyer, *The Refiner's Fire*, 97–99

Temple endowment

"Sometime previous to December 1841, an angelic messenger had revealed to the Prophet Joseph all of the details concerning the ancient temple endowment ceremony."

—Richard N. Skousen and W. Cleon Skousen, *Brother Joseph: Seer of a New Dispensation*, vol. 2, 787

Joseph administered the first full temple endowment on Wednesday, May 4, 1842. Before Joseph's death, he had trained two dozen brothers and sisters to administer the endowment.

—Truman Madsen tapes; Susan Easton Black, *Setting the Record Straight: Joseph Smith the Mormon Prophet*, 14; *Joseph Smith Papers KBYU*, September 28, 2009

Franklin D. Richards said, "He called a chosen few, and conferred upon them the ordinances of the holy endowments, so that the divine treasures of his mind might not perish from the world with his death."

—Susan Easton Black, *Setting the Record Straight: Joseph Smith: The Mormon Prophet*, 91

Temple stone used to build a jail

When the Nauvoo Temple was destroyed, they used the limestone to make the old Nauvoo jail, which was just east of Temple Square.

—LaMar C. Berrett, *Sacred Places: Ohio and Illinois*, 177

Temples all over the Rocky Mountains

"Joseph had been very anxious to get this people into the Rocky Mountains. He said . . . he wanted temples built all over the Rocky Mountains."

—Joseph Lee. Robinson, *They Knew the Prophet*, Hyrum L. Andrus, 187

Washing of feet

On March 29, 1836, the ordinance of washing of the feet was performed in the Kirtland Temple with Joseph Smith, Sidney Rigdon, Joseph Smith Sr., Oliver Cowdery, Hyrum Smith, David Whitmer, John Whitmer, William W. Phelps, and Frederick G. Williams. The next day, three hundred Kirtland Saints received this ordinance.

—*HC*, 2:430

Artifacts

Breastplate

The breastplate that was the part of the Urim and Thummim helped to hold the stones in place. His mother described, "It was wrapped in a thin muslin [a sheer cotton fabric] handkerchief, so thin that I could feel its proportions without any difficulty. It was concave on one side and convex on the other and extended from the neck downwards, as far as the center of the stomach of a man of extraordinary size. It had four straps of the same material for the purpose of fastening it to the breast, two of which ran back to go over the shoulders, and the other two were designed to fasten to the hips." After his mother examined the breastplate, Joseph put it in the chest with the Urim and Thummim.

—*History of Joseph Smith by His Mother*, 112; Bruce E. Dana, *Glad Tidings Near Cumorah*, 76–78

Egyptian Mummies

An Egyptian family from about 150 BC was buried and mummified with papyrus. Antonio Labolo spent three years in Egypt and purchased eleven of these mummies. Michael Chandler was sent to America to sell these for Labolo. He heard of a prophet who knew how to translate Egyptian, and he came to Kirtland to meet Joseph. He soon sold four or five of these mummies to the Prophet. About July 5, 1835, the mummies and the papyrus scrolls were purchased by several members of the Church for $2,400. Fifteen different accounts mention Joseph showing these mummies to individuals. The mummies were sent from Kirtland to Far West, Missouri, in July 1838, and later to Nauvoo, and in the process suffered damage. Emma Smith sold them on May 26, 1856.

—*Joseph Smith Papers, KBYU,* August 31, 2009

"There were three mummies: The old Egyptian king, the queen, and their daughter. The bodies were wrapped in seven layers of linen cut in thin strips. In the arms of the Old King lay the roll of papyrus from which our prophet translated the Book of Abraham."

—Jerusha W. Blanchard, *RJ*, 259

"Joseph Smith [Senior] . . . said the records were the writings of Abraham and Joseph, Jacob's son. Some of the writing was in black, and some in red. He said that the writing in red was pertaining to the priesthood."

—Warren Foote, *RJ*, 260

Gold Plates

The gold plates measured 6 x 8 inches and were 6 inches thick, weighing 40–60 pounds. There were engravings on both sides of each leaf, which were not so thick as common tin. The rings were on the right side because, in Egyptian, you read from right to left and from bottom to top. Elder John A. Widtsoe suggested that the gold plates had enough copper added to them to form an alloy equal to approximately 8 carat gold, so they would be hard and stiff enough to preserve inscriptions. By comparison, wedding rings are about 17 carat (45 percent gold). Pure gold (24 carat) is too soft to work with. Emma said, "It was like thick paper and would rustle with a metallic sound."

—Richard E. Turley and Lael Litke, *Stories from the Life of Joseph Smith*, 79; Norman Rothman, *The Unauthorized Biography of Joseph Smith*, 72; John A. Widstoe, *Joseph Smith: Seeker After Truth, Prophet of God*, 38; Robert V. Remini, *Joseph Smith*, 56

From the *Improvement Era* of 1966, we have the calculation of Brother Reed H. Putnam regarding the weight and composition of the gold plates. Assuming the plates were 6x8x6 inches, or 288 cubic inches, the following could be calculated: Goldsmiths of the ancient Americas worked with an alloy of gold, copper, and silver, which the Spaniards called *tumbaga*. It was 8–12 carats of gold. The sheets would be a thickness of about .02 inch, and there would be 20 sheets per inch, or 40 in the unsealed portion. If it was a solid chunk, it would have weighed 106 pounds; but because of the air between the sheets, the weight, properly calculated, would be about half of that, or 53 pounds for 8 carat gold and 86 pounds for 12 carat gold. Ancient smiths used almost pure 23 carat gold in the gilding process, to surface their work with a thickness of .0006 of an inch to help it stay bright.

—*Improvement Era*, September 1966, vol. 69, 788

Oliver Cowdery saw the gold plates in vision before he ever met Joseph Smith. Lucy Harris had a dream or vision in which she saw a personage of white, and he showed her the plates.

—Matthew B. Brown, *All Things Restored: Evidences and Witnesses of the Restoration*, 198

Liahona or directors

The Liahona, this great instrument of faith, was seen by at least four individuals: Joseph Smith, Oliver Cowdery, David Whitmer, and Martin Harris.

—D&C 17; Compiler's note

Old birch log

"In the thick woods about three miles from his home, Joseph approached the old birch log (where he had hid the plates) and found everything undisturbed. He took off a linen smock he had been wearing and wrapped the plates in it. Even though Joseph was a large and strong young man . . . the approximately sixty–pound weight was very burdensome, and he decided to take a shortcut through the woods."

—Glen S. Hopkinson, *A Faithful Life: The Story of Joseph Smith in Pictures*, 21

Records—many wagon loads in Hill Cumorah

Joseph Smith, Oliver Cowdery, Hyrum Smith, Samuel Smith, and Don Carlos Smith all went to the Hill Cumorah, went inside the hill, and saw enough plates to fill many wagon loads. They also saw the sword of Laban hung on the wall. The next time they went there, the sword was laid across the gold plates; it was unsheathed, and on it was written these words: "This sword will never be sheathed again until the kingdoms of this world become the kingdom of our God and His Christ."

—Brigham Young, *JD* 19:38; *Documentary History of the Doctrine and Covenants*, 45; *RJ*, 251

Seer stone

Joseph discussed seer stones and showed his seer stone to the brethren on December 27, 1841. Joseph gave the stone to Oliver Cowdery, saying he didn't use it any more. When Oliver rejoined the Church, he gave it to Brigham Young. In President Wilford Woodruff's journal, he records during a private dedication of the Manti Temple, "Before leaving, I consecrated upon the altar the seer stone that Joseph Smith found by revelation some thirty feet under the earth (ground), and carried by him through life." President John Taylor gave it to Wilford Woodruff, who passed it on to President Joseph F. Smith. His son, President Joseph Fielding Smith, said the seer stone is in the possession of the Church today. Joseph had two: the dark one shaped like a child's foot or shoe, and a whitish one he showed the Council of the Twelve in 1841. This was not magic—it was a miracle God provided as early as 1822 to train Joseph Smith for the Urim and Thummim, which he received in 1827.

—Bruce E. Dana, *Glad Tiding Near Cumorah*, 92–95; *A Chronology of the Life of Joseph Smith*, 126; John W. Welch, ed., BYU Studies, 126; Dan Vogel, *Joseph Smith: The Making of a Prophet*, 39, 583n22; Compiler's note

"Various sources say young Joseph had a least three seer stones. The first one was obtained by digging it out of the ground after he had seen it when using a neighbor's stone. The second was a gift, and the third he and his brother Alvin uncovered while digging a well. It was this third stone that Joseph used most extensively. With it, his mother said he could see things invisible to the natural eye. It was small and rather dark in color with light colored stripes and shaped like a hen's egg."

—Robert V. Remini, *Joseph Smith*, 33–34

Sword and artifacts

Joseph Smith, on his way to Carthage, Illinois, gave a sword to Joseph Bates Noble (1810–1900), who was one of the bodyguards to the Prophet. This family has kept the sword privately for 165 years until Howard Carlos Smith showed it publicly on October 1, 2009, in Midway, Utah. The sword is four feet long with a leather handle. It is a cavalry saber known as a wrist breaker—the blade is 35½ inches long. The hilt has a metal protector of black steel with three hand protectors. Also unveiled was the Prophet's cap, his ball musket rifle, and one of his casket canes. At this unveiling ceremony were three descendants of the Bates's family, also Michael Kennedy Jr., a great-great-great-great-grandson of the Prophet.

—Sharon Haddock, *Mormon Times,* October 10, 2009, 5

Sword given by Wilford Woodruff

It is likely that the Prophet's sword was a model M1832, custom made by the Ames Manufacturing Company.

—Howard Carlos Smith, *Keeper of the Prophet's Sword,* 61

Sword of Laban

From various early writings and tradition, it was thought that the sword of Laban was made for Joseph in Egypt and was a symbol of Priesthood lineage, passed down from Joseph in 1800 BC. In 600 BC, Laban, who was a descendant of Joseph, possessed it along with the brass plates in Jerusalem. At that time, the Lord commanded Lehi to retrieve the brass plates. After Nephi and his brothers tried to buy them and were attacked by Laban's guards, the Lord commanded Nephi to kill Laban. This sword was used for that purpose, after which Nephi took it to the New World. This same sword, now more than 3,600 years old, was shown to Joseph Smith by the angel Moroni in 1827, to the three witnesses in 1830, and later to others inside the Hill Cumorah.

—*JD*, 19:38; *Commentary of the Doctrine and Covenants*, 54

Urim and Thummim

The first person to whom he showed the Urim and Thummim was his mother. Joseph's brother William described it thus: "A silver bow ran over one stone, under the other, around over that one and under the first in the shape of a horizontal figure 8 much like a pair of spectacles. . . . [It] was attached to the breastplate by a rod which was fastened at the outer shoulder edge of the breastplate so that when the Urim and Thummim was removed from before the eyes it would reach to a pocket on the left side of the breastplate where the instrument was kept when not in use by the Seer. . . . The rod served to hold it before the eyes of the Seer." It had two smooth, three-cornered diamonds set in glass that were set in a silver bow.

—Kyle R. Walker, *United by Faith*, 250; Robert V. Remini, *Joseph Smith*, 53

Joseph used the Urim and Thummim to receive six of the first seventeen revelations of the Doctrine and Covenants.

—Compiler's note

Joseph Smith informed his mother that he had the "key" and showed it to her, and she later identified it as the Urim and Thummim.

—Susan Easton Black and Andrew C. Skinner, *Joseph Smith: Exploring the Life and Ministry of the Prophet*, 69

Elder Bruce R. McConkie wrote, "The Hebrew words *Urim* and *Thummim*, both plural, mean *lights and perfections*. Presumably one of the stones is called Urim and the other Thummim."

—Bruce E. Dana, *Glad Tidings Near Cumorah*, 79–80

Six arrests in one day

On June 28, 1830, en route to Painesville, New York, the Prophet was arrested by some people pretending debt in South Bainbridge, New York. In the hearing, no cause for action was found. After Joseph's release, he was again arrested and brought before the court, and the charges were again dismissed. He was arrested the third time, a fourth time, and a fifth time, and in each time the charges were disposed.

As he got into his buggy, a certain officer caught the lines of the horses, put his other hand on Joseph's shoulder, and said, "Mr. Smith, you are my prisoner." After this hearing, Joseph returned to Kirtland, Ohio.

Note: How does someone endure six false arrests and still be so cheerful?

—Brigham Young, *RJ*, 81

Bankruptcy

After being continually hounded by creditors, Joseph, Hyrum, and Samuel Smith filed for bankruptcy on April 18, 1842.

—*A Chronology of the Life of Joseph Smith*, BYU Studies, 131, 140–41

Rockwell's five minute jail sentence

Joseph Smith's good friend Orrin Porter Rockwell spent nine months in a Missouri prison waiting for trial. When he finally had his trial in December 1843, he was sentenced to five minutes in prison (which lasted five hours) and was then freed to walk back to Illinois. He arrived Christmas night, 1843.

—J. Christopher Conkling, *A Joseph Smith Chronology*, 185

Jail time for Joseph

Missouri

- October 31, 1838—Far West (2 days). Joseph and others slept overnight on the ground during a rainstorm while the mob guards mocked them.
- November 1, 1838—A court–martial was held. Joseph and other prisoners were ordered to be shot at 9:00 the next morning. Brigadier General Alexander Doniphan refused to carry out the order. *Note: Joseph named a son Alexander after this man.*
- November 2–3, 1838—60 mile trip to Independence (2 days). The prisoners were proudly displayed and mocked at the towns en route by General Lucas.
- November 4–6, 1838—Independence (3 days).
- November 6, 1838—En route to Richmond (3 days).
- November 9, 1838—Richmond (24 days). Put in double chains and imprisoned in the old log jail or calaboose, and then moved to the half–built courthouse.
- November 10, 1838—Richmond. An additional 56 Mormon prisoners were put with Joseph and his group.
- November 11–28, 1838—Richmond (18 days). Prisoners were kept in an unroofed courthouse under construction. Joseph rebuked the guards on November 11, as recorded by Parley Pratt. A mock trial was held for fifteen days.
- November 30, 1838—En route to Liberty (1 day).
- December 1, 1838—Liberty Jail (4 months, 10 days). Much of the time the prisoners were kept in chains.
- December 23, 1839—Joseph Smith's 33rd birthday.
- January 22, 1839—Prisoners taken to the Clay County courthouse and a trial date was set.
- January 25, 1839—Trial began in Liberty.
- April 6, 1839—Left Liberty Jail (after 128 days).

Daviess County

- April 6–7, 1839—En route to Daviess County (2 days) for another trial.
- April 8, 1839—Arrived in Daviess County, one mile from Gallatin (6 days).
- April 9–14, 1839—A "trial" commenced with Judge Morin and a drunken grand jury. A change of venue finally given to Boone County (5 days).

- April 15, 1839—En route to Boone county (2 days).
- April 16, 1839—Guards allowed prisoners to escape.

Nauvoo, Illinois

- June 24, 1844—Carthage, Illinois (3 days).

Note: The seven guards of the jail who reportedly fired blank bullets into the air are as follows: Frank A. Worrell (officer of the guard), Franklin Rhodes, William Baldwin, Levi Street, Joseph Hawley, Anthony Barkman, and Claybourn Wilson.

The nine men who were indicted by the grand jury to stand trial for the murder were Colonel Levi Williams (a Baptist minister and officer of the Warsaw militia), Thomas C. Sharp (editor of the *Warsaw Signal*), Mark Aldrich (captain of a company of Hancock county militia), Jacob C. Davis (state senator), William N. Grover (captain of a company of Warsaw, a militia under Colonel Williams), John Allen, William Voras, John Wills, and William Gallaher.

It was known that William Law, the "Judas of Mormonism," his brother Wilson, the Foster brothers, the Higbees, and others were involved in the murders, but they were never tried.

The trial was held May 19–30, 1845. The verdict of the jury was "not guilty" after everybody denied any knowledge of anything that happened. The jury members were Jesse Griffitts, Joseph Jones, William Robertson, William Smith, Joseph Massey, Silas Griffitts, Jonathan Foy, Solomon J. Hill, James Gittings, F. M. Walton, Jabez A. Beebee, and Gilmore Gallison.

—*HC*, 3:188–332; *Mormon Historical Studies,* 2.1:59–82; *A Chronology of the Life of Joseph Smith,* BYU Studies, 100–7; *History of Joseph Smith by His Mother,* 396; *Martyred,* 146,168–70; *LaMar C. Berrett, Sacred Places: Ohio and Illinois,* 208–9; Ted Gibbons, *Sealing the Testimony,* 47; *Scot Facer Proctor and Maurine Jensen Proctor, The Revised and Enhanced History of Joseph Smith by His Mother,* 467

Lawsuits

Joseph Smith was a defendant in forty-six lawsuits. He testified that he never broke the law. He had more than two hundred charges brought against him. Some of these lawsuits were

- Lucy Harris; May 1829—She tried to keep Martin from giving money to Joseph.
- Colesville, New York; June 28, 1830—Disorderly conduct. Acquitted.
- George H. Noble; August 25, 1830—Note for $190.95 for Harmony home and property by Judge Jesse Lane. Settled and paid.
- Dennis Lake; November 24, 1834—Zion's Camp member Lake said he

was promised a lot in Missouri. Joseph lost and was ordered to pay $71.67.

- Dennis Lake; May 7, 1835—For $800 debt. Dismissed.
- Calvin Stoddard; June 16, 1835—Assult. Joseph acquitted.
- Ohio Bank; January 2, 1837—$3,000.
- Martindale; February 16, 1837—$7,500. Joseph arrested and released. Settled on the debt.
- Granger v. Joseph; August 8, 1837—Joseph lost and paid $23 plus damages and court fees to Judge Frederick G. Williams.
- Usher; August 24, 1837—Joseph didn't appear. Judgment awarded.
- Geauga Bank; March 1838—$10,071. Judgment awarded against Joseph.
- State of Missouri; July 6, 1839.

—J. Christopher Conkling, *A Chronology of the Life of Joseph Smith*, 8, 15; *Joseph Smith Papers*, KBYU, interviews

"Beginning in 1826—sometimes as plaintiff, sometimes as defendant—Joseph was involved in at least 120 lawsuits."

—Rodney Turner, *Jesus and Joseph: Parallel Lives*, 150

Liquor and prejudice

At the 1838 trial in Richmond, Missouri, "there was more liquor and prejudice than testimony."

—Roy A. Cheville, *Joseph and Emma, Companions*, 75

Missouri financial damages

There have been several thousand affidavits stating the damages inflicted upon the Saints in Missouri. Hyrum said of his personal losses in June 1839, "one hundred thousand dollars would be no consideration for what I have suffered . . . and all the accumulated suffering I have been subjected to." There were between 12,000 and 15,000 Saints driven from the state and 50 murdered; 250,000 acres dispossessed, plus thousands of homes.

—*HC*, 3:XVII, 3:374

Shackles and chains

When Joseph was arrested at Far West, he was shackled, chained, loaded into a wagon, and shuttled to Independence and Richmond. He was also shackled and chained in Richmond Jail, where he rebuked the guards.

—Robert V. Remini, *Joseph Smith*, 136

Toothache

When the mob arrested Joseph on October 31, 1838, at Far West, Missouri, he was suffering with a bad toothache and a bad cold.

—*History of Joseph Smith by His Mother,* 388

Vexatious law suits

Said Joseph, "We were detained all day by malicious and vexatious law suits. About sunset I got into my carriage to return home to Kirtland; at this moment the sheriff sprang into the carriage, seized my lines, and served another writ on me."

—*HC,* 2:502

Liberty Jail

This newly built Missouri jail made of white oak logs measured 22½ x 22 feet and was 12 feet to the square. The door was 5½ x 2½ feet. The upper and lower quarters were 14 feet north to south. The dungeon was 14 feet, and 2 feet of it were under ground. The walls 4 feet thick. It was 6 feet in height and it was impossible for most of the men to stand erect. There were two benches, a small table, a couple of blankets, and a bucket for waste. Emma visited Joseph on December 8, 1838, December 20, 1838, and January 21, 1839. What an ironic name for a jail—Liberty—and to be imprisoned in a country of religious freedom pressed by jealous ministers state after state.

—Gracia Jones, *Lucy and Emma,* 131–33; *Thomas D. Cottle and Patricia C. Cottle, Liberty Jail and the Legacy of Joseph,* 74; Compiler's note; Susan Easton Black, *Setting the Record Straight: Joseph Smith the Mormon Prophet,* 46

Liberty Jail dedication as a visitors center:

On September 15, 1963, the Liberty Jail Visitors' Center was dedicated by President Joseph Fielding Smith.

—Alvin R. Dyer, *The Refiner's Fire,* 302

Liberty Jail fight proposed

In 1838, excommunicated Apostle William E. McLellin (height 6'4") asked for permission from the jailer to fight Joseph Smith (height 6'2"). The jailer agreed and proceeded to let William in for the fight. The jailer proceeded to take the shackles and chains from off Joseph so they could start the fight. McLellin protested, "No, I only am willing to fight Joseph if he is still chained up," to which the jailer said, "No, that would not be fair." Thus the fight never happened.

—*HC,* 3:32; Hyrum L. Andrus, *Joseph Smith, the Man and the Seer,* 21

Liberty jail visitors to Joseph and the brethren

Some of the visitors to the brethren in Liberty Jail in the winter of 1838–39 were

- Brigham Young
- George A. Smith
- Benjamin Covey
- Jane Blevin and daughter
- Heber C. Kimball
- Don Carlos Smith
- Orrin Rockwell
- Alansom Ripley
- Mercy Fielding Thompson
- Emma Smith and children
- James Sloan, his wife, and daughter
- Attorney Alexander W. Doniphan
- Mary Fielding Smith and three-month-old Joseph Fielding Smith

—*The Refiner's Fire* by Alvin R. Dyer, pp. 282–283

Mother and baby in Liberty jail

Mercy R. Thompson and Hyrum's wife, Mary Fielding Smith, with her eleven-week-old baby, Joseph F. Smith, were allowed to visit Hyrum in the jail. "We arrived at the prison in the evening. We were admitted and the doors closed upon us. A night never to be forgotten. A sleepless night. . . . In the morning [we] prepared to start for home with my afflicted sister [Hyrum's wife]; and as long as memory lasts will remain in my recollection the creaking hinges of that door which closed upon the noblest men on earth. Who can imagine our feelings as we traveled homewards? But would I sell the honor bestowed upon me . . . of being locked up in jail with such characters for gold? No! No!"

—Mercy R. Thompson, *RJ*, 356

Missouri enemies were real

On April 24, 1834, the Missourians spent six days "[burning] one hundred fifty houses belonging to the Saints in Jackson County." Note: Zion's Camp arrived two months later in neighboring Clay County, on June 23, 1834.

—*LDSCC*, 10

Saints killed in Missouri

Elder David W. Patten and Gideon Carter were killed at the Battle of Crooked River on October 25, 1838. At DeWitt, several died of fatigue and privation after being driven from this Missouri River site. Joseph helped to bury some on October 12, 1838. At Haun's Mill, nineteen were killed. Others died of exposure as over 12,000 Saints left the state. Almost all of the dead are in unmarked graves.

—John W. Welch, ed., *A Chronology of the Life of Joseph Smith*, BYU Studies, 98; Complier's note

Missouri's hidden things brought to light

Doctrine and Covenants 123:8 instructs that the hidden things done against the Saints should be brought to light. A partial list would be:

- Saints, including children, murdered
- Saints killed by exposure from being driven
- Women raped
- Lies
- False affidavits by apostates and Missourians
- Homes burned
- False arrests
- Prisoners held without trial

- False imprisonment
- Personal property stolen
- Land records burned in Daviess County
- Extortion
- Blackmail
- Assault

—D&C 123:13; *HC,* 1–6

Nonmembers on why others abused

"Yes, I knew them very well. They were very nice men, too. . . . What did the Smiths do that the people abused them so? They did not do anything. Why! These rascals at one time took Joseph Smith and ducked him in the pond . . . just because he preached what he believed, and for nothing else. And if Jesus Christ had been there, they would have done the same to Him."

—Thomas H. Taylor, *They Knew the Prophet*, Hyrum L. Andrus, 3

Persecution

The story of Joseph Smith "could be told as a record of continued persecution." E. D. Howe with Philastus Hurlburt, an excommunicated member, published *Mormonism Unveiled* in 1834, which became the first book against Mormonism.

—John A. Widstoe, *Joseph Smith: Seeker After Truth: Prophet of God*, 18, 76

The Prophet and the Lord spell out that to be persecuted is a sign of the true Church.

—See D&C 127:4

"[Joseph] endured the most unparalleled persecution of any man in the history of our country."

—Gilbert Belnap, *They Knew the Prophet*, Hyrum L. Andrus, 203

A minister or an apostate triggered persecution in every location the Saints ever resided: Lucy Harris (apostate) in Palmyra; Philastus Hurlbut (apostate), Symonds Ryder (apostate), Warren Parrish (apostate), and Ezra Booth (apostate) in Kirtland; Colonel George Hinkle (apostate), Sashael Wood (minister), David Whitmer (apostate), and W. W. Phelps (apostate) in Missouri; and William Law (apostate) and several others in Nauvoo.

—Compiler's note

Plots to destroy the Prophet

There were continuous rounds of plots against Joseph since the First

Vision until Carthage. Some of the major ones were:

- He was shot at (1820).
- A mob in Bainbridge, New York, determined to kill him (1829).
- He was tarred and feathered in Hiram, Ohio (1834).
- The Kirtland apostasy. The Kirtland Safety Society failed, and many apostatized after Warren Parish stole $25,000 (1837).
- The Missouri mobs (1838–1839).
- John C. Bennett, mayor of Nauvoo, was excommunicated and then tried to persuade people to kill Joseph Smith (1843).
- William Law tried to shoot Joseph, but the pistol misfired (1844).
- The martyrdom at Carthage (1844).

—George Q. Cannon, *A History of the Prophet Joseph Smith for Young People*, 200

Spit upon

Joseph Smith was arrested in South Bainbridge, New York, on false charges. The constable took him into a tavern where they spit upon him and told him to prophesy.

—Scot Facer Proctor and Maurine Jensen Proctor, eds., *The Revised and Enhanced History of Joseph Smith by His Mother*, 237

Stand against the wind

"I marvel, again, at the fact that he could stand against the wind, against all opposition, and say, I know I had a vision and I know what God expects me to do."

—Ronald Esplin, *American Prophet: The Story of Joseph Smith*, Lee Groberg and Heidi S. Swinton, 107

Tarred and feathered

On a Saturday night, March 24, 1832, a mob of fifty men attacked Joseph, beat him, stripped him, and tarred and feathered him while he was living at the John Johnson home in Hiram, Ohio. Luke S. Johnson records, "A few entered his room in the middle of the night, and Carnot Mason dragged Joseph out of bed by the hair of his head. He was then stretched on a board . . . tore off his few night clothes, for the purpose of emasculating him, and had Dr. Dennison there to perform the operation. The mob then scotched his body all over. A [man] named Waste . . . the strongest man on the Western Reserve, had boasted that he could take Joseph out [of the house] alone. Waste had a hold of one foot. Joseph drew up his leg and gave him a kick, which sent him sprawling in the street. He afterwards said the Prophet was the most powerful man he ever had hold of in his life."

—*History of Joseph Smith by His Mother*, 298–300; Hyrum L. Andrus, *They Knew the Prophet*, 33

On March 24, 1832, Joseph Smith was tarred and feathered in Hiram, Ohio. Sidney Rigdon was beaten, and father John Johnson, whose home Joseph and Emma were in, was beaten and had his collar bone broken. On July 20, 1833, in Missouri, Edward Partridge, Charles Allen, and Sidney Gilbert were also tarred and feathered. When Joseph heard this, he burst into tears and sobbed aloud.

—*HC,* 1:390–91; *History of Joseph Smith by His Mother,* 304–7

Said Joseph, "Their salary would be tar and feathers [for preaching the gospel]."

—George A. Smith, *JD,* 2:331

Temporary peace in Illinois

Joseph escaped from Missouri and found temporary peace in Illinois. Said Dimick Huntington, "I . . . saw Joseph land from the Quincy ferryboat about 8 o'clock in morning. He was dressed in an old pair of boots full of holes, pants torn . . . looked pale and haggard."

—Glen S. Hopkinson, *A Faithful Life: The Story of Joseph Smith in Pictures,* 59

Trials

"Our Prophet was at this time passing through severe trials and persecutions, but he was unruffled in his calm dignity."

—Christopher Layton, *They Knew the Prophet,* Hyrum L. Andrus, 196

According to Truman Madsen, Joseph had at least 160 trials against him. From the First Vision to his murder, that would average one trial every other month. The first one was brought by Lucy Harris when she tried to stop her husband, Martin, from helping Joseph. Later, on November 12, 1838, a fourteen-day trial commenced in Richmond, Missouri, before Judge Austin A. King. It lasted until about November 30, 1838, and most of the prisoners were released, except for Joseph and four others who were sent to Liberty Jail.

—John W. Welch, ed., *A Chronology of the Life of Joseph Smith,* BYU Studies, 102–3; Truman Madsen tapes

Weighed down and saddened with grief

"His troubles at home were more sad and harder to bear than all the trials that could be heaped upon him by outside enemies. . . . I have known him to come in with his head bowed. He would walk the floor back and forth, with his hands clasped behind him, . . . his countenance showing that he was weighed down with some terrible burden."

—Emily D. Partridge Young, *They Knew the Prophet,* Hyrum L. Andrus, 195

Weight loss

Joseph lost 45 pounds in the Liberty Jail during his four months and ten days there.

—Truman Madsen tapes

Wore a dress

Rebecca Williams, the wife of Frederick G. Williams, was six feet tall, and when Joseph needed to escape from a mob in Kirtland, he wore Sister Williams's dress and easily remained undetected.

—Compiler's note

Apostles' location at Martyrdom

Most of the leading brethren were on US presidential campaigning missions for the Prophet. The fifteen apostles' locations were as follows:

1. Joseph Smith—Carthage Jail; martyred
2. Hyrum Smith—Carthage Jail; martyred
3. Willard Richards—Carthage Jail
4. John Taylor—Carthage Jail
5. Brigham Young—Boston
6. Wilford Woodruff—Boston
7. Orson Hyde—Boston
8. Heber C. Kimball—on a train en route to Philadelphia
9. Lyman Wight—on a train en route to Philadelphia
10. Parley Pratt—on a canal boat to Buffalo, New York
11. George A. Smith—Michigan
12. Amasa Lyman—Cincinnati, Ohio
13. Sidney Rigdon—already left the Church
14. John E. Page—already left the Church
15. The fifteenth apostle was an unfilled position at that time

—*Martyred*, 205–6

Where were the other leaders

Apostles Willard Richards and John Taylor were in Carthage Jail. Brigham Young, Wilford Woodruff, and Orson Hyde were on a mission for Joseph's presidential campaign in Boston, Massachusetts. Heber C. Kimball and Lyman Wight were en route from Philadelphia to New York. Parley Pratt was on a canal boat between Utica and Buffalo, New York. George A. Smith was near Jacksonville, Michigan. Amasa Lyman was in Cincinnati, Ohio.

—Henry A. Smith, *The Day They Martyred the Prophet*, 204–6

Death held no terrors

"Death had no terrors for him although life was dear."

"He well knew that he must sacrifice his life for the principles God had revealed through him."

"I have often heard him say he expected to seal his testimony with his blood."

— Lucy Walker Kimball, *They Knew the Prophet,* Hyrum L. Andrus, 157

Didn't want to be hanged

Joseph did not want to be hanged.

—Truman G. Madsen tapes

Made it clear that he could die

In preaching at a funeral of the son of Joseph Marks on April 9, 1842, "[Joseph] enjoined the hearers to remember that he was subject to death, and that he no longer had a lease on life."

—Edward H. Anderson, *A Brief History of the Church of Jesus Christ of Latter–day Saints,* 92

Looked forward to the other side of the veil

"He anticipated great joy in meeting his [family] and friends beyond the grave. He believed that as soon as the spirit left the body we were shaking hands with and greeting our friends."

—Lucy Walker Kimball, *They Knew the Prophet,* Hyrum L. Andrus, 157

One thousand dollars for Joseph's head

Like John the Baptist, Joseph's enemies wanted his head. Missouri offered $1,000, which was equal to the wages a man could make in four to ten years. In today's dollars, it would be $250,000 to $500,000. This was a serious threat.

—Compiler's note

Reason for martyrdom

"Our candidate for this high office [President of the United States], has been butchered . . . to prevent him from being elected."

—John Taylor, "The Next President," *Times and Seasons,* August 1844

There are many reasons for the martyrdom:

- Jealous ministers from the beginning.
- Apostates who left the Church but couldn't leave it alone.
- Missouri enemies who wouldn't let their hate die.
- Mob violence.

- The Judas of Mormonism, William Law, and the secret meetings, oaths, and so on.
- Newspapers like Sharp's *Warsaw Signal* and the *Nauvoo Expositor.*
- Missouri head hunters.
- Men possessed of the devil.

—Compiler's notes

Steady the Ark

"It was now revealed to the prophet that his only safety was in flight to the Rocky Mountains and he crossed the river with a few faithful friends with a full purpose not to return. . . . With all the persons who induced him to return I was well acquainted, and I know that fearful has been the hand of the Lord to follow them from the day they sought to steady the Ark of God, which resulted in the martyrdom of his servants."

—Benjamin F. Johnson, *My Life's Review*, 91

Before Carthage

Do more on the other side of the veil

"The words of Brother Joseph began to come back to me: 'I could do so much more for my friends if I were on the other side of the veil.' "

—Benjamin F. Johnson, *They Knew the Prophet,* Hyrum L. Andrus, 109–10

Drink of water en route to Carthage

While en route to Carthage, Joseph stopped at the home of Brother Rosecrans. He asked for a drink of water. As he got ready to leave, he said to Brother Rosecrans, "If I never see you again, or if I *never come back*, remember that I love you." Sister Mary Ellen Kimball overheard this and said, "This went through me like electricity. I went in the house and threw myself on the bed and wept like a whipped child."

—Mary Ellen Kimball, *RJ*, 75

Escape to the west was feasible

"Well I remember his saying, 'Although I possessed the means of escape, yet I submit without a struggle and repair to the place of slaughter.' "

—Gilbert Belnap, *They Knew the Prophet,* Hyrum L. Andrus, 204

Five years left

Twice the Lord told Joseph that there were five years left: five years left in Kirtland and five years left in Nauvoo.

—Compiler's note

Knew he was going to be killed

Edward Stevenson said, "He was cheerful and comforting. He said, I shall not be sacrificed until my time comes; then I shall be offered freely."

—Hyrum L. Andrus, *They Knew the Prophet*, 99

Last counsel to little Julia

Before Joseph left for Carthage, he told his daughter Julia to be a good girl and never mistreat any of her playmates.

—*RJ*, 73

Last diary entry of Joseph

"I told Stephen Markham that if I and Hyrum were ever taken again we would be massacred, or I was not a Prophet of God. I want Hyrum to live to avenge my blood, but he is determined not to leave me."

—Norma J. Fischer, *Portrait of a Prophet*, 208

Last eight words

In Carthage Jail when Joseph saw that Hyrum was dead, Joseph exclaimed, "Oh dear, brother Hyrum." And as Joseph fell out of the window after being shot four times, he exclaimed, "Oh Lord my God."

—Norma J. Fischer, *Portrait of a Prophet*, 219

Last good-bye

"How does one say goodbye to his wife and children for the last time—the very last time? Finally he was astride his horse and rode with his brother and others away from his house and toward Carthage."

—Leon Hartshorn, *Joseph Smith: Prophet of the Restoration*, 57

Blood required of nation

"When alone . . . [Joseph] said, 'Well, if they kill me, I shall die innocent, and my blood will be required of this nation.' "

—Joseph B. Noble, as recorded by Benjamin Ashby, *RJ*, 375

Train my sons

Edwin Rushton's father heard Joseph ask Emma the same question three times just before he went to Carthage for the last time. He asked, "Emma, can you train my sons to walk in their father's footsteps?" She answered the same each time: "Oh Joseph, you are coming back." The Prophet then rode away to Carthage and his death.

—*RJ*, 411

Carthage Jail

The jailer at Carthage was George W. Stigall. The jail is located on the corner of Fayette and Walnut Streets. It is a 34x28–foot, two–story stone building with walls 2½ feet thick. The first floor had a doctor's room, a living room, and a dining room. The second floor had the jailer's bedroom—the room where Hyrum and Joseph were murdered—and two prison cells. On November 5, 1903, Joseph F. Smith purchased the jail for $5,000.

—*LaMar C. Berrett, Sacred Places: Ohio and Illinois*, 208–9; Ted Gibbons, *Sealing the Testimony*, 47

Carthage, Illinois—a six hour ride for Joseph's surrender

When Joseph rode to Carthage for the last time—on his favorite horse, Charlie—they left Nauvoo at 6:00 p.m. and arrived at Carthage at midnight. They found 1,100–1,200 Illinois state troops, many of whom were Carthage Grays who swore and threatened them before they checked into the Hamilton House. The next morning, they surrendered to Constable Bettisworth. The Illinois troops pulled out of Carthage and left the Carthage Grays under the command of Captain Robert Smith, a known enemy. "His [Joseph's] lovely boys, hanging onto [him] . . . cried, 'Father, O Father don't go to Carthage. They will kill you." '

—Dan Jones, *Sealing the Testimony*, Ted Gibbons, 37; *LaMar C. Berrett, Sacred places, Ohio and Illinois*, 205; Hyrum L. Andrus, *They Knew the Prophet*, 207

Visitors to Joseph Smith while in Carthage Jail

- Patriarch John Smith
- Dr. John M. Bernhisel
- John Green
- Stephen Markham
- Dan Jones
- Almon W. Babbitt
- John S. Fullmer
- Gilbert Belnap
- Cyrus H. Wheelock
- Jed S. Mills

—*Martyred*, 146,168–70; Hyrum L Andrus, *They Knew the Prophet*, 204

The Martyrdom

June 27, 1844, at 5:16 and 26 seconds was the time from John Taylor's watch. It was a very humid and rainy day. Hyrum took balls to the left side of his nose (passing into his brain), back, breast, throat, and left leg. Joseph took at least eight balls total, four while he was in the jail: one in the back, one in the right breast, one in his lower abdomen, and one to his right collar bone. A hundred or more men surrounded Joseph after he jumped from the window and landed eighteen feet below still alive, saying, "Oh Lord my God." He smiled with sweet compassion in his countenance as he gazed upon his murderers in the last moments of his life. Colonel Levi Williams, a minister, then ordered four men to shoot Joseph. Standing about eight feet from him, they shot simultaneously. His body slightly cringed as four more bullets entered him, and once more Joseph fell on his face. He lifted himself up briefly on his side and then went down. Thomas Dixon, a witness, stated that Joseph said, "God's will be done." There were reports of a shaft of light that shot "through the clouds onto Joseph, and the scene became solemnly still." William Daniels claimed the light "stopped a man from beheading Joseph with a sword."

—George Q. Cannon, *Life of Joseph Smith the Prophet*, 525; Ted Gibbons, *Sealing the Testimony*, 64; Richard Lloyd Dewey, *Joseph Smith: A Biography*, 463

The murderers

The mob of 150–500 men with painted faces and masks wanted Joseph's head for a reward in Missouri. Willard Richards stated he saw about 500 men. There are several traditions told that after Joseph was shot, a man with a knife attempted to cut off his head, but a man in a black suit stood by and forbad him and a lightning bolt struck him.

—Gary Stenhouse, *Rocky Mountain Saints*; Dallin H. Oaks and Marvin S. Hill, *Carthage Conspiracy: The Trial of the Accused Assassins of Joseph Smith*, drawing of lightning, 114

Seventeen friends rode with Joseph and Hyrum to Carthage

On June 24, 1844, Joseph and Hyrum Smith started to Carthage to give themselves up for trial. Seventeen friends accompanied them.

—LDSCC, 27

Aftermath

Last words of Emma as she viewed Joseph's body

When Emma saw Joseph's murdered body, she fell on his face, kissed him, and sobbed, "Joseph, speak to me once more."

—Norma J. Fischer, *Portrait of a Prophet*, 221

Coffin

"Early in the spring of 1844 a Nauvoo casket maker made two oak coffins or caskets. He used one–inch thick slabs for the bottom, sides and lid. No nails, every joint is tongue and groove . . . [they were] sanded, glued and polished and set aside in his shop. "The bodies of Joseph and Hyrum were brought from Carthage in these caskets with a colorful Indian blanket covering each of their bodies, escorted by Porter Rockwell and Joseph Noble with six other volunteer body guards protecting [the bodies] from the $1,000 reward for Joseph's head in Missouri. It took seven hours to get to Nauvoo. The bodies were [transferred] to pine coffins to keep their burial location a secret."

—*Howard Carlos Smith, Keeper of the Prophet's Sword,* 83–84, 91–92

Funeral of Joseph and Hyrum

Decoy caskets for the funeral were filled with sandbags to protect Joseph's and Hyrum's bodies. A $1,000 reward had been offered for the head of Joseph Smith. William W. Phelps preached the funeral service at the Nauvoo Temple.

—Norman Rothman, *The Unauthorized Biography of Joseph Smith*, 360; *Martyred,* 201

Viewing

It was estimated that between 8:00 a.m. and 5:00 p.m. on Saturday, June 29, 1844, over 10,000 people came to the Mansion House to view the bodies of the murdered Joseph and Hyrum. The bodies were then hidden in the Smith home and replaced with new coffins filled with sandbags, and the funeral procession started up Main Street to the temple. After the funeral, a staged burial was held.

—*HC,* 6:627

Fatherless children

The murders of Joseph and Hyrum left sixteen fatherless children:

- Joseph left five; Emma was four months pregnant when her husband was murdered.
- Hyrum left four.
- Samuel, who died of related causes, left seven children.

—George Q. Cannon, *Life of Joseph Smith the Prophet*, Appendix.

Back to Nauvoo with "chariots" of angels

The bodies of Joseph and Hyrum were brought back to Nauvoo with "chariots of angels and horsemen."

—Pearson H. Corbett, *Hyrum Smith Patriarch*, 428 (as noted by compiler)

According to Joseph Fielding Smith, "'The bodies of the martyred prophets were taken to Nauvoo by Dr. Willard Richards, Samuel H. Smith, and a guard of eight soldiers.' . . . Fifteen hundred Nauvoo Legion soldiers mounted on military decorated horses, sheathe swords attached, full uniform, are making their way east in meeting up with the rescue company."

—Howard Carlos Smith, *Keeper of the Prophet's Sword*, 96

Martyr's power

"Joseph Smith dead is far more potent in Mormondom than Joseph Smith alive."

—John Henry Evans, *Joseph Smith, an American Prophet*, 7

Pallbearers

An hour after the funeral for the Smith brothers at the temple, a second burial was arranged, a secret midnight burial of Joseph and Hyrum in the basement of the Nauvoo House. Those chosen as pallbearers were:

- Dimick B. Huntington
- Edward Hunter
- William D. Huntington
- William Marks
- Jonathan H. Holmes
- Gilbert Goldsmith
- Alpheus Cutler
- Lorenzo D. Wasson
- Philip B. Lewis

The guard was James Emmett, who was armed with a gun. The bodies remained there for several months until Emma had them secretly reburied in the Smith family plot.

—*Martyred*, 202

Prepared Joseph and Hyrum's dead bodies

After the bodies arrived in Nauvoo, Dimick Baker Huntington, William D. Huntington, and William Marks "washed [the martyrs' bodies] clean of blood and grime, cotton soaked in camphor was put into each wound. They were then dressed in fine white trousers and shirts, white neckerchiefs, cotton stockings and white shrouds."

—Henry A. Smith, *The Day They Martyred the Prophet*, 198

Rival clergymen praised murder

Upon hearing that Joseph Smith had been murdered, Alexander

Campbell announced in his *Millennial Harbinger* that the murder was an "act of God," because many early converts were "stolen" from his flock: "The money digger, the juggler, and the founder of the Golden Bible delusion, . . . whose career was in open rebellion against God and man." Reverend William G. Brownlow said, "Smith was killed. . . . THREE CHEERS to the brave company who shot him to pieces."

—Lee Groberg and Heidi S. Swinton, *American Prophet: The Story of Joseph Smith,* 18

Stunned with astonishment

"We hear a story of a people stunned with astonishment and grief at the news from Carthage." Reactions from the press across the nation ranged from outrage against the murders to headlines proclaiming "Thus Ends Mormonism."

—Davis Bitton, *Images of the Prophet Joseph Smith,* 200

Testators are dead

John Taylor, summarizing the martyrdom, wrote that "the testators are now dead, and their testament is in force." This was a powerful way to testify of their mission.

—See D&C 135

Voice heard by mother Smith

When mother Lucy Mack Smith saw the dead bodies of her sons Joseph and Hyrum, she cried out, "My God, my God, why hast thou forsaken this family!" She then heard a voice saying, "I have taken them to myself, that they might have rest."

—Scot F. Proctor and Maurine Jensen Proctor, eds., *History of Joseph Smith by His Mother,* 457

100th birthday party

The Sharon Township farm was purchased and a 38½–foot granite shaft was erected under the direction of President Joseph F. Smith on December 23, 1905. Also, in 1905, other property was purchased, including the Newel K. Whitney store and acreage in Far West, Adam–ondi–Ahman, and Independence, Missouri.

—*Church Almanac 2009*, 617

200th birthday party

For Joseph Smith's 200th birthday, President Gordon B. Hinckley held a telecast at his birthplace in Sharon Township, Vermont. It was telecast to 161 countries in 81 languages. President Boyd K. Packer mentioned Joseph and Emma Smith and said, "We pray now that their descendants will be gathered in." In the closing prayer by Uriah A. Kennedy, fifth great–grandson of Joseph and Emma, he said, "We pray that thou wilt give a special blessing to his descendants that the Prophet might have claim to his children once more."

—Joseph Smith Jr. Bicentennial Celebration Broadcast; *Church Almanac 2009*, 617

Birthplace monument

President Joseph F. Smith assigned Junius Wells to locate the site, procure the land, and design a monument. One hundred tons of granite was mined and shaped thirty–five miles to the north, in Berre, Vermont. The 38½–foot shaft (one foot for every year of Joseph's life) weighed forty tons, with another four pieces for the base weighing sixty tons. It took 33 days to move the granite monument to its location.

—*Joseph Smith Birthplace Memorial Pamphlet*

Brigham Young's dream of Joseph

Brigham Young was concerned about many of the brethren who wanted to go to the California gold fields. One night, he had a dream of Joseph in a wagon with some men herding sheep and goats. Some of the sheep were three and a half feet high with large, fine, beautiful fleeces, pure and white. "Then I saw some that were dark and spotted, of all colors and sizes and kinds, and their fleeces were dirty, and they looked inferior. . . .

"Joseph stopped the wagon. . . . I looked in Joseph's eye, and laughed, just as I had many a time when he was alive. . . . said I—'Joseph you have got the darndest flock of sheep I ever saw in my life; what are you going to do with them, what on earth are they for?' Joseph looked cunningly out of his eyes, just as he used to at times, and said he—'They are all good in their places.' When I awoke in the morning I did not find any fault with those who wanted to go to California."

—*RJ*, 52–53

Ensign Peak

Brigham Young had a vision in which Joseph Smith showed him Ensign Peak in the Great Salt Lake Valley. In the dream, Joseph described it to Brigham and told him, "Build under the point where the colors fall and you will prosper and have peace."

—*RJ*, 212–13

Farewell Nauvoo, Farewell Illinois

"Farewell Nauvoo. Farewell Illinois." This was what the Saints courageously said and did rather than fight the mobs and politics of 1846. This proved to be a temporary parting, however, since President Gordon B. Hinckley dedicated the Nauvoo Temple on June 27, 2000, at exactly 5:16 p.m. to commemorate 156 years since Joseph and Hyrum's martyrdom. President Hinckley noted that he knew that Joseph was there at the Nauvoo Temple dedication that day.

—Compiler's note

Mantle of Joseph went to Brigham Young

Similar to what happened with Elijah when his mantle was given to Elisha, *121* early members testified of a spiritual manifestation when Brigham Young received the mantle of Joseph Smith.

—John W. Welch, *Opening the Heavens*, 373

Mormonism only utopia that ever worked

Peter Drucker, the father of modern management, declared to Harvard University on November 19, 2009, after studying the organization of the Church carefully, that Mormonism is the only utopia that ever worked.

—Mark W. Cannon, *Mormon Times,* January 16, 2010, 6

Polished shaft

President Joseph Fielding Smith called Joseph a "polished shaft in the hand of the Almighty" at the dedication of the 38½-foot granite shaft (one foot for each year of Joseph Smith's life) on top of the monument built to honor him at his 100th birthday in 1905.

—Visitors Center at Sharon, Vermont

Shadow of Joseph

"The shadow of Joseph Smith has now gone around the world."

—Gordon B. Hinckley, Sharon Vermont commemoration, December 23, 2005

Joseph seen by others since his death in 1844

Emma Smith saw Joseph at her death.

—Buddy Youngreen, *Emma and Joseph,* 455; Gracia Jones, *Emma and Lucy,* 190

Brigham Young had a dream on February 17, 1847, in which Joseph said, "Tell the people to be sure to keep the Spirit of the Lord and follow it, and it will lead them just right." Brigham Young was shown the Salt Lake Valley and was told how to build. At his death, Brigham Young said Joseph had come to get him.

—Davis Bitton, *Images of the Prophet Joseph Smith,* 134; Compiler's note

Wilford Woodruff said, "Joseph Smith visited me a great deal after his death, and taught me many important principles. The last time he visited me was while I was in a storm at sea. . . . The night following this, Joseph and Hyrum visited me, and the Prophet laid before me a great many things. Among other things, he told me to get the Spirit of God; that all of us needed it. . . . The last time I saw him was . . . at the door of the temple in heaven."

—Wilford Woodruff, *RJ,* 215–16

Books Written about Joseph Smith

At least 730 positive books are written about Joseph and his influence for good in these last days. Sadly, about 123 misleading books have been written to tell lies and half–truths and to try to discredit him. There have been over 500 paintings and drawings made of Joseph and 40 different statues and monuments made to commemorate him.

—*Joseph Smith A–Z: "A Polished Shaft," Biographical Encyclopedia*;
Wayne J. Lewis, *Bibliography of Joseph Smith*

Joseph Smith Translation

- *Joseph Smith's Translation of the Bible: A History and Commentary: A Plainer Translation*, Robert J. Matthews, 1985, BYU Press, 468 pages.
- *Joseph Smith's New Translation of the Bible: Original Manuscript*, Robert J. Matthews, Scott H. Faulring, and Kent Jackson, 2004, BYU Religious Studies Center, 851 pages.
- *Joseph Smith's Translation: Every Revision in the Old and New Testament*, Kenneth Lutes and Lyndell Lutes, 1998, author printer, 318 pages.

Note: The Church will be indebted to Robert J. Matthews for his careful work on the Joseph Smith Translation. It seems sad that most members pay little attention to these important changes in the Bible.

Geographical locations

- *Sacred Places*, LaMar C. Berrett, Larry C. Porter, and other editors, Deseret Book, 1999, 1470 pages (volumes of New England and Eastern Canada, 195 pages; New York and Pennsylvania, 347 pages; Ohio and Illinois, 276 pages; Missouri, 652 pages).

Note: This treasure of information is a must–read for those who want the details.

Martyrdom

- *The Day They Martyred the Prophet*, Henry A. Smith, 1963, Bookcraft, 270 pages.
- *Carthage Conspiracy: The Trial of the Accused Assassins of Joseph Smith*, Dallin H. Oaks and Marvin S. Hill, 1979, University of Illinois Press, 270 pages.

Paintings

- *Joseph Smith Portraits: A Search for the Prophet's Likeness*, Ephraim Hatch, 1998, BYU Religious Studies, 112 pages.

Note: For a comprehensive display of the paintings of the Prophet Joseph Smith, see Joseph Smith Bibliography: Joseph Smith A–Z Reference Encyclopedia, vol. 1, Wayne J. Lewis, 2010, BYU and Church History Library, 331 pages.

Political views

- *Joseph Smith: Presidential Candidate: Setting the Record Straight*, Arnold K. Garr, 2007, Millennial Press, 124 pages.
- *Murder of the Mormon Prophet: Political Prelude to the Death of Joseph Smith*, LeGrand L. Baker, 2006, Eborn Books, 812 pages.

Prophesies

- *The Prophecies of Joseph Smith: Over 400 Prophesies By and About Joseph Smith, and Their Fulfillment*, Duane S. Crowther, 1983, Horizon, 413 pages.
- *The Revelations of the Prophet Joseph Smith: A Historical Biographical Commentary of the Doctrine and Covenants*, Lyndon W. Cook, 1981, Deseret, 380 pages.

Teachings

- *Teachings of the Prophet Joseph Smith*, Joseph Fielding Smith, 1969, Deseret Book, 410 pages.
- *The Teachings of Joseph Smith*, Larry E. Dahl and Donald Q. Cannon, eds., 1997, Bookcraft, 771 pages.
- *Teachings of the Presidents of the Church: Joseph Smith*, First Presidency, 2007, 587 pages.

Apostatized even after seeing the Savior

Oliver Cowdery and Sidney Rigdon saw the Savior and still apostatized.

—*HC*, 3:17 (Oliver Cowdery), *HC*, 7:268 (Sidney Rigdon)

Churches formed by apostates (partial list)

On April 28, 1844, recently excommunicated Wilson Law organized the Reformed Church with the purpose to totally destroy the Smiths and take over Nauvoo. Eighteen men started different Churches between the death of Joseph Smith and the death of Brigham Young. Out of the 50,000 or so who knew the Prophet Joseph Smith, only about 1,500 of these joined with the RLDS Church.

—Susan Easton Black, fireside, replayed on KBYU July 20, 2009

There have been dozens of splinter groups formed. Today, the RLDS (Community of Christ—about 250,000 members) and Hendrickites (about 1,000 members) are perhaps the only surviving groups still in existence.

- Northrup Sweet (1802–1881)—Baptized in 1830; apostatized in 1831. Formed Pure Church of Christ in 1831; attracted only six members and eventually died out, so they abandoned the idea of a church.
- Sidney Rigdon (1793–1876)—Baptized in 1830. After failing to get leadership in the Church, he formed the Rigdonites.
- William Smith (1811–1893): Joseph's brother. Baptized in 1830; excommunicated in 1845. Followed Strangites; associated with Lyman Wight and declared he was president of the Latter–day Saints in 1847; disbanded idea and later became RLDS.
- Grandville Hendricks (1814–1881)—Baptized in 1843; apostatized

and followed Strang and others and finally started the Church of Christ—Hendrickites (Temple Lot Church).

- David Whitmer (1805–1888)—Baptized in 1830; excommunicated in 1838. Formed Church of Christ—Whitmerites—in 1876; later disbanded.
- Joseph Smith III (1832–1914)—Baptized in 1843. Oldest living son of Joseph Smith. After several business failures, he agreed to help form the Reorganized Church of Jesus Christ of Latter–day Saints (now the Community of Christ)—RLDS—in 1861.
- James Jesse Strang (1813–1856)—Baptized in February 1844. Claimed he was successor to Joseph and formed the Strangites. He proclaimed himself King of Beaver Island, Michigan, and took an extra, secret wife, who posed as a man and his secretary. Strang was assassinated by one of his followers.
- Alpheus Cutler (1784–1864)—Baptized in 1833. Joined with other groups and finally started the True Church of Jesus Christ—Cutlerites.
- William Bickerton (1815–1905)—Never joined the Church. He joined with Sidney Rigdon in 1845 and then started the Church of Jesus Christ—Bickertonites.
- Lyman Wight (1796–1858)—Texas group.
- Francis Gladden Bishop (1809–1864)—Baptized in 1833; excommunicated and rebaptized three times. He left the Church and formed eight different churches, including the Kingdom of God.

—D&C*WW*, 149, 172; *BD*, 399 (Bishop); *BR*, 526–27 (Bishop); *BR*, 202; Internet (*People of the Time: Sample Biographies*)

Leave the Church but can't leave it alone

"Someone has observed that people can leave the church, but they can't leave it alone. And the worst persecutors of Joseph Smith were invariably those who had first been his associates and then had left his side and turned on him. Why this happened, I'm not sure. But it is not an unfamiliar phenomenon in human history."

—Elder Dallin H. Oaks, *American Prophet: The Story of Joseph Smith*, Lee Groberg and Heidi S. Swinton, 97; *HC*

Some of the obvious examples of those who left the Church but couldn't leave it alone are Ezra Booth, Symonds Ryder, Doctor Philastus Hurlbut, William and Wilson Law, Chauncey I. and Francis Higbee, Robert D. and Charles A. Foster, John A. Hicks, John C. Bennett,

William Marks, Burr Riggs, George M. Hinkle, Samson Avard, Austin W. Cowles, and Sidney Rigdon.

—Compiler's note

Leave us alone and gospel would go world wide

"Joseph [Smith] prophesied that if they would let us alone, we would spread the gospel all over the world, and if they did not let us alone, we would spread it anyhow, only a little quicker."

—George A. Smith, *RJ*, 156

Money scarce for Mormon preachers

The reason James Covill left Mormonism is that he could quickly see there was no money in being a preacher in Mormonism.

—Steve Harper, *KBYU Discussions on the Doctrine and Covenants*, October 28, 2009

Traitor George M. Hinkle's sword

Mormon colonel George M. Hinkle turned against the Church and arranged to trick the Church leaders into a meeting with Missouri mob leader General James Clark. After this act, Joseph and others were shackled, taken for a court martial, and taken on to Independence and Richmond. Hinkle was bragging about what he had done in Carrollton, Missouri, and a Missouri mob member took Hinkle's sword away from him. That sword is still housed in the Masonic Lodge at Carrollton, Missouri.

—*HC*, 3; Nancy C. Williams, *After One Hundred Years*, 121; Compiler's note

Most infamous traitors

- William Law 1809–1892
- Robert D. Foster 1811–1878
- John A. Hicks 1810–?
- William E. McLellin 1806–1883 (Also spelled: McClellan, M'Lellin, McLelland)
- Symonds Ryder 1792–1870

—D&C*WW*, 190–95

Worse than Judas

"The devil striving for empire, began to stir up, [in them] as in Judas, [desire] for the Prophet's blood." William Law, Wilson Law, William Marks, the Higbees, and Dr. Foster, "all of these and many others entered into secret covenant so much worse than Judas, that they would have the Prophet's life."

—Benjamin F. Johnson, *My Life's Review*, 88–89

City planner

Joseph conceived of a center city with wagon wheel–like spokes around it and smaller communities around this center. He envisioned a city every twelve miles or so.

—*Hyrum L. Andrus, Joseph Smith the Man and the Seer,* 107; Compiler's note

General in military

Joseph was the general of the largest army in the United States except the US Army in 1842–1844.

—Compiler's note

Letter to Congress

A letter protesting the treatment and damages of the Saints from Missouri was sent with 3,419 signatures on November 28, 1843.

—*HC,* 4:24–38, 52–74, 6:83

Mississippi River

On November 23, 1843, Joseph suggested petitioning Congress for a grant to make a canal over the falls around the Des Moines Rapids or a dam to turn the water into Nauvoo, so mills could be erected. In modern times, a dam was erected ten miles south of Nauvoo.

—John W. Welch, ed., *A Chronology of the Life of Joseph Smith,* BYU Studies, 156

Missouri damages

On March 4, 1840, Joseph Smith presented to the US Congress claims against Missouri from 491 individuals for about $1,381,000. President Martin Van Buren said, "Your cause is just, but I can do nothing for you." (If he helped Joseph, he would have lost the vote of Missouri.)

—*LDSCC,* 18; Compiler's note

Missouri extermination order

Governor Boggs's extermination order of October 27, 1838, targeting the Mormons, was officially in effect for 138 years. It was rescinded by Governor Christopher Bond with a counter order on June 25, 1976.

—Missouri Executive Order, Jefferson City, Missouri

Politics led to murder?

In the book *Junius and Joseph*, the authors argue that Joseph Smith's 1844 presidential bid had a direct connection to his assassination on June 27, 1844. "These two authors make such a persuasive case . . . their work could very well reopen the conversation about the events that led to Joseph Smith's death."

—Jan Shipps, *Junius and Joseph: Presidential Politics and the Assassination of the First Mormon Prophet*, Robert S. Wicks and Fred R. Foister (back cover note by Jan Shipps)

Political offices held by Joseph Smith

- February 1, 1841: Elected to the Nauvoo City Council.
- February 4, 1841: Elected as lieutenant general of the Nauvoo Legion.
- January 22, 1842: Elected mayor pro tem of Nauvoo at the council meeting.
- May 19, 1842: Became mayor of Nauvoo.
- March 11, 1842: As commander of the Nauvoo Legion, commanded a parade through the streets of Nauvoo.
- February 6, 1843: Reelected mayor of Nauvoo.
- September 16, 1843: Introduced as general of the Nauvoo Legion.

—Susan Easton Black, *Setting the Record Straight: Joseph Smith the Mormon Prophet*, 13; John W. Welch, ed., *A Chronology of the Life of Joseph Smith*, BYU Studies, 130, 143

Presidential candidacy

Joseph organized a third party called the Reformed Jeffersonian Democracy, Free Trade and Sailor's Rights on January 29, 1844. Sidney Rigdon was his vice presidential running mate. The Twelve Apostles appointed 337 electioneer missionaries to serve in all 26 states and in the Wisconsin Territory. Brigham Young fulfilled a nine-week electioneer's mission, while Wilford Woodruff fulfilled a nine-week mission and visited half of the states of the Union. They arranged for 47 conferences in 15 states on April 15, 1844. The other leading candidates were John C. Calhoun, Lewis Cass, Richard M. Johnson, Henry Clay, and Martin Van Buren.

—Arnold K. Garr, *Setting the Record Straight: Joseph Smith: Presidential Candidate* by, 3, 6, 9, 68; *HC*, 2:207–8

On January 29, 1844, Joseph announced his candidacy for the President of the United States and was nominated on May 17, 1844, at the Nauvoo Convention. He once said, "Come, Texas; come, Mexico; come, Canada; come, all the world. Let us be brethren, one family." His platform was to abolish slavery, lower taxes, put schools in prisons, have greater equality, and create an army to put down mobs.

—John Henry Evans, *Joseph Smith an American Prophet,* 188; Richard E. Turley and Lael Littke, *Stories From the Life of Joseph Smith*, 166

Joseph said he felt there was "oratory enough in the Church to carry me into the presidential chair first slide." A total of 586 missionaries were serving with at least 361 specifically assigned to areas to advance the candidacy of Joseph Smith.

—Arnold K. Garr, *Setting the Record Straight: Joseph Smith: Presidential Candidate*, 49–50; Compiler's note

"No one can be more fit for the task [of president of the United States] than Gen. Joseph Smith: he is wise, prudent, faithful, energetic and fearless . . . his past history shows his indomitable perseverance, and proves him to be a faithful friend, and a man of exalted genius and sterling integrity . . . prove[s] him to be a patriot and a statesman."

—John Taylor, *Religion and Politics Times and Seasons,* 15 March 1844, 470–71; As quoted in Robert S. Wicks and Fred R Foister, *Junius and Joseph: Presidential Politics and the Assassination of the First Mormon Prophet*, 97

Political views

Joseph felt the House of Representatives should be reduced from 223 to 40. A smaller body would be able to do more business than the army that then occupied the halls of the national legislature. Part of the money saved could have gone to buying slaves and freeing them. The United States population at the time was 20 million.

—Arnold K. Garr, *Setting the Record Straight: Joseph Smith: Presidential Candidate*, 43–44

Joseph Smith's Views on Government

Joseph Smith was a serious candidate and this caused fear among political leaders in Illinois, Missouri, and some in national politics.

Joseph Smith's 24-page "Views on the Powers and Policies of the United States Government" on November 4, 1843 was sent to J. C. Calhoon and Henry Clay and three other presidential candidates. Another 23-page statement was sent on January 2, 1844, making 47 pages in all.

—Joseph Smith's Views on the Powers and Policy of the Government document

Sermon to members of US Congress

In December 1839, Joseph gave a public sermon to several members of the US Congress.

—John W. Welch, ed., *A Chronology of the Life of Joseph Smith,* BYU Studies, 110

US Constitution is for all the world

"Joseph said all nations of the world [should] adopt the 'God-given Constitution of the United States as a palladium of liberty and equal rights."

—Benjamin F. Johnson, *They Knew the Prophet,* Hyrum L. Andrus, 108

World Government

Joseph said, "I intend to lay a foundation that will revolutionize the whole world." According to author Hyrum L. Andrus, the Prophet had a concept of world government. Within this was a concept of the kingdom of God and the development of a political government that would be administered under the direction of the priesthood of Zion. He organized a body of men as a nucleus of the new government: the "Special Council," "the General Council," "Council of the Kingdom," "The Kingdom of God," or the "Council of Fifty." "It will not be by sword or gun that this kingdom will roll on; the power of truth is such that all nations will be under the necessity of obeying the gospel."

—Hyrum L. Andrus, *Joseph Smith and World Government,* 1–5

Political Correspondence

Communication between the Prophet Joseph Smith and J. C. Calhoun, Henry Clay, and other Presidential Candidates.

Nauvoo, Ill., Nov. 4th, 1843.
Hon. John C. Calhoun.

Dear Sir:—As we understand you are a candidate for the Presidency at the next election; and as the Latter-day Saints (sometimes called Mormons, who now constitute a numerous class in the school politic of this vast republic) have been robbed of an immense amount of property, and endured nameless sufferings by the State of Missouri, and from her borders have been driven by force of arms, contrary to our national covenants; and as in vain we have sought redress by all constitutional, legal and honorable means, in her courts, her executive councils and her legislative halls; and as we have petitioned

Congress to take cognizance of our sufferings without effect, we have judged it wisdom to address you this communication, and solicit an immediate, specific and candid reply to "What will be your rule of action relative to us as a people," should fortune favor your ascension to the chief magistracy?

Most respectfully, sir, your friend, and the friend of peace, good order, and constitutional rights,

—Joseph Smith
In behalf of the Church of
Jesus Christ of Latter-day Saints

Similar letters were written to General Lewis Cass, Hon. Richard M. Johnson, Hon. Henry Clay, and President Martin Van Buren. The following paragraph was added to the letter addressed to Mr. Van Buren:

Also whether your views or feelings have changed since the subject matter of this communication was presented to you in your then official capacity at Washington, in the year 1841, and by you treated with a coldness, indifference, and neglect, bordering on contempt.

J. C. Calhoun's reply

Fort Hill, 2nd December, 1843.

Sir:—You ask me what would be my rule of action relative to the Mormons or Latter-day Saints, should I be elected President: to which I answer, that if I should be elected, I would strive to administer the Government according to the Constitution and the laws of the Union; and that as they make no distinction between citizens of different religious creeds, I should make none. As far as it depends on the executive department, all should have the full benefit of both, and none should be exempt from their operation.

But as you refer to the case of Missouri, candor compels me to repeat what I said to you at Washington, that, according to my views, the case does not come within the jurisdiction of the federal government, which is one of limited and specific powers.

With respect, I am, &ct., &ct.,

J. C. Calhoun.

Mr. Joseph Smith.

Joseph Smith's rejoinder to J. C. Calhoun

Nauvoo, Illinois,
January 2, 1844.

Sir:—Your reply to my letter of last November, concerning your rule of action towards the Latter-day Saints, if elected president, is at hand; and that you and your friends of the same opinion relative to the matter in question may not be disappointed as to me or my mind upon so grave a subject, permit me, as a law-abiding man, as a well-wisher to the perpetuity of constitutional rights and liberty, and as a friend to the free worship of Almighty God by all, according to the dictates of every person's own conscience, to say I am surprised that a man or men in the highest stations of public life should have made up such a fragile "view" of a case, than which there is not one on the face of the globe fraught with so much consequence to the happiness of men in this world or the world to come.

To be sure, the first paragraph of your letter appears very complacent and fair on a white sheet of paper. And who, that is ambitious for greatness and power, would not have said the same thing? Your oath would bind you to support the Constitution and laws; and as all creeds and religions are alike tolerated, they must, of course, all be justified or condemned according to merit or demerit. But why—tell me why are all the principal men held up for public stations so cautiously careful not to publish to the world that they will judge a righteous judgment, law or no law? For laws and opinions, like the vanes of steeples, change with the wind.

One Congress passes a law, another repeals it; and one statesman says that the Constitution means this, and another that; and who does not know that all may be wrong? The opinion and pledge therefore, in the first paragraph of your reply to my question, like the forced steam from the engine of a steamboat, makes the show of a bright cloud at first, but when it comes in contact with a purer atmosphere, dissolves to common air again.

Your second paragraph leaves you naked before yourself, like a likeness in mirror, when you say that, "according to your view, the federal government is one of limited and specific powers," and has no jurisdiction in the case of the Mormons. So then a State can at any time expel any portion of her citizens with impunity, and, in the language of Mr. Van Buren, frosted over with your gracious "views of the case," though the cause is ever so just, Government can do nothing for them, because it has no power.

Go on, then, Missouri, after another set of inhabitants (as the Latter-day Saints did) have entered some two or three hundred thousand dollars' worth of land; and made extensive improvements thereon. Go on, then, I say; banish the occupants or owners, or kill them, as the mobbers did many of the Latter-day Saints, and take their land and property as spoil; and let the legislature, as in the case of the Mormons, appropriate a couple of hundred thousand dollars to pay the mob for doing that job; for the renowned Senator from South Carolina, Mr. J. C. Calhoun, says the powers of the Federal Government are so specific and limited that it has no jurisdiction of the case! O ye people who groan under the oppression of tyrants! – ye exiled Poles, who have felt the iron hand of Russian grasp! – ye poor and unfortunate among all nations! Come to the asylum of the oppressed; buy ye lands of the General Government; pay in your money to the treasury to strengthen the army and the navy; worship God according to the dictates of your own consciences; pay in your taxes to support the great heads of a glorious nation: but remember a "sovereign State" is so much more powerful than the United States, the parent Government, that it can exile you at pleasure, mob you with impunity, confiscate your lands and property, have the legislature sanction it,—yea, even murder you as an edict of an emperor, and it does no wrong; for the noble senator of South Carolina says the power of the Federal Government is so limited and specific that is has no jurisdiction of the case! What think ye of imperium in imperio?

Ye spirits of the blessed of all ages, hark! Ye shades of departed statesmen listen! Abraham, Moses, Homer, Socrates, Solon, Solomon, and all that ever thought of right and wrong, look down from your exaltations, if you have any; for, it is said, in the midst of counselors there is safety: and when you have learned that fifteen thousand innocent citizens, after having purchased their lands of the United States and paid for them, were expelled from a "Sovereign State," by order of the Governor, at the point of the bayonet, their arms taken from them by the same authority, and their right of migration into said State denied, under pain of imprisonment, whipping, robbing, mobbing, and even death, and no justice or recompense allowed; and, from the legislature with the governor at the head, down to the justice of the peace, with a bottle of whisky in one hand and a bowie-knife in the other, hear them all declare that there is no justice for a Mormon in that State; and judge ye a righteous judgment, and tell me when the virtue of the States was stolen, where the honor of the General Government lies hid, and what clothes a senator with wisdom. Oh nullifying Carolina! Oh little tempestuous Rhode Island! Would it not be well for the great men of the nation to read the fable of the partial judge; and when part of the free citizens of a State had been expelled contrary to the constitution, mobbed, robbed, plundered, and many murdered, instead of searching into the course taken with Joanna Southcott, Ann Lee, the French

Prophets, the Quakers of New England, and rebellious niggers in the slave States, to hear both sides and then judge, rather than have the mortification to say, "Oh, it is my bull that has killed your ox! That alters the case! I must inquire into it; and if, and if?"

If the General Government has no power to reinstate expelled citizens to their rights, there is a monstrous hypocrite fed and fostered from the hard earnings of the people! A real "bull beggar" upheld by sycophants. And although you may wink to the priests to stigmatize, wheedle the drunkards to swear, and raise the hue-and-cry of "Imposter! False prophet! G–d–d–n old Joe Smith!" yet remember, if the Latter-day Saints are not restored to all their rights and paid for all their losses, according to the known rules of justice and judgment, reciprocation and common honesty among men, that God will come out of His hiding place, and vex this nation with a sore vexation; yea, the consuming wrath of an offended God shall smoke through the nation with as much distress and woe as independence has blazed through with pleasure and delight. Where is the strength of Government? Where is the patriotism of a Washington, a Warren, and Adams? And where is a spark from the watch-fire of '76, by which one candle might be lit that would glimmer upon the confines of Democracy? Well, may it be said that one man is not a state, nor one state the nation.

In the days of General Jackson, when France refused the first installment for spoliations, there was power, force, and honor enough to resent injustice and insult, and the money came; and shall. Missouri, filled with negro-drivers and white men stealers, go "unwhipped of justice" for tenfold greater sins than France? No! verily, no! While I have power of body and mind—while water runs and grass grows—while virtue is lovely and vice hateful, and while a stone points out a sacred spot where a fragment of American liberty once was, I or my posterity will plead the cause of injured innocence, until Missouri makes atonement for all her sins, or sinks disgraced, degraded, and damned to hell, "where the worm dieth not, and the fire is not quenched."

Why, sir, the power not delegated to the United States and the States belong to the people; and Congress sent to do the people's business have all power; and shall fifteen thousand citizens groan in exile? O vain men! Will ye not, if ye do not restore them to their rights and $2,000,000 worth of property, relinquish to them, (the Latter-day Saints,) as a body, their portion of power that belongs to them according to the Constitution? Power has its convenience as well as inconvenience. "The world was not made for Caesar alone but for Titus too."

I will give you a parable. A certain lord had a vineyard in a goodly land, which men labored in at their pleasure. A few meek men also went and purchased with money from some of these chief men that labored at pleasure a portion of land in the vineyard, at a very remote part of it, and began to improve it, and to eat and drink the fruit thereof,—when some vile persons, who regarded not man, neither feared the lord of the vineyard, rose up suddenly and robbed these meek men, and drove them from their possessions, killing many.

This barbarous act made no small stir among the men in the vineyard; and all that portion who were attached to that part of the vineyard where the men were robbed rose up in grand council, with their chief man, who had firstly ordered the deed to be done, and made a covenant not to pay for the cruel deed, but to keep the spoil, and never let those meek men set their feet on that soil again, neither recompense them for it.

Now, these meek men, in their distress, wisely sought redress of those wicked men in every possible manner, and got none. They then supplicated the chief men, who held the vineyard at pleasure, and who had the power to sell and defend it, for redress and redemption; and those men, loving the fame and favor of the multitude more than the glory of the lord of the vineyard, answered—"Your cause is just, but we can do nothing for you, because we have no power."

Now, when the lord of the vineyard saw that virtue and innocence was not regarded, and his vineyard occupied by wicked men, he sent men and took the possession of it to himself, and destroyed these unfaithful servants, and appointed them their portion among hypocrites.

And let me say that all men who say that Congress has no power to restore and defend the rights of her citizens have not the love of the truth abiding in them. Congress has power to protect the nation against foreign invasion and internal broil; and whenever that body passes an act to maintain right with any power, or to restore right to any portion of her citizens, it is the SUPREME LAW OF THE LAND; and should a State refuse submission, that state is guilty of insurrection or rebellion, and the President has as much power to repel it as Washington had to march against the "whiskey boys at Pittsburg," or General Jackson had to send an armed force to suppress the rebellion of South Carolina.

To close, I would admonish you, before you let your "candor compel" you again to write upon a subject great as the salvation of man, consequential as the life of the Savior, broad as the principles of eternal truth; and valuable as the jewels of eternity, to read in the 8th section and 1st article of the

Constitution of the United States, the first, fourteenth, and seventeenth "specific" and not very "limited powers" of the Federal Government, what can be done to protect the lives, property, and rights of a virtuous people, when the administrators of the law and law-makers are unbought by bribes, uncorrupted by patronage, untempted by gold, unawed by fear, and uncontaminated by tangling alliances—even like Caesar's wife, not only unspotted, but unsuspected! And God, who cooled the heat of a Nebuchadnezzar's furnace or shut the mouths of lions for the honor of a Daniel, will raise your mind above the narrow notion that the General Government has no power, to the sublime idea that Congress, with the President as executor, is as almighty in its sphere as Jehovah is in His.

With great respect, I have the honor to be
Your obedient servant,
—Joseph Smith

Hon. ("Mr.") J. C. Calhoun,
Fort Hill, S.C.

Reply of Henry Clay

Ashland, November 15, 1843

Dear Sir:—I have received your letter in behalf of the Church of Jesus Christ of Latter-day Saints, stating that you understand that I am a candidate for the presidency, and inquiring what will be my rule of action relative to you as a people, should I be elected.

I am profoundly grateful for the numerous and strong expressions of the people in my behalf as a candidate for President of the United States; but I do not so consider myself. That must depend upon future events and upon my sense of duty.

Should I be a candidate, I can enter into no engagements, make no promises, give no pledges to any particular portion of the people of the United States. If I ever enter into that high office, I must go into it free and unfettered, with no guarantees but such as are to be drawn from my whole life, character and conduct.

It is not inconsistent with this declaration to say that I have viewed with a lively interest the progress of the Latter-day Saints; that I have sympathized in their sufferings under injustice, as it appeared to me, which has been inflicted upon them; and that I think, in common with other religious communities, they ought to enjoy the security and protections of the Constitution and the laws.

I am with great respect,
Your friend and obedient servant,
—H. Clay

To Joseph Smith, Esq.

Joseph Smith's Rejoinder to Henry Clay

Nauvoo, Illinois, May 13, 1844

Sir:—Your answer to my inquiry, "What would be your rule of action towards the Latter-day Saints, should you be elected President of the United States?" has been under consideration since last November, in the fond expectation that you would give (for every honest citizen has a right to demand it,) to the country a manifesto of your views of the best method and means which would secure to the people, the whole people, the most freedom, the most happiness, the most union, the most wealth, the most fame, the most glory at home, and the most honor abroad, at the least expense. But I have waited in vain. So far as you have made public declarations, they have been made, like your answer to the above, soft to flatter, rather than solid to feed the people. You seem to abandon all former policy which may have actuated you in the discharge of a statesman's duty, when the vigor of intellect and the force of virtue should have sought out an everlasting habitation for liberty; when, as a wise man, a true patriot, and a friend to mankind, you should have resolved to ameliorate the lawful condition of our bleeding country by a mighty plan of wisdom, righteousness, justice, goodness and mercy, that would have brought back the golden days of our nation's youth, vigor and vivacity, when prosperity crowned the efforts of a youthful republic, when the gentle aspirations of the sons of liberty were, "We are one!"

In your answer to my question last fall, that peculiar tact of modern politicians declaring, "If you ever enter into that high office you must go into it free and unfettered; with no guarantees but such as are to be drawn from your whole life, character and conduct," so much resembles a lottery-vendor's sign, with the goddess of good luck sitting on the car of fortune, a-straddle of the horns of plenty, and driving the merry steeds of beatitude, without reins or bridle, that I cannot help exclaiming—O frail man, what have you done that will exalt you? Can anything be drawn from your life, character or conduct that is worthy of being held up to the gaze of this nation as a model of virtue, charity and wisdom? Are you not a lottery picture, with more than two blanks to a prize? Leaving many things prior to your Ghent treaty, let the world look at that, and see where is the wisdom, honor and patriotism which ought to have characterized the plenipotentiary of the only free nation upon the earth? A quarter of a century's negotiation to obtain our rights on the north-eastern boundary, and the motley manner in which Oregon tries to shine as American territory, coupled with your presidential race and some by-chance secretaryship in 1825, all go to convince the friends of freedom, the golden patriots of Jeffersonian Democracy, free trade and sailors' rights, and the protectors of person and property, that an honorable war is better than a dishonorable peace.

But had you really wanted to have exhibited the wisdom, clemency, benevolence and dignity of a great man in this boasted republic, when fifteen thousand free citizens were exiled from their own homes, lands and property, in the wonderful patriotic State of Missouri, and you then upon your oath and honor occupying the exalted station of a Senator of Congress from the noble–hearted State of Kentucky, why did you not show the world your loyalty to law and order, by using all honorable means to restore the innocent to their rights and property? Why, sir, the more we search into your character and conduct, the more we must exclaim from Holy Writ, "The tree is known by its fruit."

Again: this is not all. Rather than show yourself an honest man, by guaranteeing to the people what you will do in case you should be elected president, "you can enter into no engagement, make no promises, and give no pledges as to what you will do." Well, it may be that some hot-headed partisan would take such nothingarianism upon trust; but sensible men and even ladies would think themselves insulted by such an evasion of coming events! If a tempest is expected, why not prepare to meet it, and, in the language of the poet, exclaim –

"Then let the trial come; and witness thou
If terror be upon me, If I shrink
Or falter in my strength to meet the storm,
When hardest it besets me."

True greatness never wavers; but when the Missouri compromise was entered into by you for the benefit of slavery, there was a might shrinkage of western honor; and from that day, sir, the sterling Yankee, the struggling Abolitionist, and the staunch Democrat, with a large number of the liberal-minded Whigs, have marked you as a blackleg in politics, begging for a chance to shuffle yourself into the presidential chair, where you might deal out the destinies of our beloved country for a game of brag that would end in "Hark, from the tombs of a doleful sound." Start not at this picture, for your "whole life, character and conduct" have been spotted with deeds that cause a blush upon the face of a virtuous patriot. So you must be contented in your lot, while crime, cowardice, cupidity or low cunning have handed you down from the high tower of a statesman to the black hole of a gambler. A man that accepts a challenge or fights a duel is nothing more nor less than a murderer; for Holy Writ declares that, "Whoso sheds man's blood, by man shall his blood be shed" and when in the renowned city of Washington, the notorious Henry Clay dropped from the summit of a Senator to the sink of a scoundrel to shoot at that chalk-line of a Randolph, he not only disgraced his own fame, family and friends, but he polluted the sanctum sanctorum of American glory; and the kingly blackguards throughout the whole world are pointing the finger of scorn at the boasted "asylum of the oppressed," and hissing at American statesmen as gentlemen vagabonds and murderers, holding the olive branch of peace in one hand and a pistol for death in the other! Well might the Savior rebuke the heads of this nation with "Wo unto you Scribes, Pharisees, Hypocrites!" for the United States Government and Congress, with a few honorable exceptions, have gone the way of Cain, and must perish in the gainsayings, like Korah and his wicked host. And honest men of every clime, and the innocent, poor and oppressed, as well as heathens, pagans and Indians, everywhere, who could but hope that the tree of liberty would yield some precious fruit for the hungry human race, and shed some balmy leaves for the healing of nations, have long since given up all hopes of equal rights, of justice and judgment, and of truth and virtue, when such polluted, vain, heaven-daring, bogus patriots are forced or flung into the front rank of Government to guide the destinies of millions. Drape the heavens with weeds of woe, gird the earth with sack-cloth, and let hell mutter one melody in commemoration of fallen splendor! For the glory of America has departed, and God will set a flaming sword to guard the tree of liberty, while such mint-tithing Herods as Van Buren, Boggs, Benton, Calhoun and Clay are thrust out of the realms of virtue as fit subjects for the kingdom of fallen greatness; vox reprobi, vox Diaboli!

In your late addresses to the people of South Carolina, where rebellion budded, but could not blossom, you "renounced ultraism," "high tariff," and almost banished your "banking system" for the more certain standard of "public opinion." This is all very well, and marks the intention of a politician, the calculations of a demagogue, and the allowance for leeings of a shrewd manager, just as truly as the weathercock does the wind when it turns upon the spire. Hustings for the South, barbecues for the West, confidential letters for the North and "American System" for the east.

Lull-a-by baby upon the tree top.
And when the wind blows the cradle will rock.

Suppose you should also, taking your "whole life, character and conduct" into consideration, and, as many hands make light work, stir up the old "Clay party," the "National Republican party," the "High Protective Tariff party," and the late coonskin party, with all their paraphernalia, ultraism, ne plus ultraism, sine qua non, which have grown with your growth, strengthened with your strength, and shrunk with your shrinkage, and ask the people of this enlightened Republic what they think of your powers and policy as a statesman; for verily it would seem, from all past remains of parties, politics, projects and pictures, that you are the clay and the people the potter; and as some vessels are marred in the hands of the potter, the natural conclusion is that you are a vessel of dishonor.

You may complain that a close examination of your "whole life, character and conduct" places you, as a Kentuckian would pleasantly term it, "in a bad fix." But, sir, when the nation has sunk deeper and deeper into the mud at every turn of the great wheels of the Union, while you have acted as one of the principal drivers, it becomes the bounden duty of the whole community, as one man, to whisper you on every point of government, to uncover every act of your life, and inquire what mighty acts you have done to benefit the nation, how much you have tithed the mint to gratify your lust, and why the fragments of your raiment hang upon the thorns by the path as signals to beware.

But your shrinkage is truly wonderful! Not only your banking system and high tariff project have vanished from your mind "like the baseless fabric of a vision," but the "annexation of Texas" has touched your pathetic sensibilities of national pride so acutely, that the poor Texans, your own brethren, may fall back into the ferocity of Mexico, or be sold at auction to British stock-jobbers, and all is well for "I," the old Senator from Kentucky, and fearful it would militate against my interest in the north to enlarge the borders of the Union in the south. Truly, "a poor wise child is better than an old foolish king who will be no longer admonished." Who ever heard of a nation that had too much territory? Was it ever bad policy to make friends? Has any people ever become too good to do good? No, never. But the ambition and vanity of some men have flown away with their wisdom and judgment; and left a croaking skeleton to occupy the place of a noble soul!

Why, sir, the condition of the whole earth is lamentable. Texas dreads the teeth and the nails of Mexico. Oregon has the rheumatism, brought on by a horrid exposure to the heat and cold of British and American trappers. Canada has caught a bad cold from extreme fatigue in the patriot war. South America has the headache caused by bumps against the beams of Catholicity and Spanish Sovereignty. Spain has the gripes from age and inquisition. France trembles and wastes under the effects of contagious diseases. England groans with the gout, and wiggles with wine. Italy and the German States are pale with the consumption. Prussia, Poland, and the little contiguous dynasties, duchies and domains, have the mumps so severely, that "the whole head is sick, and the whole heart is faint." Russia has the cramp by lineage. Turkey has the numb palsy. Africa, from the curse of God, has lost the use of her limbs. China is ruined by the queen's evil, and the rest of Asia fearfully exposed to the small-pox, the natural way, from British peddlers. The islands of the sea are almost dead with the scurvy. The Indians are blind and lame; and the United States, which ought to be the good physician with "balm from Gilead" and an "asylum for the oppressed," had boosted and is boosting up into the council chamber of the Government a clique of political gamblers, to pay for the old clothes and old shoes of a sick world, and "no pledge. No promise to any particular portion of the people," that the rightful heirs will ever receive a cent of their father's legacy. Away with such self-important, self-aggrandizing, and self-willed demagogues." Their friendship is colder than polar ice, and their profession meaner than the damnation of hell.

O man! When such a great dilemma of the globe, such a tremendous convulsion of kingdoms shakes the earth from centre to circumference; when castles, prison-houses, and cells raise a cry to God against the cruelty of man; when the mourning of the fatherless and the widow causes anguish in heaven; when the poor among all nations cry day and night for bread, amid a shelter from the heat and storm; and when the degraded black slave holds up his manacled hands to the great statesmen of the United States, and sings –

"O liberty, where are thy charms,
That sages have told me are sweet?"

And when fifteen thousand free citizens of the high-blooded republic of North America are robbed and driven from one State to another without redress or redemption, it is not only time for a candidate for the presidency to pledge himself to execute judgment and justice in righteousness, law or no law; but it is his bounden duty as a man, for the honor of a disgraced country, and for the salvation of a once virtuous people, to call for a union of all honest men, and appease the wrath of God by acts of wisdom, holiness; and virtue! "The fervent prayer of a righteous man availeth much."

Perhaps you may think I go too far with my strictures and innuendos, because in your concluding paragraph you say "it is not inconsistent with our declarations to say that you have viewed with a lively interest the progress of the Latter-day Saints, that you have sympathized in their sufferings under injustice; as it appeared to you, which has been inflicted upon them, and that you think, in common with all other religious communities, they ought to enjoy the security and protection of the Constitution and the laws." If words were not wind, and imagination not a vapor, such "views" "with a lively interest" might coax out a few Mormon votes; such "sympathy" for their suffering under injustice might heal some of the sick yet lingering amongst them, raise some of the dead and recover some of their property from Missouri; and finally, if thought was not a phantom, we might, in common with other religious communities, "you think," enjoy the security and protection of the Constitution and laws. But during ten years, while the Latter-day Saints have bled, been robbed, driven from their own lands, paid oceans of money into the treasury to pay your renowned self and others for legislating and dealing out equal rights and privileges to those in common with all other religious communities, they have waited and expected in vain! If you have possessed any patriotism, it has been veiled by your popularity, for fear the Saints would fall in love with its charms. Blind charity and dumb justice never do much towards alleviating the wants of the needy; but straws show which way the wind blows. It is currently rumored that your dernier resort for the Latter-day Saints is to emigrate to Oregon or California. Such cruel humanity, such noble injustice, such honorable cowardice, such foolish wisdom, and such vicious virtue could only emanate from Clay. After the Saints have been plundered of three or four millions of land and property by the people and powers of the sovereign State of Missouri—after they have sought for redress and redemption, from the county court to Congress, and been denied through religious prejudice and sacerdotal dignity—after they have builded a city and two temples at an immense expense of labor and treasure—after they have increased from hundreds to hundreds of thousands, and after they have sent missionaries to the various nations of the earth to gather Israel, according to the predictions of all the holy prophets since the world began, that great plenipotentiary, the renowned Secretary of state, the ignoble duelist, the gambling senator, and Whig candidate for the presidency, Henry Clay, the wise Kentucky lawyer, advises the Latter-day Saints to go to Oregon to obtain justice and set up a government of their own. O ye crowned heads among all nations, is not Mr. Clay a wise man, and very patriotic? Why, great God! To transport 200,000 people through a vast prairie, over the Rocky Mountains, to Oregon, a distance of nearly 2,000 miles, would cost more than four millions! Or should they go by Cape Horn in ships to California, the cost would be more than twenty millions! And all this to save the United States from inheriting the disgrace of Missouri for murdering and robbing the Saints with impunity! Benton and Van Buren, who make no secret to say that if they get into power they will carry out Boggs' exterminating plan to rid the country of the Latter-day Saints, are "Little nipperkins of milk," compared to "Clay's" great aquafortis jars. Why, he is a real giant in humanity! "Send the Mormons to Oregon, and free Missouri from debt and disgrace!" Ah! Sir, let this doctrine go to-and-fro throughout the whole earth—that we, as Van Buren said, "know your cause is just, but the United States Government can do nothing for you because it has no power. You must go to Oregon, and get justice from the Indians!"

I mourn for the depravity of the world; I despise the hypocrisy of Christendom; I hate the imbecility of American statesmen; I detest the shrinkage of candidates for office from pledges and responsibility; I long for a day of righteousness, when "He whose right it is to reign shall judge the poor, and reprove with equity for the meek of the earth;" and I pray God, who hath given our fathers a promise of a perfect government in the last days, to purify the hearts of the people and hasten the welcome day.

With the highest consideration for virtue and unadulterated freedom,
I have the honor to be,
Your obedient servant,
—Joseph Smith

Hon. H. Clay, Ashland, Ky.

Other Facts about Joseph Smith

Age Comparison of Joseph Smith to Others

When Church Was Organized in 1830

- Joseph Smith — age 24
- Emma Smith — age 26
- Oliver Cowdery — age 24
- Hyrum Smith — age 30
- Parley Pratt — age 23
- Orson Pratt — age 18
- Joseph Smith Sr. — age 59
- David Whitmer — age 24
- Peter Whitmer Sr. — age 43
- Orrin Porter Rockwell — age 17

Not Yet Converted in 1830

- Brigham Young — age 29
- Sidney Rigdon — age 33
- David W. Patten — age 30
- Orson Hyde — age 25
- George Q. Cannon — age 3
- Newel K. Whitney — age 35
- A. Sidney Gilbert — age 40
- William W. Phelps — age 38

Martyrdom in 1844

- Joseph Smith — age 38
- Emma Smith — age 39
- Joseph Smith III — age 11

• Hyrum Smith	age 44
• Brigham Young	age 43 (baptized 1832)
• Heber C. Kimball	age 29 (baptized 1832)
• William Clayton	age 30 (baptized 1837)
• Wilford Woodruff	age 21 (baptized 1833)
• Sidney Rigdon	age 51 (baptized November 1830)
• Frederick G. Williams	age 56 (baptized October 1830)
• Lorenzo Snow	age 30 (baptized 1838)
• Joseph F. Smith	age 5
• Willard Richard	age 39 (baptized December 1836)
• George A. Smith	age 26 (baptized 1832)
• David Hyrum Smith	age –5 months (not born until November 17, 1844)

Age comparison of Joseph Smith to other famous people

A listing of those who would be basically unknown if they only lived to age 38, like Joseph Smith did, and their ages at the time of their fame.

• Abraham Lincoln	51—US President
• George Washington	49—first win as a general
• Brigham Young	43—Church President
• Thomas Jefferson	46—secretary of state
• John Adams	54—first national office
• Christopher Columbus	41—discovered American Continent
• Benjamin Franklin	50s—first prominent influence
• John F. Kennedy	43—US President
• Andrew Jackson	56—national office
• Spencer W. Kimball	78—Church President
• Gordon B. Hinckley	85—Church President
• Gandhi	52—first major influence in India
• Mark Twain	50s—first writing success
• Louis Pasteur	40s—major discovery
• Plato	40s—became known teacher
• Johannes Gutenberg	60s—successful press invention
• Muhammad	50s—first major influence
• Franklin D. Roosevelt	48—US President
• Noah	600—finished the ark
• Abraham	99—Lord changed his name from Abram
• Moses	40—received call to free Israel

- Zacharias — old (probably 80–90)—father of John the Baptist
- Lehi — probably 50s—Lord gave him a dream and call

Note: None of the above would be internationally known before the age and status indicated.

—Compiler's Notes

Days of the week

Joseph Smith's birth was *Monday,* December 23, 1805. He married Emma on *Thursday,* January 18, 1827. The Aaronic Priesthood was restored on *Friday,* May 15, 1829. The Melchizedek Priesthood (most probable date) was restored on *Thursday,* May 28, 1829. The Church was organized *Tuesday,* April 6, 1830. Joseph and Hyrum were murdered on *Thursday,* June 27, 1844.

—Internet, Church Almanacs

Dogs

Joseph Smith had a favorite dog named Major. Sylvester Smith threatened to kill it while on Zion's Camp march. Joseph also had a bulldog named Baker.

—Joseph Smith History, vol. 3; Richard Lloyd Dewey, Joseph Smith, A Biography, 162

Horse ride

Joseph rode 60 miles on Ole Charley on January 12, 1838, in fleeing a Kirtland assassination plot.

—J. Christopher Conkling, *A Joseph Smith Chronology,* 107

Horses

Joseph named a horse Joe Duncan after the father of Daniel Duncan (1790–1844), who served as governor of Missouri in 1828–1836.

—BD, 407

Joseph had many fine horses: Charlie, a black horse; Joe Duncan, purchased on July 11, 1842, and named after Jose Duncan, an Illinois Whig candidate for governor; a gray horse; and a white horse.

—RJ; Hyrum L. Andrus, *They Knew the Prophet;* Jack Welch, ed., *A Chronology of the Life of Joseph Smith,* BYU Studies, 134

Indians' painting of Joseph

"I guess you have seen the picture where Brother Joseph was preaching to the Indians. I was there at that time. The Indians were all kneeling down on the grass in front of the Mansion. . . . [I]t is a miserable picture of the Prophet."

—Rachel Ridgeway Grant, *They Knew the Prophet*, Hyrum L. Andrus, 142–43

Inventions

From the time of Jesus Christ to 1820, there was an average of thirty-nine inventions per year. From the 1820s and during Joseph's lifetime, there were four thousand new inventions per year.

—*KBYU Joseph Smith Papers*, October 12, 2009

Journal kept

Joseph's journal was kept in three ways:

- Personally recorded events.
- Words dictated to his scribes and secretaries.
- Scribes and secretaries diligently recording what he said and did.

—*KBYU Joseph Smith Papers,* November 30, 2009

Kite flying

While Joseph was supposed to be in hiding, he was actually playing in the street, flying a kite with the other boys. A man came up and asked one of the boys, Charles Stoddard, where the Prophet Joseph Smith was. Charles said, "He went to heaven on Hyrum's white horse and we are fixing this kite to send his dinner to him."

—*RJ*, 73–74

Leaky boat

Willard Richards relates, "Joseph, Hyrum, and I got Porter Rockwell out of bed. We spent about two hours locating a boat. Porter then rowed us across the river to Montrose, Iowa. The skiff was so leaky that we all kept busy bailing with our boots and shoes to keep it from sinking."

—*I Witnessed the Carthage Massacre: The Testimony of Willard Richards*, documentary, 18

Letters written

Joseph wrote at least 121 letters to various individuals.

—*HC*, Index

Maid of Iowa

On June 2, 1843, "Joseph Smith paid Dan Jones $1,375 to become half-owner of the steamboat *Maid of Iowa*." Shortly thereafter, Captain Jones (who had been baptized in the early part of 1843) "commenced running the boat between Nauvoo and Montrose as a ferry boat. When the Prophet Joseph was arrested at Dixon, the following June, Capt. Jones with a force of armed men navigated the river for the purpose of intercepting steamboats which might be engaged in kidnaping the Prophet Joseph into Missouri. In May, 1844, the Prophet bought out the interest of Dan Jones in the *Maid of Iowa*."

—John W. Welch, ed., *A Chronology of the Life of Joseph Smith*, BYU Studies, 120; *HC*, 5:417–18; *LDSBE*, 3:658

Manner of dress

He loved a front ruffled shirt, white pants, and a white scarf.

—Compiler's note

Masons

"Many of the Saints were Masons . . . [who] called attention to the spirit of brotherhood and brotherly love which are supposed to be the foundations of the Masonic fraternity. . . . This ideal agreed well with the high ideals of the Prophet for his followers. . . . Many of the prominent and influential men of the state [of Illinois] were Masons."

"Every member cheerfully gives of his time . . . to make the others happier." Joseph became a 32nd degree Mason on March 15, 1842.

—John A. Widtsoe, *Joseph Smith: Seeker After Truth Prophet of God*, 299; *HC*

The Masonic Temple of Nauvoo was dedicated April 5, 1844. About 550 members came from all over the world for the dedication.

—*LDSCC*, 25

Children named after Joseph Smith

The following is a list of children named after Joseph Smith, with the birth year, birth place, and father.

1. Joseph Smith ADAMS—1846, Little Pigeon, Iowa—Azra
2. Joseph Smith ALLEN—1840, Jackson, Missouri—James
3. Joseph Smith ALLRED—1837, Far West, Missouri
4. Joseph Smith BARNEY—1845 Nauvoo, Illinois—Lewis
5. Joseph Smith BELLOWS—*est.*1850—John
6. Joseph Smith BERRY—1843, Nauvoo, Illinois—Jesse
7. Joseph Smith BLACK—1836, Ireland—William
8. Joseph Smith BLACK Jr.—1861, Spring City, Utah—Joseph
9. Joseph Smith BURBANK—1842, Nauvoo, Illinois—Daniel
10. Joseph Smith CHAPMAN—1838, Far West, Missouri—Welcome

11. Joseph Smith CHERRY—1847, Black Hills, South Dakota—Aaron
12. Joseph Smith COOLIDGE—1843, Omaha, Nebraska—Joseph
13. Joseph Smith CRANE—1843—no other information
14. Joseph Smith DILLE—1843, Nauvoo, Illinois—David
15. Joseph Smith DOUGLAS—*est.*1845, probably Nauvoo, Illinois—William
16. Joseph Smith EGBERT—1859, West Jordan, Utah
17. Joseph Smith FREE—1868, Salt Lake City, Utah—Absalom
18. Joseph Smith FAUSETT—1838, Far West, Missouri—William
19. Joseph Smith GIBSON—1844, Mississippi—George
20. Joseph Smith GRIBBLE—1845, Nauvoo, Illinois—William
21. Joseph Smith HAMSON—1848, Council Bluffs, Iowa—George
22. Joseph Smith HANCOCK—1867, Harrisburg, Utah—Mosiah
23. Joseph Smith HANCOCK—1849, Salt Lake City, Utah—Levi
24. Joseph Smith HARRIS—1882, Salt Lake City, Utah—Thomas
25. Joseph Smith HENDRICKS—1838, Far West, Missouri—James
26. Joseph Smith HORNE—1842, Nauvoo, Illinois
27. Joseph Smith HUNTINGTON—1855, Salt Lake City, Utah—Dimick
28. Joseph Smith HYDE—*est.* 1859, Salt Lake City, Utah—Orson
29. Joseph Smith KIMBALL—1851, Salt Lake City, Utah—Heber C. (Joseph Smith Kimball was a twin and died before age twelve.)
30. Joseph Smith LAMB—1836, New York—Abel
31. Joseph Smith LEAVITT—1860, St. George, Utah—Jeremiah III
32. Joseph Smith LEE—1839, Payson, Illinois—Alfred
33. Joseph Smith LITTLEFIELD—1838, Far West, Missouri—Waldo
34. Joseph Smith MAJOR—1845, Nauvoo, Illinois—William

35. Joseph Smith MAXFIELD—1847, Bedeque, Canada—John
36. Joseph Smith MCFATE—1845, Nauvoo, Illinois—James
37. Joseph Smith MENDENHALL—*est.*1858, probably Council Bluffs, Iowa—James
38. Joseph Smith MILLER—1847, Council Bluffs, Iowa—Daniel
39. Joseph Smith MURDOCK—1831, Kirtland, Ohio—John and then Joseph (adopted twin)
40. Joseph Smith NELSON—1836, Caldwell County, Missouri—Edmond
41. Joseph Smith ROBISON—1864, Salt Lake City, Utah—Lewis
42. Joseph Smith SCHOFIELD—1809, New York—Elijah
43. Joseph Smith SHARP—1840, Calhoon, Illinois—James
44. Joseph SMITH—1838, Iowa—John
45. Joseph SMITH—1843, Nauvoo, Illinois—George
46. Joseph SMITH—1848, Pompton, New Jersey—James Henry
47. Joseph SMITH—Iowa—William
48. Joseph Smith SNOW—1873, St. George, Utah—Erastus
49. Joseph Smith STEVENS—1845, Tioga, Illinois—Lyman
50. Joseph Smith TANNER—1833, New York—John
51. Joseph Smith TURLEY—1846, Winter Quarters, Nebraska—Theodore
52. Joseph Smith WHITEHEAD—1845, Nauvoo, Illinois
53. Joseph Smith WOOLSEY—1844, Nauvoo, Illinois—James
54. Joseph Smith WORTHEN—1845, Nauvoo, Illinois—Samuel

Note: It is likely that hundreds of families named a child with the first name of Joseph or Hyrum after the two brothers were murdered. At least sixteen families named a child with the name of Hyrum Smith. Seventeen named a child Joseph Hyrum.

—ELDS; Early Journals; Far West History.com; Nancy C. Williams, *After One Hundred Years*, 173

Nauvoo tornados

Joseph and early Mormons mentioned tornados in Nauvoo. Other tornados in the history of Nauvoo include:

- 1850: A tornado hit the Nauvoo Temple and knocked down its walls.
- 1876: A tornado hit the St. Peter and St. Paul Catholic church and ripped off the 140-foot-high steeple.

- October 6, 1903: A tornado hit Nauvoo and tore off roofs and did considerable damage.
- 1995: Tornados damaged fifty-five buildings in Hancock County.
- 2001: A tornado that came through Nauvoo while the temple there was being reconstructed. It barely missed the temple but damaged a few structures as it ripped through town.

—Glenn Guerden, *Images of America: Nauvoo*, 63, 75, 85, 116

Nauvoo Legion oath

"I do solemnly swear that I will support the Constitution of the United States, and this State, and that I will not be engaged in dueling, either directly or indirectly, during my continuance in office; and that I will faithfully discharge the duties of ____________(rank), in the Regiment of the Nauvoo Legion of Illinois militia, to the best of my skill and understanding so help me God."

—*Keeper of the Prophet's Sword* by Howard Carlos Smith, 52

Nauvoo Legion parade

"I saw the Nauvoo Legion on parade with the Prophet (then General Joseph Smith) with his wife, Emma, on horseback at the head of the troops. It was indeed an imposing site. He's so fair, and she so dark, in their beautiful riding-habits. He was in full military suit, and she was trimmed with gold buttons, a neat cap on her head with a black plume in it, while the Prophet wore a red plume in his, and a red sash across his breast. His coat was black, while his white pants had red stripes on the outside seams. He also wore a sword at his side. His favorite riding-horse was named Charlie, a big black steed."

—Eunice Billings Palmer, *They Knew the Prophet*, Hyrum L. Andrus, 172–73

Prices in Nauvoo

Cost of goods in Nauvoo (from the daybook of the Red Brick Store):

- shovel $1.25
- cradle scythe $1.50
- three dozen eggs 19¢
- whip $1.50
- yard of ribbon 13¢
- 1 pound of sugar 10¢
- pair of shoes $2.25
- boots $4.50

—Matthew B. Brown, *Joseph Smith: The Man, The Mission, The Message*, 82

Rebuke to a customer

"Not long after the Mansion [house] was open as a hotel, a stranger came and registered. Just before supper he insulted one of the hired girls. The Prophet heard of it after the stranger had retired. The next morning he met him as he came down from his room and said, 'Sir, I understand that you insulted one of the employees of this house last evening.' The stranger began to make all kinds of apologies, but nothing would answer the purpose. The Prophet told the stranger to get his baggage and to get. . . . The man offered to pay his bill . . . 'I want none of your money, or any other man's of your stamp.' Upon that, the stranger struck a lively exit."

—William Homes Walker, *They Knew the Prophet,* Hyrum L. Andrus, 168

Serenaded

Joseph and Emma were serenaded on the morning of December 25, 1843, by Sister Lettice Rushton's family. On December 31, 1843, about fifty musicians and singers performed William W. Phelps's New Year's hymn under Joseph and Emma's window. "When [the Prophet] was in hiding . . . he would request my father and mother to come to sing for him."

—Eunice Billings Snow, *A Chronology of the Life of Joseph Smith*, BYU Studies, 157; *HC*, 6:134, 153; John W. Welch, ed., *Opening the Heavens,* 158; Hyrum L. Andrus, *They Knew the Prophet*, 171

Shoes

Pairs of shoes in the time of the Prophet were made identical; there was no left shoe or right shoe. They were made the same, and with perhaps some pain, the person who wore them made them a left or right as the feet forced the leather to mold accordingly.

KBYU Joseph Smith Discussion by Keith Perkins, January 3, 2010

Sicknesses

In 1839, Joseph had a violent illness and stayed at the Johnson home in Ramus, Illinois. Benjamin F. Johnson cared for him for almost two weeks. "As Emma was in no degree able to care for him, it wholly devolved upon me. Both day and night through period of a little less than two weeks I was hardly absent from his room. Almost his only food was gruel, and about the only treatment he would accept was a flush of the colon with warm water, perhaps tinctured slightly with capsicum or myrrh, or a little soda and salt, both of which were prepared and administered by me."

—Hyrum L. Andrus, *They Knew the Prophet*, 102

Sleigh ride

On December 2, 1835, Joseph went on a sleigh ride with his family to Painesville, Ohio.

—John W. Welch, ed., *A Chronology of the Life of Joseph Smith,* BYU Studies, 76

Smith name

An interesting coincidence is that the doctor who operated on and saved Joseph's leg at age seven was Nathan Smith.

The printing press that Grandin purchased just before Joseph Smith needed it to print the Book of Mormon was the Smith Patented Improved Press.

Robert Smith was captain of the Mormon hating mob or militia of the Carthage Greys.

—Ted Gibbons, *Sealing the Testimony*, 58; Compiler's note

Spectacles

"The prophet did in fact own a pair of spectacles, but they were not for practical use. The lenses were made of ordinary glass."

—Matthew B. Brown, *Joseph Smith: The Man, the Mission, the Message*, 13; *Ensign*, January 1984, 36

Spelling in Joseph's day

Joseph lived before the standardization of the English language. These are a few of the words that were spelled incorrectly by Joseph's scribes and associates of the 1830s and 1840s. This was done by almost all the brethren, including Dr. Frederick G. Williams, William Clayton, Willard Richards, and Brigham Young. Some examples of spelling are:

- brotheren, breatheren
- bishopwrick, bishopwreck
- hart
- journy
- Thirsday
- chilldren
- instructid
- oh clock
- intiligence
- dreem
- cittys
- litle
- watter
- stedfast
- Wensday
- kees
- bennifit
- complyance
- trecheous
- decreeeth
- saught
- baught
- leters
- mooved

- immedeately
- thir (their)
- imprest

—Scott H. Faulring, ed., *An American Prophet's Record: The Diaries and Journals of Joseph Smith*, 1–15, 42–44; Mark L. McConkie tapes

Stagecoach heroism "John Wayne" style

"On a trip to Washington, D.C. in December 1839, a stage driver stopped in to get a drink. The horses became spooked and ran at full speed. Joseph opened the door of the stage and climbed up the side of the coach until he made his way to the driver's seat. He somehow got a hold of the reins and brought the horses to a halt after they had run for two or three miles." Some of the grateful passengers, who were members of Congress, proposed the idea of mentioning the Prophet's act of bravery in a session of Congress. However, when they found out that their hero was Joseph Smith "the Mormon prophet," their enthusiasm quickly diminished. "I heard no more of their praise, gratitude or reward," said the Prophet.

—Susan Easton Black, *Setting the Record Straight: Joseph Smith the Mormon Prophet*, 16; *A Chronology of the Life of Joseph Smith*, BYU Studies, 110; *HC*, 1:271

Tall black hat

"Joseph's spirited black horse, when he attempted to mount him, made a start, wheeling partly around, but the Prophet with a sudden spring gained the saddle minus his tall black hat, containing, as was customary in those days, his papers, etc. There being at the time a light wind, hat and papers went flying around."

—Samuel Miles, *They Knew the Prophet*, Hyrum L. Andrus, 111

Tanned a wolf skin

Wilford Woodruff's first introduction to the Prophet was in 1834 in Kirtland. "[Joseph] brought out a wolf-skin and said, 'Brother Woodruff, I want you to help me tan this.' So I pulled off my coat, went to work and helped him, and felt honored in so doing. . . . He wanted this wolf-skin to put upon his wagon seat [to go to Zion's Camp], as he had no buffalo robe."

—Hyrum L. Andrus, *They Knew the Prophet*, 90–91

Teenage pranks

Joseph tipped over an outhouse.

—Kenneth Godfrey, BYU Lecture, 1969

Telegraphs

On May 27, 1844, just two months before Joseph was murdered, Samuel F. B. Morse sent the first telegraph with this message: "What hath God wrought?" This was a perfect question as to what God had wrought through this mighty prophet.

—Gorton Carruth, *A Chronology of the Life and Events in America*, 282

Train ride

On December 21, 1839, Joseph took a train ride from Washington, DC, to Philadelphia, where he preached to many congregations, and after a month returned to Washington, DC, at the end of January 1840.

—Arnold K. Garr, *Setting the Record Straight: Joseph Smith: Presidential Candidate*, 18; Smith, *HC*, 4:47

Travel

Joseph might have traveled 5,000 miles in his lifetime, which was a lot for his time. However, with modern means, some of our leaders have traveled several hundred thousand miles. For instance, in 1998, President Gordon B. Hinckley traveled 77,000 miles and visited 16 countries. President Monson has traveled millions of miles in 160 countries. President Boyd K. Packer stated at the 2012 Worldwide Leadership Conference that he had traveled 2.5 million miles in church service.

—*Church News*, 18 February 2012

Treasure hunting in 1820s

There were at least 500 respectable men who were engaged in treasure hunting, according to the Palmyra Herald of July 24, 1822.

—Robert V. Remini, *Joseph Smith*, 16

Trip to Salem, Massachusetts

Jonathan Burgess, a Church member living in Barnstable, Massachusetts, knew where there was a large sum of money hidden and abandoned in a home in Salem. Joseph decided to investigate this claim. He left Kirtland on Monday, July 25, 1836, with Sidney Rigdon, Hyrum Smith, and Oliver Cowdery. Jonathan couldn't seem to locate it because the city had changed so much. However, over a hundred converts were baptized in this area within five years.

—Richard N. Skousen and W. Cleon Skousen, *Brother Joseph: Seer of a New Dispensation*, vol. 2, 590–91

University of Nauvoo

Officers of the University of Nauvoo on December 16, 1840:

John C. Bennett: Chancellor

William Law: Registrar

Board of Regents:

- Joseph Smith
- Hyrum Smith
- Samuel H. Smith
- Newel K. Whitney
- John T. Barnett
- Don Carlos Smith
- Vinson Knight
- Elias Higbee
- James Adams
- Samuel Bennett
- John Snider
- Lenos M. Knight
- Sidney Rigdon
- William Marks
- Daniel H. Wells
- Charles C. Rich
- Wilson Law
- John Greene
- Isaac Galland
- Robert D. Foster
- Robert B. Thompson
- Ebenezer Robinson
- George Miller

—*HC*, 4:313

Allowed in the Nauvoo Charter: Don Carlos Smith and Vinson Knight were on the Board of Regents; James Kelly was elected President of the University on February 9, 1841. "[Joseph] did more than help administer the school; he was a student as well. He attended music classes taught . . . by Professor Gustavus Hills."

—Knight, D&C*WW*, 86; *Joseph Smith Papers Book 2 Revelations and Translations*, 663; Matthew B. Brown, *Joseph Smith: The Man, the Mission, the Message*, 61

Vocabulary of Joseph

Joseph used between 2,000 and 3,000 words in his written publications. *The Book of Mormon* had 2,896 general words, 245 personal names, and 166 place names. The Doctrine and Covenants had 2,445 ordinary words, 230 persons' names, and 47 place names.

—John A. Widtsoe, *Joseph Smith: Seeker After Truth: Prophet of God*, 69–71

Washington DC trip

On October 29, 1839, Joseph left Nauvoo and arrived in Washington, DC, on November 28, 1839. He met with President Van Buren on November 29th. He arrived back in Nauvoo on March 4, 1840, after a trip of four months and seven days.

—J. Christopher Conkling, *Church Almanac: A Chronology of Joseph Smith*, 137–41

Wickedest man on earth came to call

"On one occasion a man by the name of Joseph Jackson called. Not finding Joseph at home, I heard him say to Mrs. Smith, 'You tell the Prophet that the wickedest man on earth called to see him.' "

—William Homes Walker, *They Knew the Prophet*, Hyrum L. Andrus, 167

Broke a leg while wrestling

While wrestling with the Prophet, Howard Coray broke his leg some three inches above the ankle joint. Said Brother Coray, "He (Joseph Smith) immediately carried me into the house, pulled off my boot, and found at once that my leg was decidedly broken . . . then got some splinters and bandaged it. A number of times that day he came in to see me. . . . The next day when he happened in to see me, after a little conversation, I said: 'Brother Joseph, when Jacob wrestled with the angel and was lamed by him, the angel blessed him. Now I think I am also entitled to a blessing.' To that he replied, 'I am not the Patriarch, but my father is. . . . I'll have him bless you.' Then looking very earnestly at me, he declared, 'Brother Coray, you will soon find a companion . . . whom you will be satisfied with. She will cling to you like the cords of death; and you will have a good many children.' " He soon married Martha Knowlton and said of her, "A more intelligent, self-sacrificing, and devoted wife and mother few men have been blessed with."

—Hyrum L. Andrus, *They Knew the Prophet*, 153–54

About Wayne J. Lewis

Wayne J. Lewis was born in Mesa, Arizona. He served a mission in Virginia and North Carolina. He received his BA in political science in 1969 and his master's degree in history in 1981, both at Brigham Young University. He taught seminary in Mesa and Snowflake, Arizona, and also taught classes in the College of Religion Education at BYU. His master's thesis identified 6,700 names of Latter-day Saints who lived in the state of Missouri during the 1830s and also identified the property that many of these early Saints owned there. He also pursued work toward a PhD in the College of Family Sciences.

He worked for the Presiding Bishopric Office of the LDS Church and was assigned to the LDS Philanthropies for twenty years to assist in financing various projects of the Church and BYU. He assisted in some of the priority needs with the College of Religion, BYU Sports, and Ezra Taft Benson Agricultural Institute, and served as assistant dean in the College of Biology and Agriculture at BYU.

Wayne and his wife, Maren Barraclough, were married in the Mesa Arizona Temple and have twelve children, fifty grandchildren, and three great-grandchildren. He has served as a bishop and has served in numerous other positions in the Church.

Wayne has collected books written about Joseph Smith for over forty-five years and has over five hundred books about the Prophet Joseph Smith in his personal library.

In 2009, Wayne compiled the first complete bibliography of the Prophet Joseph Smith. In 2010, he printed a second edition entitled *Joseph Smith Bibliography, Joseph Smith A–Z Volume 1, Reference Encyclopedia*.

About Jana Lee Cox

Jana Lee Tiffany Cox lives in Mesa, Arizona, with her husband, Max, and two daughters, the youngest of their six children. Max and Jana were married in the Mesa Arizona Temple in March 1984 and are active members of The Church of Jesus Christ of Latter-day Saints.

Jana received an Associate of Arts in Psychology from MCC in 1984 and went on to earn a second degree in creative writing in 1986. She has worked for over thirty years in the printing industry, specializing in computer layout and design. Jana and Max work together as partners in their own printing business, Legend eXpress Publishing, where she has been instrumental in the production of over one hundred books, from life and family histories, works of fiction, and poetry and art to business manuals and educational material and workbooks. Although she has provided editing assistance to a number of first time authors, *Joseph Smith A–Z* and *500 Little Known Facts about Joseph and Emma Smith* are her largest editing ventures to date.

0 26575 15242 5